A Letter to Jacqueline

E. Wright

My Detroit
Childhood Memoirs

ISBN 979-8-218-64160-3

Self-Published by: Eric Wright
Edits by: Eric Wright
Cover Design by: Eric Wright
Stories Written by: Eric Wright
Research by:: Eric Wright

ChatGPT AI technology.
No copies of pictures were used but generated
by ChatGPT AI technology.

Table of Contents

Introduction

"A Letter to Jacqueline: My Detroit Childhood Memoirs"

Is a poignant and evocative journey back to a bygone era, painting a vivid portrait of a young boy's experiences growing up on the vibrant streets of Detroit. Combining heartfelt storytelling with a deep sense of nostalgia, this memoir explores themes of resilience, family, and community, inviting readers to relive the author's formative years through the lens of their own cherished memories.

With a remarkable blend of humor, tenderness, and raw honesty, **"A Letter to Jacqueline"** transports readers to a time filled with innocence, joy, and the boundless possibilities of youth while illuminating the indelible imprint that childhood leaves on the person we eventually become.

Proverbs 22:6 (NIV):
"Start children off on the way they should go, and even when they are old they will not turn from it."

My Life's Journey Has Been a Trip and a Half.

The United States Constitution grants us Freedom of Speech, and in this book, I will exercise that right. I will say what I want, how I want to say it, and recount whatever I remember as a child. Everything I share will be factual. I refuse to escape from the truth, though I also understand that some truths don't always need to be spoken.

There will be moments in these stories that may touch a nerve or stir emotions in some readers—that is not my intention. My goal is to share a little history, some truths, and lessons I've learned along the way.

This book contains short stories about my childhood. Growing up on Detroit's West Side on Dumbarton Street, later moving to the Northwest Side to the Smith Home Projects, and navigating the struggles and joys of life's journey. These stories reflect the hardships, the bonds of family, and the close connection I shared with my mother.

Through these pages, you'll find tales of love, compassion, the good old days, music, racism, religion, the physical and emotional pain, the arguments, the difficult relationships, and the fights that shaped me into the man I've become.

The God within me has blessed me with the gift of memory and music. For over 35 years, I've thought about writing this book. I don't know how much time I have left on this Earth now that I'm on the other side of sixty, but I figured it's finally time to share my story.

I want to take you back to my early years in Detroit while also giving you a glimpse of the city's history. Let me take you on a journey, sharing childhood memories that even my dear mother never knew about her oldest son.

I was a pure mama's boy and this is
my history, my own experiences, my true story

Love you, Ma. Continue to rest in peace.

Dedications and Acknowledgments

Dad, there are so many things I want to thank you for. My early years with you were so much fun. I was around 7 or 8 years old when I thought I could outrun you. You pulled ahead of me, then tripped and fell. I immediately stopped to see if you were okay, but you tricked me! Suddenly, you got up and beat me to the corner store. Dad, you cheated! I also remember the time you took me to the store, and we met the legendary wrestler, Bobo Brazil. I was about 5 years old, and I couldn't believe how enormous his hand felt when he shook mine. And what about the time I won second place in an essay contest in elementary school? I won a $5 check but lost it the same day. I was so devastated, but you replaced the money and took me to get candy.

So many precious childhood memories come to mind.

You were such a great dad, husband, and provider when I was a toddler. But within a few short years, things changed. The world seemed to shrink for you, and doors began to close, even though you were so talented, athletic, smart, and could fix anything.

I discovered early on that you were also very artistic with your drawings. However, you had two things working against you in this cold, cruel world—being a Black man and dealing with a hearing impairment. You were partially deaf, and I know how frustrating that must have been for you.

Mom, you were the strongest woman I've ever known—caring, compassionate, loving, and funny. You endured so much in your life. You couldn't hear or speak; you were completely deaf. Back then, people used to call it "deaf and dumb." I hated that term with a passion because you weren't dumb at all. You were incredibly intelligent and taught us all how to communicate using sign language.

You were a breast cancer survivor, and I've always tried to emulate your strength. Thank you for giving me life. I know it must have been difficult to make the decision to kick your oldest son out into the world, but I understand why you did it.

My oldest sister, Ms. Brainiac, I'm so proud of you—the bookworm of the family. You were the first person to go to college and graduate. Man, you were so smart in school. I still remember your report cards. After all you've been through, you never stopped reaching your goals.

You could have easily given up and taken the wrong turn in life, but that was never in your DNA.

Instead, you kept striving for excellence, had a promising career, and traveled the world. Congratulations on your future retirement! Looking back, while I was busy playing the big brother, I should have paid attention to what you were doing and followed your lead, big sis.

My brother, Mr. Business Man, I'm so proud of you. You've become a great provider, an excellent husband, an amazing father, and an awesome human being. But things could've gone differently. You could've gotten into the drug game or committed unlawful acts that might have landed you in prison. The streets could've swallowed you whole.

You were too smart for that, and I couldn't sit back and let that happen. Growing up, I called myself protecting you from those evils, even if it meant we had to fight about it.

When we were kids, I knew you were watching my every move. Everywhere I went, you weren't too far behind. That's why I tried my best never to do anything negative around you. I wanted to set the best example I could. But instead of giving in to the streets, you made up your mind and went into the armed services.

There, you met your lovely wife, had children, and together you built a very successful business. You didn't do too bad for yourself, brother.

My middle sister, Ms. Sweet and Concern, I can't say enough about you. You're a book novel all by yourself. While all of us flew out of the nest, you stayed behind and took care of Mom. But while caring for her, you also had to find your way through life. Looking back, it was so unfair to leave you in that situation, but you were so good at dealing with life's struggles.

I'm so proud that you came out on the other side of those struggles. You took care of yourself, Mom, and my nephew James at the same time while becoming a businesswoman in your own right.

This is why I consider you the second strongest woman I know. I can never forget the email you sent to each of us.

At one point, we were so far apart as a family—failing to connect and not checking on each other. I'll admit, it was ridiculous, and I can only blame myself for my part.

We've seen enough examples of family members not speaking to each other on both sides. But that email you sent told the truth and made us all feel so bad. And look at us now. You brought this family right back together. Yes, you did that. Thank you, my amazing sister.

My baby sister, Mrs. You Play Stupid Games and You'll Win Stupid Prizes, the stylist of the family. I remember holding you as a baby and rocking you to sleep. Maybe that's why I felt we were the closest. But we all protected you.

I'm still mad, though. I'm mad because we got our butts beat, and you hardly ever got any whippings. You could do something wrong and always got away with it. Still, I'm so proud of you, little sis. You've become a devoted mom and wife.

I love how you interact with your kids, making sure they don't experience what we went through. With all your physical setbacks over the years, life seems to be trying to sit you down.

But you've overcome those difficulties and continued doing whatever you set your mind to—and you do it well. Love you, sis. We're still close. You just act like we're not. Just kidding!

I would like to take this time to acknowledge **myself**. I've done almost everything in life I wanted to do. I've broken down barriers, faced my fears, and conquered many things people said I couldn't do. I avoided prison and stayed far away from drugs.

I had one failed marriage but learned from my imperfections. I now have an awesome marriage to my best friend. I had a daughter who never wants to see me again, but I also have another daughter who thinks the world of me.

I've made many mistakes in life, but those mistakes have made me a better man, husband, father, brother, and friend.

I want to thank the God within me for keeping me focused and alive. I still have so much more to do, but time is running out. Now that I'm on the other side of sixty, I have a few more things to cross off my bucket list. But to be honest, right now, I could leave this Earth with a smile on my face.

To my aunts and uncles on both sides of our family, thank you for putting smiles on our tiny faces and adding genuine love and happiness to our hearts.

Thank you for teaching, protecting, and caring for us.

I also thank you for my nicknames. On my mom's side, I was called **Pookie**. On my dad's side, I was called **Pokie**. I don't know where those nicknames came from, but I'm never ashamed to be called either.

They were given to me by very special family members, and I cherish both names to this day.

To my auntie, you were also like a mother to us. My life with you was so much fun. You took us on motorcycle rides, taught us how to fish, fly kites, and took us to the drive-in.

You showed me how to play basketball properly, and you took us to Edgewater Amusement Park and Boblo Island.

I want to thank you for the love you had for us. And you already know—I absolutely love you back.

To my other auntie, you were also like a mother to me.

Those times we spent with you on Trumbull in the high-rise apartments are some of my most unforgettable memories. I want to thank you for everything.

Continue to rest in peace.

To my other auntie, in your heyday, I thought you were so beautiful. You should have been a model instead of a nurse. Continue resting in peace.

To my other auntie, you also played a mother's role in my life. Spending weekends with you and my cousins was always so much fun. I got my musical taste from you, and I still remember some of your playlist: Phyllis Hyman, Phoebe Snow, Brenda Russell, Roberta Flack, Nick Ashford and Valerie Simpson, Patti Austin, Angela Bofill, Dionne Warwick, Deniece Williams, Nancy Wilson, Minnie Riperton, Regina Belle, and

Roberta Flack—just to name a few. I thank you.

You are part of the reason why I love music so much.

To my uncle, I wanted to be like you. I wanted to sing and walk like you. I wanted to dress like you. I wanted my hair cut like yours. I wanted the cars you had when I was finally able to drive.

I looked up to you and wanted to clone you.

You were also so good to my mother.

Thank you for being a positive role model for me to look up to and for being an awesome brother to your sister.

To my other uncles and aunties, you absolutely showed your sister (my mother) love and support. She never asked for much, but whatever she needed, she got. Thank you for always being there for her.

To my eight uncles, you treated my mother as if she were your biological sister. Thank you for making her laugh and smile.
Thank you for teaching us, playing with us, looking after us, visiting us, spending time with us, and being patient with us.

Some of the pranks you all played on us were pretty cruel, but hey, we were your kids for all those summers. Christmas and Thanksgiving with all of you were amazing memories.

To my cousins on my mom's side, we had so much fun together. Delray was like Disneyland to us.

To my cousins on my dad's side, man, I wish I could turn back the hands of time. We worked so hard on Grandma's farm together, but we played even harder. Talladay Road was another Disneyland for us as kids. I also have fond memories of Detroit's Vinewood and 25th Street.

Last but not least, **to my grandparents**, Ngiyohlala ngikuthanda kuze kube phakade. Futhiuyohlala usenhliziyweni yami. Qhubeka uphumule ngokuthula. **(In the South African language of Zulu or Bantu)**

I can never thank you enough. I truly and deeply miss the three of you. You were—and still are—everything to me.

My childhood memories with you were so amazing. And Grandma, to this day, I've never had better homemade strawberry cake or peach cobbler. Grand Dad, Your brim hats fit my head so perfect.

You three were the most wonderful grandparents a child could ever have. Let me stop now; I'm crying as I write this.

Today, you will always be the center of my spiritual universe.

To all the Smith Home Project mothers, thank you for keeping us out of trouble and believing in the term "it takes a village."

To my closest homies from the Smith Home Projects, we were the cool kids. We were the ones parents wanted their kids to hang out with and look up to.

We were popular in middle school, high school, and in nightclubs all over the city of Detroit. We had the prettiest and baddest girlfriends. We were the shit, and we knew it.

(Those Suited Up Boys)

P.S. Sorry for kicking all your butts on the basketball court for so many years. You can blame that on my auntie—she taught me how to punish any opponent in front of me. (laughing)

February 18, 2023

Today, I needed some motivation to write in my memoir, a project that has been both a labor of love and a journey of self-reflection. I decided to get my family together and take a ride to Detroit's West Side. When I was a small child, I lived on a street called Dumbarton, now renamed Heritage Place.

The block looks incredibly different today. Even **McShane Playground**, which we lived across from, doesn't look the same. It used to be fenced in, a place that felt both secure and familiar, but now it looks so modern. The charm and character of the past seem to have faded. All the apartment buildings are gone except for two
—one still occupied and the other standing eerily empty, a silent relic of what once was.

The Prekindergarten and kindergarten school, **Little Angell**, is also no longer there. I remember it as a tiny school that held just 69 kids and two teachers. Despite its size, it was such an essential part of our early lives. Sadly, it was demolished in 2004, leaving behind only memories.

Curiosity got the best of me, and I decided to Google Map my way to my elementary school, **Big Angell**. I couldn't quite recall the walking route I used to take as a child, but as we arrived at the location where the school once stood, I was stunned. It was now nothing but a vacant field—just another Detroit school erased from the map, a piece of the past gone forever.

As we continued driving through my old neighborhood, I couldn't help but notice the deplorable state of the housing conditions. House after house stood empty on each block. Trash was strewn everywhere.

Many roofs had massive holes, some completely torn down to the porches, which were either missing entirely or reduced to scattered bricks in the front yards.

Yet, amidst this decay, people still lived in many of these homes.

Seeing all of this today brought back vivid memories of how this side of **Grand River** looked during the **1967 Detroit Rebellion**, a harrowing 56 years ago. It's almost as if time stood still in some of these areas. There's been no bulldozing, no remodeling, no upkeep.

While **Downtown Detroit** now resembles something out of the space age with its modern architecture and revitalization, the neighborhoods

I remember as a child still look like **Martial Law** is in effect.

The racial tension back in those days led to the burning and destruction of this side of town, and sadly, it still bears the scars. The liquor store that once stood on the corner of our street is now boarded up. The church where I was baptized no longer exists. I can even recall riding my **Big Wheel** one block over to **Petoskey Street**, just to see my crush play in her yard. Her house doesn't exist anymore either, and there are maybe four homes left on that entire block.

The saddest part is knowing that these communities were ravaged and never rebuilt. What the **1967 Rebellion** didn't destroy, the flood of drugs that came in afterward finished off. By the 1970s, though, these same communities began to thrive. Blacks owned laundromats, markets, cleaners, gas stations, clothing stores, pharmacies, restaurants, ice cream parlors, doctor's offices—you name it. Everything you needed to make a community viable and self-sufficient was there.

Then, we started selling off everything. We left for the suburbs, not realizing the true cost of our decisions. In many ways, we sold out—not just the businesses, but the soul of the community.

Today, these are no longer neighborhoods. They're just **HOODS.**

Driving through this place today was both shocking and painful.

It reminded me of the vibrant community that once existed here and the stark contrast to its current state.

But through these memoirs, I will bring this neighborhood to life again.

Please forgive me if my memories seem all over the place. I intentionally chose to write these short chapters in this way. As a child, my thoughts didn't come in any specific order, and this book reflects that.

Whatever I remembered, I turned into a story.

This part of **Grand River Avenue** is now considered historic. And Dumbarton Street? It's now called **Heritage Place**.

The Year I Was Born

The year I was born marked a pivotal moment in boxing history, a time when the heavyweight division witnessed a monumental shift in dominance. That was the year the hard-hitting Sonny Liston defeated Floyd Patterson to claim the world boxing title. The fight was a spectacle, showcasing Liston's sheer power, precision, and dominance in the ring. Patterson, a respected and skilled champion, was no match for the relentless force that Liston brought to the bout.

Liston had been a feared contender for years, and many believed he was long overdue for a title shot. His reputation as a knockout artist, with devastating power in both hands, struck fear into opponents. When the match against Patterson was finally set, anticipation built to a fever pitch. Many doubted whether Patterson could withstand the onslaught that Liston was known for delivering.

The fight itself was shockingly brief, a vivid demonstration of Liston's overwhelming strength. Patterson, who had successfully defended his title multiple times, was floored by Liston's punches in the very first round. The bout ended in a mere two minutes and six seconds, leaving no question about who the superior fighter was that night. Liston's victory was as decisive as it was brutal, cementing his place at the top of the heavyweight division.

This victory not only crowned Liston as the world champion but also set the stage for one of the most iconic rivalries in boxing history. His dominant performance against Patterson caught the attention of a young and brash contender who was rising through the ranks—**Cassius Clay**, later known as **Muhammad Ali**. Clay, known for his charisma and bold proclamations, began calling out Liston, referring to him as a "big ugly bear" and mocking his stoic demeanor. The contrast between the two fighters couldn't have been more striking: Liston, the feared and silent champion, and Clay, the flamboyant and outspoken challenger.

Liston's crushing defeat of Patterson put him on a collision course with Clay, a fight that would eventually redefine the sport of boxing.

While Liston represented raw power and an intimidating presence, Clay embodied speed, strategy, and a psychological edge. The bout that would follow between them not only showcased their contrasting styles but also marked a cultural and generational shift within the sport.

Liston's victory over Patterson was more than just a title fight; it was the catalyst for the heavyweight division's transformation. It set the tone for an era of unforgettable matches, culminating in his historic encounter with Muhammad Ali—a fight that would change boxing forever.

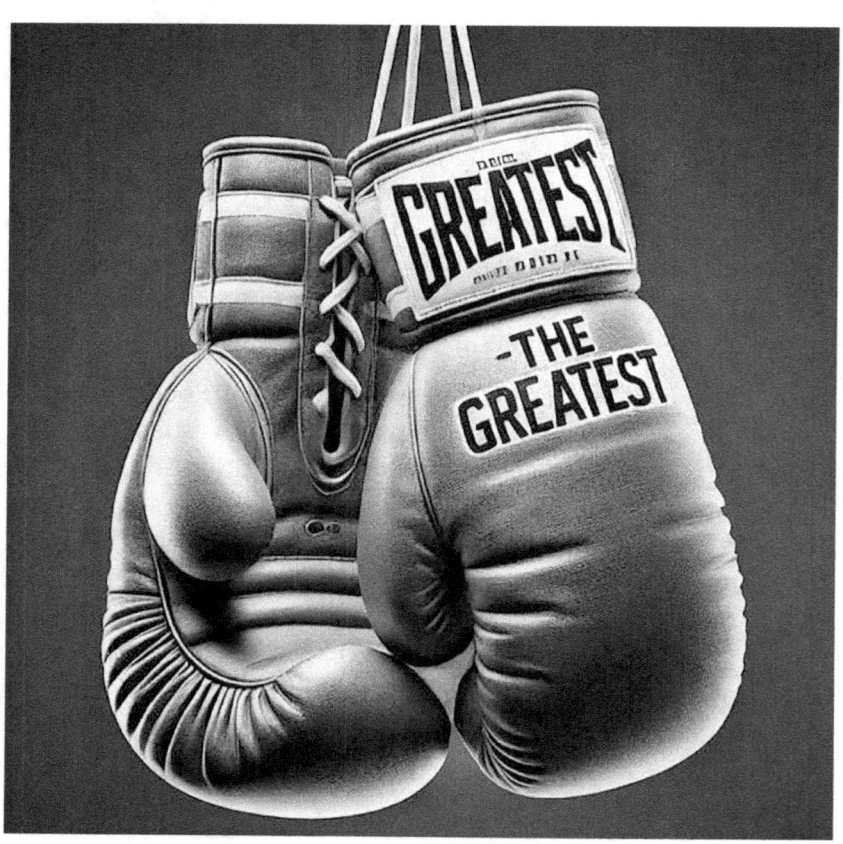

Chapter 1

Let Start With a Little Detroit History
The Rebellion of 1967 (Not a Riot)

Before I begin writing about my childhood, let me share a little Detroit history with you.

My beloved city of Detroit was once one of the most admired cities in America. In fact, in 1963, the mayor at the time, **Jerome Patrick Cavanagh**, was preparing a bid for the 1968 Olympics, even beating out Los Angeles in the early stages. Officials planned to break ground for the games at the Michigan State Fairgrounds, with **Wayne State University's campus** serving as the Olympic Village. However, Detroit ultimately lost the bid to Mexico City.

Despite these grand plans, 1967 became a boiling point for the city, marking an unstable and frightening time for many. For people of color, it was particularly harrowing, as nothing seemed fair, and the situation grew increasingly frustrating. The root causes of the tension included a lack of economic job opportunities, insufficient job training programs, housing discrimination, subpar education systems, failed infrastructures, judicial inequities, and, perhaps most significantly, the mistreatment and intimidation by the **Detroit Police Department**.

At the time, the police force operated by its own set of rules, frequently terrorizing and harassing members of the Black community without cause. They routinely targeted citizens for beatings and unjust arrests, fueling mistrust and resentment among residents.

Detroit's schools were far less diverse than they are today, yet the city had its bright spots.

The car manufacturing industry was booming, and the **Motown Sound** dominated the charts, bringing global recognition to Detroit's cultural vibrancy.

25

It all began on a Sunday, July 23rd, at the intersection of **12th and Clairmount Street**. A homecoming celebration for two Vietnam veterans was being held on the second floor of the Economy Printing Company, which doubled as an illegal after-hours club and gambling spot—what the police referred to as a **Blind Pig**.
Two Black undercover officers were sent in to make a drug buy. After the transaction, the police broke through the front door with a sledgehammer and raided the club.

Outside, three or four paddy wagons waited to transport the 80 to 85 attendees who were arrested. Word of the raid spread quickly, and Detroit's simmering anger began to boil over. Bottles and bricks were hurled at police cars. Fires erupted. Law and order began to break down as the community's long-standing mistrust of the police ignited into full-blown rebellion.

This event marked the beginning of the **Rebellion of 1967**—the most severe civil disorder in Detroit's history and one of the darkest chapters in the city's timeline. From July 23rd to July 28th, the chaos engulfed many parts of Detroit. By the time it ended, over 1,000 people were injured, and 43 lives were lost—33 Black and 10 white.

As pandemonium escalated, the **National Guard** was called in by Governor **George W. Romney** to assist the Detroit Police in quelling the fires and looting. A command post was set up in the very hospital where I was born, **Herman Kiefer Hospital**.
National Guard troops also used **Detroit Central High School's football field** as their campsite.

The situation grew so dire that President **Lyndon B. Johnson** had to deploy the **82nd and 101st Airborne Divisions**.

The rebellion spilled over from Detroit into neighboring cities like **Highland Park** and **Hamtramck**, with looting, fires, and the torching of vehicles becoming widespread.

The events of those days left an indelible mark on Detroit, its people, and its history.

Volunteer free food pantries began opening all over the city to help people who had lost their homes during the destruction. These pantries became a lifeline for those who had been displaced and left without basic necessities.

At the time, there were no Black firefighters in Detroit, and only 5 percent of the police force was Black.

The racial tension within the force itself was so severe that Black officers were being shot at by their own comrades during the rebellion.

A few days into the uprising, the jails became so overcrowded that law enforcement had to transport prisoners to **Belle Isle**, temporarily holding them in the park's bathhouses. The chaos led to a shortage of blood supplies for victims, both Black and white, leaving hospitals struggling to care for the injured.

Snipers hid in vacant buildings, targeting law enforcement under the cover of night. To counter this, police used tear gas to flush out the snipers, often filling entire buildings with gas to regain control. Meanwhile, some stores that were unaffected by the destruction began **price gouging**, exploiting the chaos and desperation of the five-day atrocities.

Most Black business owners were unable to recover after the devastation. Insurance claims for property damage were often denied, and many couldn't afford to make the necessary repairs. As a result, countless Black-owned stores and shops were lost forever.

Five days of fear, violence, and destruction completely unraveled this once-model city.

Something else unfolded during and after the 1967 rebellion that further devastated Detroit—it marked the beginning of the **exodus**, commonly referred to as **White Flight**.

At one time, Blacks and whites lived together in harmony throughout many neighborhoods.

But by the 1940s and 1950s, **90 percent of Detroit's population was white**, while most Black residents were confined to poorer areas like **Detroit's Black Bottom** due to a practice called **Redlining**. This systemic discrimination excluded Black families from purchasing homes or living in predominantly white neighborhoods. Economic threats, physical intimidation, and outright violence were used to keep them out.

During the rebellion of 1967, over **one million white residents** began packing up and leaving urban Detroit in droves, moving their families and businesses to the suburbs.

Steel industries, car manufacturers, and small local businesses followed, relocating outside the city limits. The mass departure left Detroit's Black population without jobs, training opportunities, or adequate education, forcing many families onto welfare.

By the mid-1970s, Detroit had become a majority Black city.

Here's an interesting fact I discovered while starting this book: right before I was born, African Americans had to pay a $2 poll tax just to vote in elections. This was a deliberate form of voter suppression designed to keep Black citizens from participating in democracy.

I honestly didn't know about this until now, and it underscores why we need our books to remain accessible in schools today.

This history must not be erased.

Personal Timeline 1965

It happened.

While addressing an audience inside a grand ballroom, this brilliant man, a beacon of truth and empowerment, was brutally assassinated. The world lost a revolutionary voice that day. Just one week before, his home had been firebombed in a heinous act of hatred and intimidation.

At the time, I had no interest in studying the Muslim religion. Yet, as the years passed, his teachings began to resonate with me, shaping my perspectives on truth, justice, and equality. He was a man who fearlessly confronted the injustices of his time, even when he knew his life was at risk.

Many years after his death, my father started reading the **Holy Quran**, and soon, copies of the **Muhammad Speaks** newspaper began finding their way into our home. Curiosity led me to pick up those newspapers, and I found them profoundly informative. The articles opened my eyes to a world of knowledge and ideas that I had never considered before.

Who was this brave man who knew his end was near and yet continued to speak truth to power until he was abruptly silenced on February 21, 1965?

Malcolm X.

Make no mistake about it—Malcolm X was not just a man. He was a movement, a force of nature who challenged the status quo and demanded dignity and equality for his people. His words, though often controversial, pierced through the lies of the time, leaving behind an enduring legacy that still influences me today.

My dad worked tirelessly to provide for his wife and children, and he did an outstanding job.

But life has a way of throwing unforeseen challenges, and I trulybelieve the **1967 rebellion** played a significant role in shaping the struggles that followed.

For my family, 1967 was a dream-killing year. It wasn't just the material losses—it was the ripple effect on a young, growing family's aspirations. For many years, I struggled to understand why our family's hardships seemed to linger, why it felt like we were stuck in an endless loop of challenges.

But as I grew into adulthood, the clarity came.

I began to see the invisible threads connecting our struggles to the societal upheaval of the time. I began to understand why my family became who we are today.

We were rich—not in money, but in determination. That unshakable will to endure and overcome was, and still is, a defining family trait.

Without a family setback, there can be no family triumph. This is not just a story. It's a vital family memory—a piece of who we are.

— **Eric Wright**

Chapter 2

Detroit's Dumbarton Street:
A Childhood in Chaos

My dad said we'd have to move as soon as possible. Our apartment building was next in line to be demolished on the block. It had been constructed sometime between 1923 and 1924, after the city removed the railroad that once passed through the area. Over the years, black mold and asbestos had overtaken the structure, making it uninhabitable. It wasn't safe for anyone to live there anymore.

We were among the last tenants to leave. We didn't have much, but Dad managed to find us a new place and moved what few belongings we owned to our next destination.

Before we left **Seville Court**, I had to process and sort through all the memories—both good and bad—that I couldn't leave behind. I also had to give away my two Cocker Spaniel puppies, **Chico and Rico**, because the new place didn't allow pets. That was tough. Everything I knew, everything I was familiar with, was here on

Dumbarton Street.

The memories of that old building and the surrounding neighborhoods ran deep. I was the firstborn in my family, and so much of my early life unfolded within those walls. My parents and I initially lived in the basement of the building before moving to the fifth floor and, later, to the third floor. **Apartment B5** is where it all began for me.

I recall being a very sick child. I was born with a heart murmur, rheumatic fever, and a mysterious skin virus that caused sores and scabs to cover my body, leaving my skin peeling away in painful patches. I vividly remember my dad carrying me up a flight of stairs, rushing me into the car, and taking me to the hospital. I must have been about three or four years old.

My mom later told me how she had to soak me in a warm bath with prescribed medicine to help my skin heal. It amazes me that I can still remember this part of my life so clearly.

Life in the basement quarters wasn't easy, but my parents taught me important lessons during that time. They didn't have a high chair to teach me and my sister how to feed ourselves. Instead, they spread newspapers on the floor, placed us in the center, and set a plate of food between our legs. That's how we learned to eat on our own. Our favorite snack was **Cracker Jacks**—I loved the thrill of finding the prize hidden inside the box.

Learning to tie my shoes was another challenge. It took me ages to master, and my dad often grew frustrated with my slow progress. I must have been a mischievous kid because I also remember getting disciplined quite harshly. Yes, I got my butt whipped with an **extension cord** at an early age. The welts would stay on my tender skin for days. Today, that kind of punishment would undoubtedly be considered child abuse. How times have changed.

My memories take me to one sweltering summer in **July 1967**, a time when all hell broke loose on Dumbarton Street. By then, my younger sister, my little brother, and my baby sister—who had been born just a month earlier—were all living with us in the same apartment.

We didn't understand why we could no longer go across the street to play at **McShane Park** or why the nights were filled with so much noise and chaos. As a curious child, I wanted answers.

One night, I decided to jump onto the couch, stand on the headrest, and pull myself up onto the window ledge to get a better view. What I saw left me in utter disbelief.

The night skies were painted blood red. Buildings and houses all around us were engulfed in flames, burning to the ground.

People ran frantically through the streets, screaming in terror and shouting profanities. Police cars and fire trucks were stationed everywhere, their lights flashing against the smoky backdrop.

Army tanks and armed National Guards were stationed right in front of our window.

It was a chilling sight that added to the already overwhelming tension. We had to turn off all the lights and sleep on the floor, fearing stray bullets that might ricochet through our apartment.

It was an uneasy and terrifying time, and as a child, I couldn't fully understand why people were so angry and upset.

Dumbarton Street and the surrounding neighborhoods were engulfed in flames. The destruction seemed endless.

Within a couple of days, my dad and uncle brought home a brand-new television and record player console. Later in life, I discovered the truth—they had participated in the looting that occurred during the rebellion. Looking back, I can't entirely blame them for their choices, but it's still something that sits uneasily in my memory.

There was a strict **curfew** in place, keeping people off the streets between 9 p.m. and 5 a.m. It was the first and only time I personally witnessed **Martial Law** in Detroit. The rebellion left devastating numbers in its wake: 43 lives lost, over 1,000 injured, more than 7,200 arrested, and over 2,000 buildings damaged or destroyed. Entire city blocks were reduced to ruins, leaving hundreds of families homeless. It was far worse than the racial riots Detroit had experienced in **1943**.

My dad didn't need to be among those counted in the looting statistics, though. We had it good during those turbulent times.

My family was part of the **middle class**, and we had the best of everything. My dad provided for us well, ensuring we had nice clothes, reliable transportation, and memorable holidays.

I still remember his station wagon with the wood grain panels on the doors—it felt like a symbol of stability and pride. On special occasions, my brother and I wore little suits, while my sisters were dressed in tiny beautiful dresses.

Christmas was always magical in our house. My parents had a tradition of hiding our gifts in trash bags under an old baby bed mattress. Every year, they told us we wouldn't be getting anything for Christmas, but we always knew better.

My siblings and I had discovered their hiding spot long ago and would sneak a peek at what each of us was getting. By the time Christmas morning came, we were pros at pretending to be surprised!

My dad worked for **Ford Motors** before later transitioning to a job at the **Eastern Market Meat Packing House**. One time, he took me on a guest tour of his workplace.

Before entering the massive walk-in refrigerators, I had to wear little rubber boots and a child-sized lab coat. When the doors opened, I was hit with a sight I'll never forget. Blood covered the floors, and skinless cows and pigs hung upside down from giant hooks. The metallic smell of blood was overwhelming, and the scene was like something out of a nightmare. I panicked, crying and screaming for him to get me out of there. My dad thought it was hilarious and laughed so hard it seemed like the joke of the day to him.

Another vivid memory interrupts my thoughts—this one about my mother. My mom was deaf, unable to hear or speak, but she communicated with us through **sign language**.

She often asked me to accompany her to the laundry room, which was just down the hallway from our apartment.

One Saturday morning, we went to wash a few loads of clothes. Back then, washing machines didn't have rinse cycles. Instead, there was a large porcelain wash basin on four legs with two electric rollers on top.

The process was labor-intensive: you washed the clothes in the basin, fed them through the rollers to squeeze out the soapy water, dipped them into clean water, and then ran them through the rollers again before putting them into the dryer.

I was a curious and mischievous child, always finding ways to get myself into trouble. That day, while my mom wasn't paying attention, I decided to see if my hand could pass through the rollers and come back out again. It couldn't. My tiny hand and wrist were caught, and the machine continued pulling me forward.

I screamed for my mom, but she couldn't hear my cries of agony. My forearm kept feeding through the rollers, and no matter how hard I pulled, I couldn't free myself.

Desperate and terrified, I yelled even louder, the pain becoming unbearable. Suddenly, my mom looked over and saw me trapped and in despair.

She dropped everything, rushed over, and hit the button to stop the unsafe contraption of a machine. My mom saved me that day, and from that moment on, she has always been my **Super Shero**.

Personal Timeline 1966 and 1967

The years 1966 and 1967 were pivotal, brimming with cultural, social, and historical milestones that continue to resonate today. In the world of music, **The Beatles** released their groundbreaking album **"Revolver"** in 1966. Widely regarded as one of the most innovative albums of all time, it featured hits like "Eleanor Rigby" and "Yellow Submarine." The album showcased the band's creative evolution, blending rock with orchestral arrangements and experimental techniques. Meanwhile, the legendary **Temptations** had their own moment on the music charts with **"Beauty is Only Skin Deep."**

The song, written by the iconic Motown duo **Norman Whitfield** and **Eddie Holland**, became a soulful anthem, emphasizing the importance of inner beauty over outward appearances. It further solidified the Motown Sound as a defining force in the music industry.

By 1967, **Aretha Franklin** released her empowering hit

"Respect," which quickly became an anthem for both the civil rights and women's liberation movements. Originally written by Otis Redding, Aretha's rendition added an undeniable strength and urgency, transforming the song into a universal call for dignity and equality.

In sports history, **January 1967** marked the birth of a new era with the very first **Super Bowl**. The Green Bay Packers, led by legendary coach **Vince Lombardi**, faced off against the Kansas City Chiefs. The Packers emerged victorious, cementing their place in football history and laying the foundation for what would become one of America's most celebrated annual events.

The political landscape also saw groundbreaking change in 1967, with **Thurgood Marshall** making history as the first African American appointed to the **U.S. Supreme Court**.

Known for his work as the lead attorney in the landmark **Brown v. Board of Education** case,

Marshall's appointment was a monumental step forward for racial equality and justice in America.

The arts and entertainment world were also thriving. The rise of **psychedelic rock** brought artists like **Jimi Hendrix** and bands like **The Doors** into the spotlight, reshaping the music industry.

Movies like **"The Good, the Bad, and the Ugly"** captivated audiences, while TV shows like **"Star Trek"** and **"Batman"** became cultural phenomena.

These two years were a mix of innovation, rebellion, and triumph. Music, sports, and politics reflected the changing times and helped lay the groundwork for future generations to break barriers and redefine possibilities.

Chapter 3

Dumbarton: April 4th, 1968

1968 was a tense and difficult time for me to understand, to say the least. One day, my uncle came over to show off what looked like a new fountain pen. He bragged that he had ordered it from a weapons magazine. Back then, you could purchase all kinds of unusual items from the back pages of magazines.

But this wasn't your typical ink pen. It was a **tear gas pen**, likely a relic from World War II. My father examined it briefly before firmly telling my uncle to put it away and keep it far from his kids.

After a few drinks, my uncle got up, went to the restroom, and locked the door behind him. Forty-five minutes to an hour later, a strange odor began filling the air, followed by smoke seeping from under the door. My dad knocked but got no answer. After a few moments of silence, he made the decision to break down the locked door. Inside, he found my uncle unconscious on the bathroom floor. My dad dragged him out and quickly realized the cause—my uncle had set off the tear gas pen.

Just a few days later, on **Thursday, April 4th**, my uncle returned to our apartment to apologize to my parents for the incident. As they sat in the kitchen talking, a news bulletin interrupted the program on our black-and-white television.

"Dr. Martin Luther King has just been shot."

The announcer's voice carried a tone of shock and sorrow. I'll never forget the sadness that filled the room. My uncle cried openly, and the look of disbelief on my parents' faces left an indelible mark on my memory. At my young age, I couldn't fully grasp the weight of what had just happened.

About an hour later, another news bulletin flashed across the screen.

"To all our viewers around the country, we have received terrible news.

Civil Rights Leader and peacemaker Dr. Martin Luther King has died. He passed away at 7:05 pm. this evening."

My parents and uncle's sadness turned to pain and anger.

Their grief seemed to swell as they sat at the kitchen table, drinking and discussing the tragedy that had just unfolded.

Meanwhile, I remained glued to the television, still trying to process everything. On the screen, I saw a woman of remarkable strength—a widow who had just lost her husband, standing strong for her children and her community.

That woman was **Mrs. Coretta Scott King**.

Even in the face of unimaginable tragedy, she radiated dignity and grace. Her presence on the screen was captivating, a beacon of calm amidst chaos. In that moment, I didn't fully understand the magnitude of her role, but I could see her strength. Over time, I came to realize that Coretta Scott King was more than the wife of Dr. King—she was a powerful force in her own right.

Born in Alabama, Coretta was deeply involved in the civil rights movement alongside her husband. She was an accomplished singer and musician, often using her talents to raise funds for the cause.

After Dr. King's assassination, Concetta carried on his legacy with unwavering determination. She became an advocate for nonviolence, economic justice, and racial equality, cementing her place in history as a leader in her own right.

Her courage in the face of loss inspired millions, including me. As I watched her on that television, I saw not just a grieving widow, but a woman who embodied resilience, strength, and hope.

Looking back, the memories of those days in **Apartment B5** remain vivid. From getting whipped with extension cords to sitting on newspapers to learn how to feed myself, from struggling to tie my shoes, to witnessing the chaos of the Detroit rebellion—these moments are etched into my mind.

But the events of April 4th, **1968**, stand out.

The deaths of **Dr. Martin Luther King, John F. Kennedy, Bobby Kennedy, Malcolm X, Medgar Evers**, and so many other civil rights leaders shaped my understanding of the world. They were tragedies that unfolded before my young eyes, often on our black-and-white television. Yet, amidst the pain and loss, there was a glimmer of hope and beauty in **Mrs. Coretta Scott King**. For me, her strength was nothing short of extraordinary.

Personal Timeline 1968

Just fifteen months after the rebellion that left Detroit scarred and divided, the city found a reason to come together in celebration. The Detroit Tigers won the World Series, defeating the St. Louis Cardinals in a thrilling seven-game series.

At that moment, it wasn't about race relations, political strife, or the wounds that had been inflicted upon the city just a year before. For a brief and beautiful time, the city of Detroit became united in victory. People of all races, neighborhoods, and walks of life celebrated together as if nothing else mattered. The Tigers' triumph on the field wasn't just a win for the team—it was a win for the city.

That series showcased the talent and determination of players like **Denny McLain**, who had an incredible season with 31 wins, and **Mickey Lolich**, who pitched his heart out and earned MVP honors for his performance in the World Series.

Willie Horton, one of Detroit's own and a key player, became a symbol of pride for the city's Black community.

Horton, who grew up in Detroit, was more than just a baseball player—he was a hometown hero.

Game seven, played on October 10th, **1968**, was unforgettable. Mickey Lolich pitched on short rest and led the Tigers to a 4-1 victory over Bob Gibson, the Cardinals' ace. When the final out was made, a sense of euphoria swept through Detroit.

People poured into the streets to celebrate, cheering, hugging, and waving Tigers pennants.

In that wonderful moment in time, Detroiters weren't Black or white—they were simply champions. The wounds of the past were momentarily forgotten, replaced by a shared joy that transcended racial and economic barriers. For those few days, the city wasn't divided by its struggles; it was united by its triumph.

We had all become champions.
Every single one of us.
Detroiters made it to become number one.

— Eric Wright

Chapter 4

The Move to the 5th Floor

1970 was a challenging year, as I remember it. The basement in our apartment building had started flooding every week. Eventually, all the tenants living down there were forced to relocate to the upper floors. For my family, this meant moving to **Apartment 507 on the 5th floor.**

Now, with four children and another on the way, we had to squeeze into an even smaller apartment. It was one of the few units left available at the time. All the larger two- and three-bedroom apartments were already taken. My parents slept in the one bedroom, while the rest of us shared the living room, sleeping on roll-away folding beds.

My brother and I stored our bed in a closet, while my sisters folded theirs and leaned it against the wall each day. Looking back, the living conditions were cramped and far from ideal, but as kids, we didn't realize how congested things were. To us, this was normal. We made the best of it, turning our tiny home into an imaginative playground.

We had endless fun, leaping from one bed to another, running up and down the hallways, and finding adventures on the elevator. The limitations of space didn't dampen our spirits—if anything, they fueled our creativity and energy.

While we were busy being kids, my mother was facing unimaginable challenges. Expecting her fifth child, she received devastating news from her doctors: she had breast cancer. I can only imagine how difficult this pregnancy must have been for her, balancing the physical toll of carrying a child with the emotional weight of her diagnosis.

The day finally came for my youngest sister to enter the world.

I remember my dad leaving my mom at the hospital to undergo surgery to remove the cancer.

When he returned home, he brought with him a beautiful baby girl, with a head full of curly, jet-black hair.

I adored my baby sister. Holding her in my arms, I loved running my fingers through her soft curls. To my older sister, she was like her very own human baby doll. We all marveled at how beautiful she was. To this day, the smell of baby oil still brings back memories of my little sister as a newborn.

While Mom recovered in the hospital, my dad took on the full responsibility of caring for us. He made sure we took our baths, wore clean clothes, and made it safely across the street to school every morning. Braiding my sisters' hair was a particular challenge, and feeding us often became an adventure of its own.

One morning, Dad decided to make us breakfast. He served scrambled eggs—with beer mixed in for flavor. Yes, you read that right. Scrambled eggs with beer. To this day, I still wonder what made him think that combination would work. It was the nastiest meal I've ever eaten in my life. But despite the culinary mishap, he did the best he could.

That year was tough for him too. He had just been laid off from his job. First, he lost his position at **Ford Motors**, and now, his job at the **Packing House** was gone as well. Still, he kept his spirits high.

"Don't worry, I'll get another one," he reassured us. "Right now, I just need to get your mother back home and well."

We faced so many challenges that year, but we got through them together. My parents applied for government assistance to help us get by, and somehow, we managed. As kids, our attention spans were too short to grasp the full extent of our financial struggles.

We were happy with what we had—our living room playground and plenty of toys to keep us occupied.

One toy in particular stood out: our **Close 'n Play phonograph record player**.

We loved that little machine and played the only record we owned over and over again.

"A B C, it's easy as 1 2 3, as simple as do re mi… A B C, 1 2 3, baby, you and me!"

That **Jackson Five** song became the soundtrack to our lives in that tiny 5th-floor apartment. It was a reminder that even in tough times, joy could always be found in the simplest things.

The moral of this story is that resilience, love, and togetherness can help a family overcome even the most challenging circumstances. Despite financial struggles, cramped living conditions, and health hardships, the family found ways to adapt and persevere.

The children discovered joy in simple things, while the parents prioritized their well-being and worked tirelessly to keep them safe and cared for. This chapter reminds us that, even in the hardest times, hope, creativity, and love can flourish, shaping us into stronger and more compassionate individuals.

Personal Timeline 1970

My parents were married on **July 25th, 1970**. My dad was 32, and my mom was 28. Out of all the social events I remember from my childhood, it's funny that I can't recall what we did as a family or even the mood on their wedding day. What I do find amusing is that my mom didn't have to change her last name when she married my dad—she was already a Wright.

Now, let's see. What else happened that year?

On **October 31st, 1970**, three and a half years after being stripped of his championship title for refusing to register for the Vietnam War, my dad's favorite sports figure and humanitarian, **Muhammad Ali**, finally made his triumphant return to the ring.

Ali, who had become a symbol of courage and conviction, regained his boxing license and fought **Jerry Quarry** in **Atlanta, Georgia**. In true Ali fashion, he stopped Quarry in the 3rd round.

They met again on **June 27, 1972**, for a rematch, and this time Ali finished Quarry in the 7th round. My dad followed Ali's career religiously, and over time, it became something special that bonded us. Watching Ali's fights on **ABC's Wide World of Sports** became one of our favorite things to do together.

I'd sit on the couch, and my dad would settle into his favorite chair. Together, we dissected every round, analyzing Ali's footwork, his famous "rope-a-dope," and, of course, his unmatched charisma. Those moments became some of the best father-son memories of my life.

Ali wasn't just a sports figure to us. He was a larger-than-life humanitarian, and one of his quotes has stayed with me:

"Service to others is the rent you pay for your room here on earth."

— Muhammad Ali

On another note, my dad had a second favorite icon: Elvis Presley. I always thought that was a bit unusual, but it never failed to entertain us. He'd crack us up trying to dance and sing like Elvis. He wasn't even close (laughing)

Chapter 5

The Making of a Small-Time Hustler

Two years after the Detroit rebellion, my neighborhood still bore the scars of annihilation and the aftermath of bruised city blocks. What was once a middle-class area had turned into a ghetto in a matter of days. As a child, I couldn't understand why people would destroy their own property. It seemed senseless to me. Burning down perfectly good homes and apartment buildings accomplished nothing except making our streets look like a war zone.

Even at that young age, I didn't agree with the destruction. But it would take years for me to understand the pain, frustration, and suffering that drove people to such extreme measures.

Walking down **West Grand River Avenue**, the devastation was undeniable. Abandoned storefronts and boarded-up food markets stood as grim reminders of what had been lost. Many of these structures were unsafe to stand near, with debris still falling from their crumbling facades. On street corners, grown men stood smoking half-finished cigarettes, reminiscing about the loot they had taken from the stores they once supported.

The negatives were glaring—it had taken only five days to tear the city down, but rebuilding would take decades. However, amidst the pain, loss, and racial divide, I discovered a surprising positive: an opportunity to make money from the devastation and destruction.

One morning, I found an old grocery cart in the back alley. As I strolled up the block, a brilliant idea came to me. I started collecting fallen bricks from abandoned and burned-down homes in the area, loading them into the cart. When I got home, I asked my dad if he had any extra sandpaper lying around. I used it to smooth the bricks down and began turning them into ashtrays.

Because the heat from the fires had partially shaped the bricks, they were easy to work with. I used a paint set I had received the previous Christmas to add color and detail. To finish them off, I sprayed them with a glossy coating using my dad's old spray cans.

The very next day, I went door to door selling my handcrafted ashtrays. Pretty creative, huh? No other kid thought of doing something like that. It was brilliance in the making.

It's amazing how resourceful the mind can be when you're motivated by the desire for penny candies, 25-cent Fay-go sodas, and 10-cent bags of chips.

Eventually, I grew tired of painting and selling ashtrays, so I came up with another idea to make a profit. At the time, you could order garden seeds from the back pages of certain magazines. A case contained fifty variety packs of flower, vegetable, and fruit seeds. I started walking door to door, selling these seed packets to neighbors. It was a good time to sell because, after the rebellion, people were trying to regrow their own food or redo their front yards.

I would collect all the money, place it in a special envelope provided with the case, and mail it back to the company. In return, the company sent me a small percentage of the sales. For a while, I was honest and followed the rules. But then I came up with a shady scheme.

I filled out the order form with a fake name and used the same building address but listed an unoccupied apartment number. I would sit at the end of the hallway each day, waiting for the package to be delivered. Back then, it was easy to pull off. I would receive the seeds, sell them door to door, and keep all the money.

This went on for weeks until my dad figured out what I was doing. Boy, did I get my butt beat. My dad didn't play when it came to dishonesty in any shape or form.

It's probably the reason why I try so hard to be honest today. My dad was as strong as an ox, athletic, and heavy-handed.

He would hold me upside down by one leg and whip the life out of me. My mom hated to see me punished like that. It broke her heart to see her firstborn son get into trouble time and time again. You could see the sadness in her eyes.

Yet, as much as it pained her, she eventually decided to add whippings to her own repertoire. Thinking back, I can't blame her one bit—I was definitely a handful. Those harsh punishments from both my parents gradually set me on the right path. Though painful at the time, they helped shape me into the person I would become.

The moral of this story is that life's challenges, even those rooted in adversity, can fuel creativity and resourcefulness. It shows how necessity can drive innovation, as a young mind turns devastation into opportunity. However, it also teaches the importance of honesty and integrity. While shortcuts may seem tempting, they come with consequences that shape us in profound ways. Through discipline and love, even the toughest lessons from family can guide us toward becoming better, more responsible individuals.

There's absolutely nothing wrong with someone older teaching you valuable lessons about life. However, when the person you choose to trust has a negative ulterior motive, it can leave a devastating and lasting impact on your life.

If you keep the pain bottled up and don't talk about it, it will change you forever. Never be afraid to tell someone what has happened or is happening to you. **Get help.**

Here are some important resources that are available 24/7:

- **Substance Abuse and Mental Health Helpline:** (800) 662-HELP (4357)
- **Suicide & Crisis Lifeline:** Call or text 988 (formerly 800-273-TALK)
- **National Sexual Assault Hotline:** (800) 656-HOPE (4673)
- **National Street Harassment Hotline:** (855) 897-5910
- **National Runaway Safeline:** (800) RUNAWAY (786-2929)
- **National Human Trafficking Hotline:** (888) 373-7888 or text HELP to 233733

When you reach this part of the book, write these numbers down and keep them in a safe place. Share this information with someone you believe might be in need or trouble. **You could be saving someone's life.**

Pay attention to the signs. If you suspect something is happening to a child, don't be afraid to ask if they've been touched inappropriately by an adult. Sometimes, all it takes is someone to listen and care to make a difference.

Chapter 6

A Playful S.A.

This is a part of my life that I never shared -not even with my mother.

All these years I kept it blocked from my memories. As a child, these events damaged and took a lasting effect on me for a very long time. After everyone was forced to move to the upper floors from the basement, I kept going down there to see if I could find a few things that tenants left behind.

One day I found this old cassette player with a dusty cassette tape next to it. It was the James Brown's classic and 1965 hit, Papa's Got a Brand New Bag. I put it in the tape deck and it still worked. I listened to the song until suddenly I hear another voice in the basement with me. "Hey what are you doing down here" he asked. It was a guy in his late teens, maybe twenty years old. I explained that I often come down to see what old things I could find that people left behind. Well you shouldn't be down here by yourself. It's dangerous and you never know who else is down here. I suggest you never come down here again. This person sounded very concerned for my safety and made sure I got the hell from down there.

The very next day as I was getting ready to walk to the store, I saw the same person in the apartment lobby. Good morning. How are you? Where are you on your way to? I told him I was walking to the store. "If you don't mind, I'll walk with you" he says to me. This went on for several weeks as I gained his trust and was sure that he was friendly enough to hang around with.

One late evening I came off the elevator and as the door opened, he was once again waiting for me in the lobby.

Hey! Where you going? I told him I was going outside to play with some friends. Sit down on these stair for a minute with me. The subject of bullies came up.

Do you get picked on by any bullies in school? No not really. Well do you know how to defend yourself if someone tried to bully you? I think so. Well let me show you some wrestling techniques to use just in case.

I became curious and stepped off the staircase onto the carpeted floor with him. He showed me a few arm and neck locks. He even showed me a few flips. Afterwards, I told him I had to be home by 8pm. Hey, I understand. I'll see you tomorrow. Then, you can show me what I taught you. As he walked toward the lobby doors, I took the trip up the sometimes working elevator.

Around 12 am the next day, we finished our chores and my mom kicked us all out to go across the street to play on the playground. This time the elevator wasn't working so, we all ran down the flights of stairs. Once I got to the lobby, the same guy was waiting for me again. Hey little buddy, how are you. You ready to show me those moves?

As my siblings left me, I couldn't wait to show him the arm twist. Oh wow! That's awesome. I'm going to show you something new today. What would you do if I grabbed you from behind like this? How would you get out of this hold? I tried to break loose from his tight grip when suddenly I felt him rubbing his genital against me. I felt him humping me. This person who I thought was my friend, a big brother, someone who I began to trust, wouldn't let me go until he had his orgasm. I knew this was a terrible thing that he had done to me and even though this wasn't my fault. It made me feel dirty.
I finally broke free from his grip. In that moment, I thanked God that the situation hadn't escalated further, despite the unsettling nature of what had happened.

This could've been far worse if he went any further. I frantically ran back up the staircase, hoping that he wouldn't try and chase me down. Once I got home my mother could see the fear on my face. She asked me what was wrong and I told her I didn't feel like playing on the playground today and that I'd rather stay home and help her around the apartment.

I was to embarrassed to explain what just happened to me. I was still trying to process why he chose me to take full advantage of. What I really wanted was my mother's love and protection. I thinks that's when I became a mama's boy. For weeks I stayed home with her. I felt protected.

Once I finally got the courage to go outside again, I didn't see a trace of this stranger that took advantage of me. In my mind, I was finally comfortable enough to say that he was gone forever. I was back to my playful self again. Going across the street to the park, walking to school or anywhere else I wanted to go by myself.

So, we couldn't do the family's laundry in the basement anymore because of the flood and it was also just too dangerous to even go down there. Besides, the building removed all the washing machines and dryers. We had to go to the next building over to clean our clothes.

There was a few times where my mom let my sister do the family laundry. I used to run passed the other building's basement windows, knock on them and run. Teasing my sister that she had to clean our clothes as one of her household chores. She was starting to do this on her own every couple of weeks.

One day she was cleaning our clothes and when I looked inside the window this time, the child molester was in the laundry room with her. Seeing him engaging in a conversation with my sister shook me to the core. I pounded on the thick glass window and screamed as loud as I could for him to get the fuck away from her.

I suddenly got the courage to tell him that if he didn't leave I was going to run and tell my dad what he had already done to me. He disappeared and this time, I never saw him ever again.

I'd like to think that he moved away or he came across the wrong kid or person, sending him off to prison or better yet, to his death.

Moral of the Story, Sometimes life puts us in situations where we must choose between staying silent or finding the courage to speak out. Protecting yourself and those you love takes bravery, even when the fear feels overwhelming. Painful experiences may shape us, but they don't have to define us. There is always strength in standing up for what's right, seeking help, and ensuring others don't face the same harm. Let this serve as a reminder: you are stronger than you realize, and speaking out can be the beginning of healing and change.

Chapter 7

The Most Beautiful Bully I'd Ever Seen

Well, that bully finally came into my life in elementary school, but this bully didn't come as a dominant, young male figure.

As a small child, my mother didn't allow me to play beyond Dumbarton. We lived in the front part of the building, so she could always see where I was or what I was doing. However, I can also remember that once she wasn't in the window, I would always manage to wander off on my Big Wheel, a block over to Petoskey Street, just to see this little girl play in her yard. The curiosity of a pretty girl started at an early age.

Once we got to Big Angell Elementary School, which was on Holmur Street between Euclid and Virginia Park, things changed. This person I had been admiring for a couple of years decided that she wanted to embarrass and harass me every chance she got. For some reason, she didn't like me. I never knew why, but she chose to become my bully. Maybe she wasn't into boys. Maybe boys were yucky to her.

I tried to offer her my penny candy, but she would slap the candy out of my hand. On cupcake day at school, I tried to buy her one, but she would slap that out of my hand as well. This pretty girl was very mean to me.

One day, she and some friends saw me walking home from school. They all ran to catch up with me. "Watch this," she said to the other girls. She slapped all my books out of my hands, and they all laughed. When I tried to pick up the books, she kicked them into the street. Her friends laughed even harder.

I knew that if I retaliated, I would feel terrible. After all, I still had a major crush on her. I didn't want to do anything that would tarnish that. I knew I could hurt her—I just didn't want to.

Walking to and from Big Angell Elementary School became a struggle for me. Picking my books up off the ground became a daily ritual.

But no matter what she did, my feelings for her never wavered. Eventually, this annoyance had gotten to a point where enough was enough. She had to be stopped, and the laughter had to come to an end. Kicking my books further into the street had gone way too far by this point.

One day after school, the leader and her pack of girlfriends pointed me out and ran to catch up with me. The bully walked closely behind me, pushed all my books out of my arms, and, once again, kicked them into the street.

I'd had enough. I immediately grabbed her arm and twisted it behind her back. At the same time, she suddenly slipped off the curb, fell, and broke her arm. I was stunned. I couldn't believe what had just happened. Seeing her in so much pain really traumatized me. First, I had just committed bodily harm to my crush. Second, I had used the very arm twist that my molester taught me.

I didn't know what else to do, so I left her there crying in pain, picked up all my books, and ran home.

The next day, her parents came over to tell my dad what I had done. What I didn't know was that this girl was also my sister's best friend and classmate. I tried hiding from the situation, but that's how her parents found out exactly where I lived—my sister had provided that information.

My dad had taught me at an early age to never hit a girl, no matter what. When he explained the situation to my mom, she was devastated.

It was the very first time my mom decided to whip me. I was also suspended from school for two weeks, and my bully hated me even more. The very next time I saw her was about four months later.

The cast had been removed from her tiny arm, and she was finally able to leave her front yard, walk a block over to Dumbarton, and play with my sister. On one of her visits, we all decided to play hide and seek.

Our building had plenty of places to hide—anywhere in the front lobby or outside in the flower court. At the time, bushes lined up in front of the building made for an excellent hiding spot. Somehow, we both ended up behind those bushes.

As we sat there, she looked at me with disgust on her face. It was a very awkward situation for both of us. We just sat there in silence, waiting for someone to find us. The sooner, the better. I wanted so badly to tell her how sorry I was, but I was afraid she would hit me. Finally, I built up enough courage.

"I'm very sorry I made you break your arm," I said to her. Then, in the stupid bravery of a young boy, I kissed her on the cheek. I closed my eyes, waiting for the smack or the punch, but nothing happened. To my surprise, she didn't react at all. Encouraged, I apologized again and kissed her on the cheek a second time. She sat there quietly, still saying nothing.

To me, that silence meant everything. Without a word, I felt she had accepted my apology. We just sat there until someone finally found us. I felt amazing, like a weight had been lifted off my shoulders.

From that day forward, she still acted as if she didn't like me, but she never bullied me again. I can remember feeling satisfied with just that. After all, I had managed to kiss her without getting slapped in the face. Today, when I visit her Facebook page, I can see all the wonderful accomplishments she has had in her lifetime.

As an adult, she has become such a kind, inspiring, and wonderful human being. The world is lucky to have her in it.

She's still the most beautiful bully I've ever seen.

Chapter 8

My Childhood Introduction to the Word Stress

- *A difficult strain and tension of mental as well as physical pain.*
- *A demanding high level of circumstances.*
- *A cause for worry through difficult challenges or coping with unexpected events.*
- *A human, natural response to what could be a life threat.*
- *An enduring emotional pressure or tension in an uncontrolled situation.*
- *Can cause a lot of sleepless nights.*
- *Can cause a person to indulge in drugs, alcohol, or chain smoking.*

As a young kid, I found out firsthand what the word **stress** really meant. At this point, my mom had five children she still had to clothe, feed, and send off to school. She still had to pay the monthly rent, and my dad still hadn't found a decent-paying job yet. We were receiving government assistance, but it was not enough money for a family of our size to live on. On top of all that, my mom was going through chemotherapy every week.

My mom was a social drinker, but with all the stress, she began to drink more than usual. I could see the worry on her face; she was not herself. Something was wrong, and I didn't like what she was going through. I wanted, somehow, to assure her that things would be okay. As her firstborn, I wanted to protect her as much as she protected me.

One early afternoon, I noticed she was getting pretty intoxicated. I suddenly came up with the idea of hiding her cocktail glass from her.

When she wasn't looking or left the room, I would pick up herglass and put it in a different place in our home, hoping she wouldn't find it and take another drink.

56

But she eventually found the glass, filled it with more alcohol, and placed it back beside her on the table. Undeterred, I would hide it again and quickly run to my bed, slipping under the covers.

Eventually, she got tired of me hiding her drink. Out of frustration, she threw the glass at me.

At that moment, I didn't realize that I was only adding to her stress. The game I thought I was playing with her had become way too much for her to bear. I ducked as the glass shattered against the wall behind me. A large piece of it pierced halfway into my back.

Miraculously, she sobered up instantly. She turned me on my stomach and carefully pulled the glass from my back. She carried me to the bathroom, cleaned the cut, dabbed rubbing alcohol on it, and placed a large patch over the wound. She kept apologizing, assuring me that this would never happen again. Then she hugged me and showered me with kisses.

The very next day, she surprised me by taking me to the old Riviera Theater on Grand River and Joy Road. (Built in 1925 and demolished in 1996.) I was about 7 or 8 years old when this happened. Today, I still have the scar on my back to remind me that life can get very stressful. Stress happens to everyone. You just have to know how to deal with it and stay calm.

Even years later, my dad never managed to secure a good-paying job. Doors kept closing for him. He eventually realized that he had two things working against him: he was hearing impaired, and he was a Black man.

Yes, the color of his skin kept him out of the workforce.

Not long after the rebellion, jobs began moving out of Detroit and into the suburbs.

Once those jobs moved, only a very small percentage of Black men were hired. Despite being young, smart, strong, and athletic, he still couldn't get the jobs he applied for.

Family stories have it that when he was in high school, he was an extremely talented pitcher. He even had a chance to try out for the Detroit Tigers but was turned down for the same reasons: a hearing handicap and being Black. In those days, a Black pitcher was almost unheard of—just like Black quarterbacks in the National Football League back in those days.

So, we stayed on welfare and government assistance. But my mother, God bless her soul, made sure she used the money and food stamps wisely. Back then, you could get a lot of food for a hundred dollars—six or seven paper grocery bags full.

The rent was paid every month, we got nice clothes from the Salvation Army, and every school year, we had brand-new S. S. Kresge plastic-bottom gym shoes to start school with.

We were dirt poor, but at times my mother didn't make it feel that way. She was good with money and always tried to give us what we liked. She sacrificed so much to keep her children happy.

Moral of the Story, resilience is often born out of struggle, and love shines brightest in the darkest times. Despite the obstacles, including systemic racism, poverty, and personal hardships, the strength of a family and the sacrifices of a devoted mother can create moments of joy and stability. Life may deal unfair challenges, but perseverance, resourcefulness, and love can transform even the harshest circumstances into enduring lessons and cherished memories.

Personal Timeline 1970

The classic song from William DeVaughn, "Be Thankful for What You Got," resonated deeply within the Black community when it was released in 1970. Its smooth, soulful rhythm and heartfelt lyrics captured the spirit of resilience and pride that many African Americans held onto during a time of struggle and societal upheaval.

The imagery in the lyrics—**"Diamond in the back, Sunroof top, Diggin' the scene with a gangsta' lean"**—wasn't just about material possessions. It was a metaphor for aspiration, pride, and dignity. For a community that faced systemic racism, economic struggles, and daily adversities, the song was a reminder to appreciate what they had and to celebrate their strength and creativity.

Owning a car, even one that wasn't brand new, but adorned with "gangsta' whitewalls" and "TV antennas in the back," symbolized making the most out of limited resources. It represented self-expression and pride in individuality. The song's message urged listeners to find joy and satisfaction in their lives, no matter their circumstances.

At its core, **"Be Thankful for What You Got"** became an anthem for a community striving for more but refusing to let poverty or discrimination rob them of their humanity and hope. It was about creating beauty and value in their lives and holding their heads high, even in the face of adversity.

It's remarkable how much time has changed the school system.

Throughout the years, with all the governmental changes, life in some ways hasn't gotten any better. In fact, some decisions have set us back fifty years.

When I was in school, I had the privilege of learning both anthems: **The National Anthem** and **The Afro-American Anthem**. We were taught how to pray, and we actually prayed in class.

When I misbehaved, my teacher disciplined me with rulers, paddles, or anything flat—whether bending me over for a spanking or tapping my hand. And there was no backlash from my parents. They trusted the teachers. Now, in some states, we can't even allow certain books to be read in classrooms. Parts of history are being omitted entirely.

Mass school shootings were unheard of back then. Today, we are the only country that refuses to confront the issue of guns and how to protect our children in schools. For so long, teachers have been underpaid and overburdened, dealing with increasingly difficult challenges.

More parents today are too busy to stay involved in their children's lives. Yet, if a teacher tries to discipline their child—even verbally
—some parents are ready to gear up for battle, coming to the school as if they're prepared for war.

You have to ask yourself: with all these decisions, rulings, and laws, are we really better off? I don't think so—not even close. Look around. We're living in the digital age, where technology has made our kids both spoiled, angry and a bit lazy.

I truly believe that when prayer in schools stopped, when teachers lost the ability to discipline children the way parents once disciplined us, that's when the crime rate started to rise. And it hasn't stopped rising since.

Chapter 9

There's Levels To Brilliance:
The First Essay I Ever Wrote

By the time I reached fourth grade, I was a terrible kid. I didn't take school seriously, I stopped doing my assignments, and I never did my homework. My attention span in class became worthless. Instead, I became a class clown. I thought that being funny was more important. My mom would send me off to school every day, not knowing that I was falling behind all the other kids in my classes.

I sucked at math, had no interest in science, and language arts—forget about it. The classes I did like were history, social studies, and art. But even in those classes, I was hard-headed. I didn't do the work, but I could sure make you laugh. Every once in a while, I tried making an effort in doing my schoolwork.

One day in my history class, we were assigned to write a report on the life of Dr. Martin Luther King Jr. We had to complete the report over the weekend and turn it in the following Monday. I knew the assignment, but I decided to write about Coretta Scott King instead.

I was infatuated with this woman. She was intriguing, and I thought I knew every single thing about her. That Monday, I turned in my report. When the teacher finally came across it, the look on her face was puzzling.

"Eric, can you stand up, please?" she asked.

I froze.

"I thought I asked you to write about Dr. Martin Luther King Jr. Why did you turn in a report on Coretta Scott King?"

I answered honestly: "The Reverend King is always talked about, but no one ever talks about what his wife went through before and after her husband's assassination." The teacher nodded slowly.

"Eric, this is a really nice report, and what you're saying is very true. But I'm afraid you will be receiving a D-minus for a grade." Her response stung. My teacher gave up on me.

"Eric," she added, "one day, you will learn to pay attention in class. You finally managed to turn in your homework this time, but it's the wrong assignment."

I failed her class that semester. Worse, I failed the whole fourth grade. I had always told my parents I lost my report card, but this time, it was mailed directly to them. My dad took one look at it. All he saw were D's and E's. I got my butt whipped so bad for having so many bad grades, and my mom was deeply disappointed in me.

She didn't speak to me for a while. But you know what? I could easily put some of the blame on my parents too. They never came to the school to see how I was doing. They never even asked. I never had anyone sit down and help me with my homework. No one ever came to a parent-teacher conference, either. I kinda understand why they didn't now. They didn't for so many personal reasons.

The following year, I returned to school to retake the very same classes, while everyone else moved ahead of me. My ex-classmates didn't see me as a class clown anymore. They surely didn't laugh at my jokes. They saw me as a failure.

I got teased on the playground and during lunch breaks. It was humiliating for a child to go through, but it was absolutely my fault.

I had caused this embarrassment for myself. Still terrible at math, I worked harder to do much better in all my classes. I focused this time, turning in all my homework assignments correctly.

I found myself alone a lot. Reading and writing became my solace. Eventually, this became my favorite thing to do, and at an early age, I realized I was becoming good at it.

One week, there was an Afro-American History contest at school. Students could write about any person they admired and enter their essays into the contest. I immediately remembered my report about the beautiful Coretta Scott King from the prior year.

Though the original report had a glaring red **D-minus** scrawled across the top, I decided to rewrite it.

I added a few more details about her life, polished the content, and submitted it as my contest essay.

A week later, I was called over the loudspeaker to appear in the school auditorium. As I walked in, I saw students from fourth to eighth grade standing on stage. Each grade would have three winners, and I represented the fourth grade. My heart pounded with anticipation. Then, to my amazement, my name was called— I had won **second place** for my essay on Coretta Scott King!

The very same essay that earned me a **D-minus** the year before now won me a **$5 check** and an honor certificate.

I was overjoyed! Back then, five dollars could buy a lot of candy. I tucked my check and certificate carefully between the pages of a book and dashed home, eager to show my parents what I had accomplished.

Once I got home, I opened the book to retrieve my prizes.

The certificate was still there, but the check was nowhere to be found. My heart sank. I must have lost it on the way home.

I was devastated.

Tears streamed down my face as I thought about how much this achievement meant to me and how badly I wanted my parents to be proud. My dad, seeing how heartbroken I was, handed me a five-dollar bill and took me to the store to buy as much candy as I wanted.

That moment became a turning point for me. It wasn't just about winning second place or the five-dollar check—it was about discovering a passion that would stay with me forever.

I was just a tiny kid, but deep down, I knew I would grow to love writing short stories.

Writing gave me a sense of brilliance, even though I was still one hard-headed child.

Moral of the Story: Sometimes, success comes from revisit in past failures with a fresh perspective. What may seem like a setback can become a stepping stone toward discovering your true passion. Persistence, creativity, and the courage to try again can transform failure into triumph—and sometimes, a little encouragement from those who care makes all the difference.

Chapter 10

The Tragic Ending of a Beautiful Soul

I can still remember the tragedy that unfolded when one of my sister's best friends tragically passed away. My recollections remain vivid to this day. A new family had just moved across the street into the apartment building right next to McShane Park. If I'm not mistaken, we were the very first kids they met.

There was a young girl, about 8 or 9 years old, her shy younger brother, maybe 6 years old, and a baby brother around 6 months old. The little girl, with her beautiful Afro and radiant dark complexion, was sweet and polite. Her younger brother, always by her side, seemed hesitant and reserved.

We ran up to introduce ourselves. "What's your name?" my sister asked. She politely told us her name. My sister then turned to her little brother. "And what's your name?" she asked. Still sucking his thumb, he seemed too shy to respond and hid behind his big sister.

"Boy, tell them your name," she said, but he still didn't answer. My sister then asked, "Would you two like to go to the playground with us?"

"Sure, but I have to ask my mom first," the little girl replied. The two disappeared into their apartment building to ask for permission. After about ten minutes, they reappeared.

"My mom said yes, but we have to be back in two hours. We have somewhere to go later," she explained. From that day forward, she and my sister became inseparable, more like sisters than friends.

She had a beautiful smile and laughed at everything. Even if something wasn't particularly funny to the rest of us, life seemed to tickle her endlessly. She was such a happy kid, full of energy and enthusiasm. The bond between her and my sister grew stronger over time.

She would sometimes spend the night with us, a rare privilege since my parents rarely allowed other kids to stay over.

Trust between our families was never an issue. In fact, my sister spent so much time at her house that her mom gave my sister her very first job: helping to babysit her two younger brothers on weekends.

The job paid twenty dollars, which they split. Afterward, we would all walk to the store, excited to spend the money on bags of penny candy, ten-cent chips, and twenty-cent cans of soda.

Allegedly, on a particular Saturday, the girl's father went to work only to discover he'd been fired from Ford Motors. Whether it was due to the economic ripple effects of the 1967 rebellion or another reason, the devastating news hit him hard. Distraught, he decided to drown his sorrows at the nearest bar.

Overwhelmed with misery that soon turned to anger, he drove home, parked the car, and walked inside the apartment building. He took the elevator ride to the fourth floor, filled with the intent to destroy everything in his life.

When he opened the door, he saw my sister sitting on the couch. "You have to go," he told her. She left, unaware of the horrific events about to unfold.

"I'll see you tomorrow," she said as she left. It was the last time she would ever see her best friend.

Staggering to his 6-month-old son, the man picked up the baby and walked to the nearby window. In a moment of unspeakable violence, he threw his infant son out the window. Miraculously, the child survived the fall by landing on the grass below.

Then he grabbed his six-year-old son. At this point, I can only imagine his oldest daughter desperately trying to stop her father from throwing her little brother out next. Despite her efforts, he approached the window again, holding the boy.

Finally, he tossed him out as well.

Miraculously, with a few broken bones, the boy survived the fall and landed on the grass below.

Now, he turned his focus to his oldest daughter. She struggled, desperately trying to stay far away from that window.

Closer and closer they moved. I can imagine her putting up a brave fight, doing everything she could to stop what was about to happen. As she dangled on the window ledge, she clung tightly, holding on to her father. But he didn't stop. He finally let her go.

She fell headfirst. She never made it to the grass below. Instead, her head struck the concrete stairs leading to the basement. She died instantly as blood streamed down the crumbling staircase.

On what had been a sunny, hot day, the neighborhood was suddenly filled with silence and grief. The cheerful sounds of children playing—the ringing of hula hoops, metal skates dragging across concrete, noisy big wheels racing across chalk drawings— vanished. Even the man in the park singing doo-wop fell silent.

Instead, we heard people screaming and crying. Police and ambulance sirens pierced the air. We quickly gathered ourselves and ran down the street to see what all the commotion was about. As my sister and I approached, we saw the police arresting the girl's father. When they cuffed him and brought him out, he was completely nude.

Later, we learned what had happened.

My sister's best friend was gone.

It was a senseless and tragic loss of life.

I had the chance to attend her funeral, but I decided not to go. Even though it was a closed casket, I couldn't stop imagining what she would look like inside that box. The thought gave me nightmares for years.

It would have been my very first funeral, but at the time, I was too young to understand death.

I was just too afraid to attend the service.

Even now, I still see her cute face and remember how kind she was to others. I can only imagine how incredible she would have been as an adult. And after so many years, I still feel this terrible loss.

Though it has been many, many years, I know she will continue to rest in peace, our old childhood friend.

Chapter 11

Before This Dirt Road Became
(Detroit's Jefferies Freeway)

Before I-96 was completed on Detroit's west side, it was nothing but dirt hills and a wide-open, unpaved dirt road. My best friend and I, along with a few other kids from the neighborhood, used to get together each day to play this game called "Dodge 'Em Rocks." It was such a stupid and dangerous game, but let me explain how it was played.

Five or six of us would spread out along the top of the dirt hills. The person standing in the middle of the dirt road below would make a run for it as fast as he could while dodging the rocks that were thrown at him. The very first person on the hill to hit the runner with their rock would win the game. Then, the winner would take their turn as the runner, switching places with the person who got hit.

One day, we all got together for another round of Dodge 'Em Rocks. At this particular time, I was the runner. My best friend picked up a boulder and threw it at me. I saw this huge thing coming, but I couldn't escape it. All I could do at that moment was close my eyes and hope for the best. The boulder split my head wide open and knocked me out cold.

From what I understand, all the kids got pretty scared after seeing the bloody gash in my head, and they all ran home. The only person who didn't leave me lying there unconscious was the person who had cracked me upside the head—my best friend.

After being stretched out for a while, I finally woke up from my short coma. My buddy took his shirt off, wrapped my bleeding head, helped me up, and together we climbed the steep hill. I leaned on him, my arm around his neck, as he tried to walk me across Grand River, down Dumbarton, and back to the apartment.

He knocked on the door, and when someone opened it, he led me straight to the kitchen.

I sat in a chair as my dad asked him what had happened. "Mr. Wright, I threw a rock and made the mistake of hitting him in the head," he said.

My dad explained to my mom, using some aggressive sign language, what had happened. She became more furious by the minute that her son had been seriously hurt. As my mom carefully wrapped a new bandage around my head, I had to stick up for my best friend. I explained to her that he didn't mean to hit me in the head. To be honest, I thought she was going to find a leather belt and whip him with it. But she knew better than to hit someone else's child. I still think she at least considered it, though.

After that day, we became inseparable. We were more like brothers. As far as I was concerned, he was my brother. We shared everything and did everything together. We even got in trouble together.

Every other week, I would walk over to Martindale Street and have dinner with his family. His mother loved me like another son, and my mother loved him like he was hers. When his dog had puppies, he gave me two of the most beautiful Cocker Spaniels. I named the pups Chico and Rico.

We made a promise that no matter what happened to us, we would never break our brotherhood. Even if one of us moved away, we would somehow reconnect.

A few years later, I kept that promise. I visited him at the market where he worked bagging groceries. I waited until he got off work, and we hung out just like we did in the early days.

For many years, I searched for my childhood best friend, hoping he would be absolutely excited to reconnect after all this time.

In November **2022**, I finally found him on a social media platform. I sent him a friend request, and to my delight, he accepted. I introduced myself, brought up cherished childhood memories, and he remembered everything.

I even asked if he recalled how upset my mom was when I got hit in the head with a boulder, and he said he did. Seeing the older version of him and pictures of his wife and kids made me happy—it felt like a piece of the past had come alive again.

But soon, I noticed that our conversation wasn't going as I had hoped. I was doing all the talking, and his responses were short and dry. He didn't seem excited to hear from me after all these years. My happiness quickly turned into sadness and regret. It became clear that adulthood had changed him, and the brotherhood we once shared had been broken long ago.

Disappointed, I made the difficult decision to delete him from my friends list and never contacted him again. He was my brother, and we had a special bond. But I don't understand it—I just don't get why people change sometimes.

Moral of the Story: Life often takes us down different paths, and the bonds we once held dear may not always stand the test of time. While it's natural to long for connections from our past, it's important to remember that people grow, evolve, and sometimes drift apart. Cherish the memories for what they were, and accept that not everyone will carry the same sentiment forward.

Reconnecting with old friends can bring joy, but it can also reveal how much life has changed. The true lesson lies in appreciating the moments you shared while understanding that some relationships are meant to remain in the past.

Letting go doesn't diminish the value of what was—it simply makes room for new connections and growth.

Chapter 12

Let's Call This What it Actually Was.
Black Flight

For a while, my mind had been playing tricks on me. But after doing my research, my faint memories of the past became a crystal-clear truth. Detroit's Grand River Avenue and the surrounding areas were starting to have their own version of Black Wall Street. A few years after the rebellion of 1967, people began creating golden opportunities to rebuild and own businesses for themselves.

Suddenly, abandoned properties were being reconstructed, cleaned up, and repainted. Before long, new places to shop began to emerge—soul food restaurants, nightclubs, hardware stores, meat markets, barber shops, record shops, cleaners, beauty supply stores, motels, gas stations, ice cream parlors, dry cleaners, liquor stores, and pharmacies. Places like Lindy's Supermarket, Gateman's Meat Market, Gene's Motel, Kirk's Barbecue, Superior Beauty and Barber Supply, White Tower Hamburgers, and Action Hardware, just to name a few, became household names.

Detroit's Grand River Avenue and the surrounding areas began to flourish again, just as they had before the rebellion. As a small child, I can remember that many of these places were Black-owned establishments, and Grand River was officially reborn. Rising from the ashes was an amazing thing to witness.

Even the neighborhoods began their own cleanup movement. This was also the first time people started putting bars on their doors and windows for security. More families bought dogs to protect their front and back yards, just in case another rebellion happened.

The Jefferies Freeway construction was nearing completion on this side of town, adding to the renewed energy and optimism.

I can vividly recall walking with my mom from our apartment to Grand River Avenue, visiting several of these newly renovated businesses that were now mostly owned and operated by African Americans.

Those evening walks were unforgettable—stopping for ice cream cones, bringing home hot, steamy fries covered in mounds of ketchup and lying in red-and-white checkered paper boats.

My father would take me and my brother to the Barber School for discounted, fresh cuts. The aroma of barbecue ribs, fried fish, and shrimp filled the air. Every Wednesday and Sunday afternoon, the late Mother Waddles gave away free baked goods to those in need.

I remember short walks to the supermarket just to see my childhood best friend, who worked as a grocery bagger. There were curious glances inside the Moon Glow or Swans bars, and Cookie's Record Shop became a popular hangout spot, where we listened to the latest Detroit hits. The late radio personality Martha Jean "The Queen" could be heard blaring from store-front speakers.

Penny candy shops popped up everywhere. We indulged in candies like Now and Later, Boston Baked Beans, Mike and Ike, Hot Tamales, Milk Duds, Mary Janes, Squirrels, Pop Rocks, Bottle Caps, Jawbreakers, Blow Pops, Laffy Taffy, Good & Plenty, and Pixie Stix—just to name a few.

As a birth child of the fourth-largest city in America at the time, I was in the middle of it all. I witnessed the growth, development, and resilience of our community. I lived it. I remembered it.

This was a time of pride and hope—a moment when our community came together to create a thriving economic infrastructure and opportunities to own property along Grand River Avenue and beyond.

So, believe me when I say this: we were proud owners of so much. In my mind, this was the beginning of Detroit's own version of Black Wall Street.

But something profound happened during the early and mid-70s. Redlining—a discriminatory practice that confined Black residents to specific neighborhoods—began to wane, allowing people to move from the slums into better neighborhoods. Yet, even as this change unfolded, the promise of equality remained elusive.

Property taxes and insurance premiums were still exorbitantly high, making it incredibly difficult for many Black business owners and homeowners to maintain their livelihoods and properties.

The white flight that had followed the rebellion only compounded these challenges, leaving behind an economic void. Jobs paying decent wages were scarce, and opportunities to rebuild a stable life grew increasingly limited. In desperation, business owners began selling off their properties. Those who couldn't find buyers were forced to shutter their businesses, boarding up windows and doors for good. Black-owned establishments that had once thrived along Grand River Avenue became rarer with each passing year.

Homeowners, too, faced a grim reality. Unable to sustain the financial burden, many put their homes on the market. Families packed their belongings, gathered their children, and left Detroit in search of better opportunities. For others, it wasn't about hope—it was simply about survival.

The completion of the west side section of the Jefferies Freeway provided a literal and figurative escape route, ushering Black Detroiters toward the suburbs.

This mass exodus marked the onset of what I call "Black Flight."

It was a stark reversal of the progress made in the years following the rebellion. Grand River Avenue, once a symbol of resilience and rebirth, began to succumb to neglect and decay.

For many years, homes sat empty, abandoned to the elements and time. Apartment buildings that were left behind, never bulldozed, became haunting reminders of a brighter past.

As Black families moved out, a new wave of residents moved in.

This group, whom I refer to as "The Hood Rats," seemed indifferent to the community's legacy or its upkeep. The neighborhood fell further into disrepair—overgrown grass, garbage-strewn lots, and junked cars became common sights. Old tires and mattresses were dumped in open fields, while porches and staircases crumbled into ruins. Broken windows stared out from roofs that sagged and eventually caved in.

Graffiti became the language of the streets, scrawled across homes and buildings that once exuded pride.

Gangs took root in the vacuum of leadership and community cohesion. People lingered aimlessly at all hours, and crime escalated. The crack epidemic, a devastating plague of the 1980s, slowly crept into these already struggling neighborhoods, choking whatever hope remained.

Grand River Avenue reflected this downward spiral. The once-great Grande Ballroom, a cultural landmark, closed its doors.

The Riviera Theater, where my mother took me to watch Bruce Lee movies, shut down for good. Restaurants, bars, stores, shops, motels, and hotels—many of them once Black-owned—were boarded up, their contributions to the community now just memories.

Yet, even amidst this decline, there were glimmers of hope.

Many families refused to leave, standing firm against the wave of poverty and neglect. I vividly recall beautiful, stately homes with neatly trimmed yards and vibrant flowers growing in front gardens. Some of these homes, built in the early 1900s, looked like small castles. In certain pockets of the neighborhood, life seemed untouched by the violence and destruction of the past.

Still, Grand River Avenue would never be the same. Its energy,

its vibrancy, and its spirit had been eroded. The area that had once symbolized a thriving Black Wall Street was now a shadow of its former self.

Looking back, I can't help but ask: Why didn't the city of Detroit intervene? Why didn't city officials invest in these neighborhoods, especially given their proximity to downtown? Why were so many blighted properties from the '60s and '70s allowed to stand, untouched and deteriorating, for decades?

It's a bitter truth to confront.

The city turned its back on these neighborhoods when they needed help the most, leaving them to bear the weight of neglect, poverty, and systemic racism. Grand River Avenue deserved better— Detroit deserved better.

Some Places That No Longer Exist on West Grand River Avenue and the Surrounding Areas

- **Olympia Stadium**: Opened in 1927, closed in 1980, and demolished in 1987.
- **Burger Chef**: Located across from Olympia Stadium, demolished in the 1980s.
- **The Riviera Theater**: Built in 1924, demolished in the 1990s.
- **The Beverly Theater**: Opened in 1937 and closed in 1964.
- **The Grande Ballroom**: Established in 1928, abandoned in 1972.
- **My preschool Little Angell**: No longer exists.
- **My elementary school Big Angell**: No longer exists.
- **Jupiter Discount Store**: Discontinued operations in the early 1980s.
- **The Graystone Ballroom**: Demolished in 1980.
- **Seville Court Apartments**: Located on Dumbarton Street, demolished in the early.
- **Mother Waddles Mission**: Operated in the area, remembered for its charitable outreach, now discontinued.

- **Genes Motel**: Served travelers along Grand River, eventually shut down.
- **Kirk's Barbecue**: Known for its signature ribs and soul food, now a memory.
- **Cookie's Record Shop**: A hub for Motown and R&B records, closed decades ago.
- **Lindy's Supermarket**: A key neighborhood grocery store, no longer operational.
- **Gateman's Meat Market**: A community staple, now defunct.
- **Action Hardware**: A one-stop hardware shop for locals, also gone.
- **Swans Bar**: Once a bustling nightlife spot, now just a recollection.
- **Moon Glow Bar**: A neighborhood watering hole that has since closed.
- **Superior Beauty and Barber Supply**: A vital resource for the community, now out of business.

Chapter 13

An Unusual Baptism

At an early age, I became very curious about religion. I wanted to understand what started the evolution of so many things on this place we call Earth. Why do things grow and why do things have to die? What is the significance of Easter Sunday? Why do we need the Ten Commandments? What does it mean when the Bible says you have to be born again and have all your sins forgiven before entering the gates of heaven?

My understanding at the time was simple yet terrifying: if you did bad and evil things in life, you would end up in the fiery pits of hell. It didn't matter how old you were—if you didn't live life the "right way," eternal fire awaited. That thought scared me as a young child. It pushed me to steer far from my mischievous ways and strive to become a better person.

For the most part, I became a good kid. I tried to be a positive example for my siblings and other kids my age. Knowing right from wrong came naturally to me. Of course, I still did what most young kids do—mostly from peer pressure—but the word of God and those frequent butt whippings from my dad quickly put me back on the straight and narrow.

I would never, in life, do what the older kids around me were doing—getting into trouble that could land them in the juvenile system. Selling drugs, breaking into homes and cars, or joining gangs? Oh no, not me. Petty crimes were not in my nature.

Meeting the Grand River Prophet

As my friends and I played up and down Grand River every day, we always noticed an older gentleman with a long gray beard, wearing a skull cap and a camouflage army jacket.

He carried a Bible in his hands and passionately preached the word of God to anyone who would stop and listen.

One day, curiosity got the better of us, and we stopped to hear what he was saying. Most adults ignored him, walking briskly past his sermons, but we lingered. He answered our questions with a mild-mannered demeanor and a voice so low we could barely hear him.

He gestured often as he spoke, never looking us directly in the eyes. Despite his peculiar nature, he was kind to us. We gave him the nickname "The Grand River Prophet."

One Sunday afternoon, we saw him again, walking up and down the block, preaching. This time, he mentioned that after he finished, he would head home to teach Sunday school at his house. "You're more than welcome to come," he said. "Other kids will be there too."

At first, we hesitated. Even back in those days, it was a huge no-no for kids to voluntarily go to a stranger's house—especially without telling our parents or getting their permission. But something about the old man felt trustworthy, and eventually, we agreed to follow him.

Sunday School on Arcadia Street

We walked a couple of blocks to Arcadia Street. When we entered his home, we met his wife, who was just finishing up dinner. Just as he had said, other kids from the neighborhood were already sitting on the couple's living room floor.

We quickly learned that every Sunday, the couple offered dinner before Bible study. Going into their home without my parents' knowledge was one thing, but eating their food and drinking their Kool-Aid?

That was something I was reluctant to do for the first few Sundays. After the dinner was prepared, his wife called us kids around the kitchen table. The old man said a prayer over the food. I must admit, the fried chicken looked and smelled incredible. For a moment, I almost caved in, but I quickly came back to my senses. After dinner, we all gathered back in the living room, sitting cross- legged on the floor.

The old man encouraged us to introduce ourselves to the other kids before beginning the Bible study. Despite our initial hesitations, we soon found ourselves settling into a routine.

After several weeks, most of our nervousness faded. The old man and his wife earned our trust with their kind demeanor and genuine care for us. Their explanations of Bible chapters and verses captivated us, making complex scriptures easier to understand. They had a way of connecting the teachings to our young minds, and before long, I found myself looking forward to these Sunday sessions.

One Sunday, the discussion turned to forgiveness and salvation. The old man passionately explained the importance of being "born again" and having our sins washed away in Jesus' name. He then shared his plan to baptize us himself, right there in his home.

"The process is simple," he began. "I'll fill the bathtub with warm water, and each of you will stand in the middle of the tub. I'll hold your head, say a prayer, and gently lower you backward until you're submerged for a couple of seconds.

Then, you'll rise, cleansed of your sins." He concluded his explanation with a question: "So, who wants to be cleansed today?"

To my surprise, two or three kids eagerly raised their hands. I, on the other hand, felt an overwhelming sense of discomfort. Something about the entire situation didn't sit right with me.

Unease and a Personal Resolve

The old man directed the willing participants to follow his wife into another room to change into long t-shirts provided for the baptism. Watching this unfold triggered a flood of memories I had buried deep inside. Flashbacks of my childhood trauma raced through my mind. I had made a solemn promise to myself after that dark experience: I would never allow anyone to touch or coerce me into doing something against my will ever again.

I couldn't bring myself to go along with it.

The thought of stepping into someone else's bedroom, changing out of my clothes, and putting on their shirt filled me with unease. As much as I wanted to believe this couple meant no harm, I knew deep in my heart that what they were doing wasn't right. They hadn't spoken to any of our parents about their intentions, and that realization solidified my decision.

I left their home that day and never went back.

Finding a New Path

Determined to find a legitimate church, I began searching on my own. My journey led me to a church on Grand River Avenue, where the pastor welcomed me with open arms. This church became a cornerstone in my life.

The pastor was serious about preaching the word of God, but he also knew how to connect with us kids. He gave several of us jobs cleaning and organizing the church after Sunday services.

It felt good to contribute and to be part of a community that genuinely cared for us. Eventually, I was baptized in that same church—the right way, with the consent and presence of my family.

That day, I felt a profound sense of renewal and belonging. The pastor's kindness extended beyond the church walls.
He took us on trips and shared information about places like Mother Waddles' Mission, where free baked goods and clothing were distributed every Wednesday and Sunday afternoon.

The Impact of Mother Waddles

Speaking of this remarkable woman, Mother Waddles' generosity touched countless lives, including mine. At that time, my family was struggling more than ever. We were dirt poor, barely making ends meet, and in desperate need of help.

Mother Waddles' mission was simple: to provide for those in need, free of charge. Week after week, her selfless efforts made life a little more bearable for families like mine.

She gave hope when it felt like there was none.

To this day, I marvel at her unwavering dedication. Detroit's "Mother of Hope" deserves to be remembered and celebrated. Her work was a testament to the power of compassion and the impact one person can have on an entire community.

When I was a kid, I made a surprising discovery about my dad. He had a hidden talent besides excelling in sports and being able to repair just about anything. He loved to read, and he always had books lying around or inside these boxes.

One day, out of curiosity, I picked up one of his books, and something told me to check the back of it.

To my astonishment, I found a drawing of a man's face. It was incredibly detailed and lifelike.

Intrigued, I grabbed another book and looked inside the back cover. Sure enough, there was another amazing pencil drawing.

One book after another, I uncovered more of these realistic portraits. I couldn't believe my dad had this kind of talent. I asked him how he did it and whether he could teach me.

He told me, "Find a picture you like, take a blank piece of paper, and place it over the picture.

Trace the outline carefully. Keep practicing this technique, and one day, you won't need to trace at all. You'll be able to draw freehand just by observing the picture."

I took his advice and started practicing every day. I would trace, sketch, and draw until I improved. By the time I got to middle school, I had become really good at drawing, painting, and even sculpting. I was often the talk of my art classes.

Although writing became my second favorite hobby, art always held the top spot. Until now, I never shared with anyone where I learned this skill.

Thanks, Dad, for showing me another way to be creative.

Chapter 14

Witness to an Unnecessary Murder

Asbestos was taking over our building, and tenants were quickly moving out. The top floors were nearly empty, and word had it that soon we would all have to relocate. Our building was slated for demolition, with plans to replace it with townhouses. The remaining tenants were forced to move to one side of the building, specifically the second and third floors. This marked our third move within the same structure.

We no longer faced the park across the street, where my mother used to keep an eye on us as we played. Instead, our apartment now faced Blaine Street. From this vantage point, my mom could partially see us crossing the alley entrance and walking up the block to school, but it wasn't the same. Our station wagon was always parked directly under our window, near the side door we now used.

One Saturday, after getting paid from my church job, I decided to take my little brother to the store for some candy and other treats. Afterward, we walked to the playground, settled ourselves on a wooden bench, and listened to the old men parked on the street talking smack to one another. This had become a favorite pastime of ours. We couldn't resist eavesdropping on their heated arguments, hilarious jokes, pranks, and even their discussions about personal matters. We were curious kids, and their conversations were endlessly entertaining.

That day, a homeless man showed up, as he often did, offering to run store errands for the old-timers in exchange for a little cash. They would send him for whatever they needed, letting him keep the change. It was how he managed to buy cheap liquor and meals every day.

On this particular day, one of the regulars—a man who rode a motorcycle—asked the homeless man to fetch him a pack of cigarettes and one other item.

I remember him handing the man a ten-dollar bill.

When the homeless man returned, he handed over the items and attempted to walk away.

"Hey, man, where's my change?" the biker demanded.

"Sorry, you didn't have any change," the man replied nervously.

"Motherfucker, what the hell do you mean? I gave you a ten-dollar bill!"

The homeless man stammered, "The guy behind the counter must've forgotten to give me the change back."

As my little brother and I continued sitting on the park bench, we couldn't take our eyes off the brewing altercation. Things escalated quickly.

The biker, now enraged, pulled out a pistol. "Man, if you don't give me my fuckin' change, I'm going to take it out of your ass!"

The homeless man pleaded, trying to explain as he circled a ticketed, junked car parked on the side of the street. The first shot missed, but instead of running away, the homeless man ducked under the car for cover.

The biker, showing no remorse, laid on the ground, aimed, and fired again. This time, the shot hit its mark.

My brother and I were hiding under the park bench, trembling with fear. We couldn't believe what we had just witnessed. The biker showed no regret for what he had done. He and the other men hurriedly gathered their belongings, got into their vehicles, and sped off, leaving the homeless man to bleed out in the middle of the street.

We could see the man lying motionless, blood pooling and slowly streaming from his lifeless body. In a panic, my little brother and I scrambled out from under the bench and ran as fast as we could across the street, back to our nearly empty apartment building.

For the first time, I was grateful that no one lived in the front part of our building anymore.

My mom couldn't see us playing in the park, and there were no other witnesses to this unnecessary murder—no one walking by, no cars passing through. It felt like we were the only two people in the world who had seen what happened.

We were the only witnesses, unless someone living in the Viceroy Apartments across Blaine Street or the houses behind the park on Petoskey Street saw what happened.

From our side window, we couldn't see the front of the park, but we heard the police sirens and the ambulance arrive. A crowd was beginning to gather outside.

My mom didn't realize the commotion that was going on, and we decided to keep our mouths shut about what we had seen. Fearful that those men might come after us, we stayed indoors, avoiding the park and sticking close to home for the rest of the summer break.

After a couple of weeks, we cautiously returned to the park. By then, everything seemed back to normal, and the group of men had vanished as if they'd never been there.

Chapter 15

So Hard to Say Goodbye

1972

1972 was a challenging year for me and my family. The tenants in our building were now given a final deadline to leave. My parents scrambled to find a suitable place for low-income families. Though we didn't own much, my dad spent the entire week transporting boxes, bags, and everything we had to our new home. The moment had finally arrived—it was time to say goodbye.

We were moving from the west side to the northwest side of Detroit, and the change was overwhelming for me. Leaving behind everything familiar—Grand River Avenue and the surrounding area—was heartbreaking. It had shaped so much of my young childhood. The thought of changing schools and trying to make new friends filled me with dread. We were an impoverished family, and I hoped that somehow, things would change for us.

There was so much I would miss.

I would miss my best friend and the brotherhood we had built. We had promised each other that as we got older, I would find him again and reconnect. Before I left, I asked if he could take back my Cocker Spaniel puppies, Chico and Rico, since pets weren't allowed where we were moving. Saying goodbye to my puppies felt like losing a part of myself.

I would miss the girl from a block over who used to bully me. Though she teased me relentlessly, she was part of my life. I would also miss my sister's best friend—the one I secretly hoped would one day become my girlfriend. She was so beautiful, but I was always too shy and scared to share my feelings, worried she might reject me or laugh.

She was my first love, even though she never knew. I would miss my pastor and Sunday school.

Those lessons about faith, the friendships I made with the other kids, and the joy of giving my life to Christ—all of it felt like leaving a piece of my soul behind.

I would miss swimming at the Boys and Girls Club, those late evening walks to the Dairy Queen, and the aroma of barbecue ribs and fried shrimp that filled the air on warm evenings.

I would miss walking to the corner store, seeing familiar faces, and hearing the laughter of neighbors.

The walks to school, surrounded by a sea of kids, the classrooms, my teachers at Big Angell Elementary—they were all part of my daily life that I would never get back.

McShane Park would haunt my memories the most. The swings, the monkey bars, the seesaw, and those summer days spent on the grass and dirt—all of it would now be just a memory. Even the soulful doo-wop crooners who gathered under the streetlights to sing old tunes would no longer be part of my evenings.

Family trips to Burger Chef across from Olympia Stadium, Sunday dinners, and the laughter of the neighborhood—it was all slipping away.

Most of all, I would miss the corner of Dumbarton and Blaine Street—the place where my life began.

That corner wasn't just an intersection; it was my home, my childhood, and my entire world.

My family was a part of history on this side of town. We survived the rebellion of **1967**. From the beginning to the end, we witnessed it, lived through it, and came out the other side.

A few days before the moving deadline, we packed up the last of our belongings into my dad's trusty station wagon. With the car loaded to capacity, we piled in and left the neighborhood for good.

I can still remember the weight of not wanting to leave—my heart heavy with the knowledge that I had no say in the matter.

My world was being uprooted, and my heart was broken.

As we drove away, everything I cherished—every corner, every memory—flashed before my eyes.

The playground, the park benches, the familiar faces, the street corners, and the laughter of the neighborhood all faded into the distance, leaving behind an emptiness I couldn't describe.

Though we moved just 25 minutes away, it felt like we were leaving behind a lifetime. It wasn't just a place we left—it was a piece of who I was, a chapter that had been closed too soon.

Personal Timeline 1972

I specifically remember my mom taking me to the theater to see Blacula in 1972. It was a horror-blaxploitation film that stood out for its unique story and cultural significance.

The movie followed Mamuwalde, an African prince, played by William Marshall, who traveled to Transylvania in the 18th century with his wife, Luva, to seek Count Dracula's help in ending the transatlantic slave trade. Instead, Dracula mocked Mamuwalde and cursed him, transforming him into a vampire and imprisoning him in a coffin. Centuries later, in 1970s Los Angeles, Mamuwalde is accidentally freed and reborn as "Blacula."

In Los Angeles, Blacula encounters Tina, a woman who resembles his lost wife, Luva. Convinced she is her reincarnation, he becomes consumed with love for her while struggling with the torment of his curse. His vampiric existence leaves a trail of victims, drawing the attention of Dr. Gordon Thomas, a pathologist who works to uncover the truth and stop him.

The story concludes tragically as Mamuwalde, overwhelmed by his torment, chooses to end his existence in the sunlight.

Blacula wasn't just a horror film—it was a blend of romance, tragedy, and social commentary.

It re-imagined the vampire genre by infusing it with black culture and exploring themes of love, loss, and racism.

I left the theater amazed, and that movie has stayed with me ever since, not just as a fun memory with my mom, but as a significant piece of cinematic history.

Also in 1972, my dad was as vocal as ever with his kids about the state of America, particularly how the country had turned its back on him and worked against him so profoundly. For a man who only wanted to live the American dream and provide for his wife and children, the fading economic opportunities plunged him into a long and deep depression that lingered for many years.

The doors of opportunity continued to close, while racism reared its ugly head high and often.

It's probably why, in that same year, he turned to the Muslim faith —to seek some form of mental relief, personal understanding, and comfort. An overload of drinking alcohol also came into play. I vividly remember my comic book collection, a treasure trove of milk crates filled with my favorite superheroes. One day, my dad looked at me and said, "You'll never learn anything from reading these damn comic books. Everything in them is fake.

It's just like believing in Santa Claus." Without hesitation, he gathered my entire collection, threw the books in the trash, and handed me the Muslim Quran.

"Open and read this every day," he said firmly. "It will open your eyes to a lot of things and change your life." Change my life? At the time, I was only ten years old.

How much change did I need at that age?

Now, decades later, I can't help but wonder how much that good-conditioned comic book collection would be worth today.

My mom, on the other hand, never sat me down to discuss her struggles as a person of color growing up in the late 1940s, 50s, and 60s.

Perhaps her family did an extraordinary job of shielding her from the world's evils because of her handicap.

Neither of my parents ever had a serious conversation with me about the challenges I would personally face in the early and mid-**1970s**.

I never had the "Son, you need to be careful out there" talk. Nor did I receive the discussion about police brutality or how to safely navigate encounters with law enforcement. I had to figure it out on my own. I watched a lot of black and white television as a kid and saw all the examples of brutality.

As I got older, I realized it was now my generation's turn to endure the blatant trauma and hatred that seemed to be passed down through time. I also had no idea that moving from Detroit's West Side to the Northwest Side in **1972** would bring such a drastic change to our lives.

The world was changing around me, but some things stayed painfully the same.

And now part 2 of my memoirs. My early teenage years.

Reflecting on the Journey So Far

Chapters 1–15: A Foundation of Memories and Milestones

As we pause to reflect on the first 15 chapters, it's remarkable how each page has painted a vivid portrait of resilience, transformation, and the enduring power of memory. These stories, rooted in the streets of Detroit and the trials of a young boy navigating an uncertain world, serve as a testament to the strength of family, community, and personal growth.

Themes and Moments That Stand Out:

- **A City's Turmoil:** From the rebellion of 1967 to the slow rebirth of Detroit's Grand River Avenue, these chapters capture the beauty and heartbreak of a city in flux.
- **Family Dynamics:** Through moments of love, discipline, and struggle, the family bond remains the backbone of these memories.
- **Childhood Innocence and Challenges:** Whether it's playground antics, encounters with bullies, or difficult lessons in trust, these stories remind us of the complexities of growing up.
- **Faith and Redemption:** From unique Sunday school experiences to finding spiritual refuge in a church on Grand River, faith weaves through these pages as a guiding force.
- **Resilience in the Face of Change:** The move from the west side to the northwest side of Detroit marked a shift not just in geography but in life perspective, as new challenges arose and old ones lingered.

A Message for the Reader:

The journey through these chapters has been as much about uncovering the beauty in hardship as it has been about celebrating the joy in small victories. These stories aren't just mine—they are universal in their themes of love, loss, and hope.

As we turn the page to what comes next, I invite you to carry forward the lessons learned and memories shared so far.

Chapter 16

Detroit's John W. Smith Homes Housing Projects

Looking back, I guess we were somewhat like the family on the hit television show Good Times. I could relate to J.J. Walker—the goofy, skinny older brother who loved art. The main difference? They had five family members, and we had seven. Both families, however, shared similar struggles.

"DYNOMITE!"

Within 25 minutes, we arrived at our new home: 14337 Crescent Drive, nestled between Lyndon Street and Evergreen. Driving into the complex, we saw beautifully kept yards, vibrant flowers, and neatly trimmed bushes.

Historically, the entire complex was initially built for post-World War II defense workers. On December 1, 1942, the first 10 low-income families moved in. It was named after John W. Smith, Detroit's 52nd and 57th mayor, who also served on the city council for many years. Smith even ran for governor, though he lost the race. He passed away on June 17, 1942, at the age of 60.

When we moved in, in 1972, we were probably the 11th or 12th Black family to call the complex home. At the time, there were 157 units in total: 83 two-bedroom homes, 45 three-bedroom homes, and 29 four-bedroom homes. With the size of our family, we were fortunate enough to get a four-bedroom unit.

The projects were surrounded by beautiful middle-class homes, churches, stores, and a nearby school. My parents had a surprise waiting for us once we finished moving in our belongings. While we didn't have much furniture or a stocked kitchen just yet, we were excited to see what they had in store.

"Run up the stairs and check it out!" my mom said.

We bolted up the staircase to discover three bedrooms upstairs. One for my parents, one for my sisters, and one for me and my brother.

It was such a thrill to see bunk beds in our room and our own closets and dressers. Up until then, we had never had such a setup, so it was a pleasant and much-appreciated surprise.

The bathroom was next to our room and right across from my sisters' room. There was even an additional bedroom on the lower level near the staircase. My dad claimed that space to store his equipment and work on his television repair studies.

As we unpacked our boxes and bags, unfortunately, some unwelcome guests from our old apartment building came along for the ride—roaches. It wasn't that we were a dirty family; my mom made sure we lived in a clean home. But the infested building we left behind had been a breeding ground for those critters, and they managed to hitch a ride with us.

Determined to get rid of them, my dad immediately went to the store and bought several roach motels, placing them strategically throughout the house. Within a few months, we were finally roach- free and back to living in a clean environment.

We didn't have much at first. The place came with a refrigerator and stove. Eventually, we managed to buy a used washing machine, but we couldn't afford a dryer. Instead, we dried our clothes on lines outside in the backyard or inside the hot furnace utility room. Little by little, we furnished our home. We finally got a kitchen table with chairs and rented some living room furniture from a rental store, though it felt like it took forever to pay it off.

We didn't have enough dishes, glasses, or silverware, so my parents went to the Salvation Army to purchase what we needed.

When it came to breakfast, lunch, and dinner, my parents initially signed us up for the Commodity Supplemental Food Program (Government Food). I remember how awful that stuff tasted.

Powdered eggs, powdered milk, butter, juice, cereal, corn syrup, oatmeal, and canned pulled meat—most of it was terrible. But the canned peanut butter and the block of cheddar cheese?

Those were the absolute best. We spent many nights making peanut butter cookies and world- famous grilled cheese sandwiches.

Sundays were special in our household. That was the day we could enjoy a good meal. My mom's spaghetti was amazing, and her fried chicken, greens, and macaroni and cheese were a real treat.

Salmon was inexpensive back then, and her salmon burger patties were incredible. I still have her recipe. We ate a lot of hot dogs, homemade french fries, and pot pies, too. Whenever mom made meatloaf, we knew she had hidden some money somewhere for a slightly better meal.

I'll never forget one day when my dad brought home a cow tongue from the supermarket. He placed it in a pot and told us it was for dinner. Curious, I lifted the lid and saw this massive, bumpy tongue floating in the boiling water—it scared the living daylights out of me! If I remember correctly, most of us skipped dinner that night.

Six blocks away from us was Warren G. Harding Elementary School, named after the 29th President and opened in 1923. Although my parents couldn't communicate directly with the school staff due to their hearing impairment, my oldest sister and I used sign language to translate, which allowed us to get registered and attend the school.

For school clothes, we often rode the bus downtown with our mom to shop at S.S. Kresge or Woolworth. We'd get plastic-bottom tennis shoes, which were fine until you ran too much—the sides would rip open.

Occasionally, when my mom managed to save a little extra money, she'd take us to Hansel and Gretel Children's Shoe Store to buy better school shoes. My mom always sacrificed her needs to make sure we had what we needed, and I'll always admire her for that.

One Saturday morning, I signed out bush trimmers and a two-wheel manual lawn mower from our community center to do some yard work. While I was working, a kid walked up and introduced himself.

"Nice to meet you and welcome to the projects," he said. "After you're done, I can show you around if you like. I live over there in the horseshoe."

"The horseshoe?" I asked.

"Yeah, there are homes that curve around and bring you back to Crescent Drive. The back-streeters have one too," he explained.

"The back-streeters?" I asked, even more confused.

"Yeah! That's what we call everyone who lives on the other side of the projects," he said. We talked a bit more, and I asked if there was a store nearby.

"Yeah, Dave's. It's right across from the projects on Evergreen," he replied.

I quickly finished my chores, and the kid gave me a tour of the projects. Afterward, we walked to Dave's store together, and from that day on, we became the best of friends. He was my very first best friend in the projects.

Monday morning rolled around, and it was the first day of school. My sisters' hair was nicely braided, and my dad had given me and my brother fresh haircuts. We wore our brand-new S.S. Kresge white tennis shoes and school clothes, ready to head out the door. Other kids joined us as we walked to Harding Elementary.

As we passed other units, I noticed the mean looks some tenants gave us. Something felt off.

A woman watering her plants glanced at us with a look of disgust. It didn't sit right with me, and I wondered why we were met with such unkindness in our new neighborhood.

Men sat on their porches, staring at us as if, given the chance, they would harm us all. I knew I hadn't done anything to deserve such hatred, but the looks they gave us were piercing. It was the strangest thing I'd ever experienced, and it's something I've never forgotten to this day.

Even the six-block walk to school was filled with tension.

Cars would creep by slowly, windows rolled down, and the vile words they hurled at us hit hard. "Don't you have another school to go to?" they'd shout. "We don't want you here."

This was the first time someone had said something so hateful directly to me.

The walk down Lyndon to Burt Road was dangerous, but the walk back home after school was far worse. Cars would wait at the corners, their occupants ready to torment us. At those moments, we had three choices:

- Take a chance and run down a different block to get home.
- Stay at school and wait until the coast was clear.
- Walk past the cars and risk being hit with zip lock bags or plastic bags filled with urine.

One time, a white kid living across the street from one of these dangerous corners spoke up for us. He asked the skinheads to leave us alone, but his bravery came at a cost. They jumped him for standing up for us. Despite what happened, that same kid later became one of my closest friends.

Within a year, I noticed a drastic change in the Smith Homes Housing Projects.

More African American families moved in, while white families moved out in droves. The same thing happened at our elementary school.

The transformation was undeniable, but the hatred lingered, its roots deep and persistent. It was clear that, suddenly, no one wanted to live among us blacks.

Moral of the Story

Life often challenges us with circumstances that test our resilience, character, and courage. Moving to a new place, facing hostility, and navigating a world of prejudice are not easy burdens to bear, especially for a child. Yet, in the face of hatred and adversity, we learn the importance of standing tall and seeking connection with those who choose kindness over cruelty.

This chapter reminds us that courage is not just about defending yourself but also about enduring the hardships of change and holding on to hope. It teaches us the value of finding allies in unexpected places, like the brave kid who stood up for justice. Ultimately, it's about persevering through the trials of life while never losing faith in the possibility of better days ahead.

Chapter 17

How I Met My Second Best Friend in Smith Homes

I was just a shy kid who didn't know too many people at school yet. I mostly kept to myself. One day, as I sat in my art class, I noticed the other children gathering around another student's table. All hour long, he had the whole class in awe. The way he drew a picture captivated them. "I wish I could draw like that," some of the students said.

I, on the other hand, didn't want to bring any attention to myself. I would hide my drawings in my desk or tuck them between book pages. But one day, I was sketching a picture when a kid happened to look over and saw what I was doing. "Hey, everyone, come see what Eric just drew!" he shouted.

Suddenly, all the kids ran over to my desk, leaving the "best artist in the class" abandoned. Children have no filter—they'll say whatever comes to mind, regardless of whether it hurts someone's feelings. Words can be humiliating sometimes. The more compliments I got, the higher my pedestal rose.

"I think he's the best in our class," one student said. "I want to draw like him," another chimed in.

Even our teacher gave me a lot of praise. To be honest, I started enjoying all the new attention I was getting. But at the same time, I noticed the kid who had captivated everyone before was now sitting in the corner, alone and shedding tears. His whole world had come tumbling down. He was no longer considered the best in our class.

I never meant for that to happen, and I felt pretty bad about the whole ordeal. I was shy, but I also had a heart. The art teacher decided that the two of us should sit next to each other and work on projects together.

It turned out that we had something in common—we both loved art. Eventually, we both transformed into the best artists in the entire school.

By the end of the semester, we were the best of friends. By the end of the school year, we were more like brothers.
His family was much smaller than mine. He had two brothers, and his mom became like a second mother to me.

Here's One of My Art Class Memories

I created a winter portrait featuring a child shoveling snow, decorating a Christmas tree, Christmas caroling, and snowboarding down a snowy hill. My art teacher bought a large wooden frame and a picture easel for it. She entered my portrait into J.L. Hudson's Downtown Holiday Arts Contest.

Several weeks later, I found out that, out of hundreds of paintings, sketches, and chalk drawings, my portrait had won second place in the statewide contest.

The only problem was, my portrait was never returned to me. It was said that somehow it had gone missing after the contest.

But I know my art teacher stole it. I'm absolutely sure of it.

To this day, I truly believe she took it home and kept it for herself. I thought, when she bought that nice picture frame and easel, she was just being nice to a kid. But no—she was a damn thief. She made my contest picture one of her prized possessions.

Moral of the Story: Sometimes, unexpected challenges or rivalries can lead to lifelong friendships and shared success. Always stay humble, and remember, true talent shines brighter when it's shared rather than compared. Supporting and uplifting others not only builds bonds but also inspires everyone to grow and achieve their best. Genuine kindness and collaboration often leave a lasting impression far beyond personal victories.

Chapter 18

Evident Change (1972–1973)

1973 was fast approaching, and things were changing at a rapid pace, especially in Smith Homes Housing Projects and the surrounding areas. More Black families were moving into Brightmoor, Grandmont, Rosedale Park, the Old Redford communities, and beyond. White families quickly moved out of the projects while the majority of Black families settled in. Smith Homes became a protection zone for the younger kids running home from school, while the older teens protected them from any harm caused by skinheads driving by or any racial violence.

I can still remember one particular night when an unknown person sped through the projects, scaring the kids playing on the block and calling them every racial name he could yell out of his car window. That same person later had the audacity to stop in the projects and ask some teens if he could buy marijuana from them. A kid frantically yelled to the teens that he was the one who had been terrorizing the whole block. The teens quickly grabbed him, pulled him out of his car, and held him on the ground. One teen grabbed a hula hoop from a child, lit it with a lighter, and melted the hot plastic onto the man's back. After receiving several burns, they let him go, and he never came back yelling racial slurs again.

The community had a playground and a full basketball court attached to what the residents called "the big field."

I can also remember one late night playing on the court with a few of my friends. Suddenly, we heard a car speeding through the projects, the sound of thick chains clinking together, and skinheads in the car screaming, "We're going to kill a nigger tonight!" We continued playing our game and thought nothing of it at first.

Ten minutes later, the car came through again, and this time, we heard them yell, "The first nigger we see, we're chaining him up and dragging him down Evergreen Road!"

We dropped the basketball, ran deeper into the field, and hid ourselves in the tall grass.

Thinking about those moments now, I still can't believe we had to go through that. This wasn't the South. This wasn't Alabama, Georgia, Mississippi, or Kentucky. No, this was Detroit, Michigan, back in the early '70s.

Warren G. Harding Middle School was changing as well. Bussing from Detroit's Isaac Crary and Mettetal Middle Schools to our school began. I don't remember the specific reasons why. Either we had room for more students and those two schools were overcrowded, or they wanted to racially balance the white and Black students between the three schools. All I know is that getting along with each other was a bit rough. Those students didn't want to be a part of our school, to say the least. I'll never forget the group of bullies who stepped off that school bus every morning. They thought they could run and terrorize our whole school.

I had one of these bullies in my art class. At the time, I was the teacher's pet—well, actually, I had a crush on her, too. She was a young, beautiful Jewish teacher with long hair that nearly reached the back of her feet. Whenever the class got too loud, I was the one who helped her quiet my classmates down. I also assisted her with all the art projects.

One particular day, I was showing everyone how to use the oven for their ceramic vases. In the background, I could hear the class bully say, "I feel like beating up a nigger today." I turned around to see who he was talking to, and he was pointing directly at me.

He balled up his fist and kept smacking it into his other hand. "I'll be waiting for you after class," he told me.

I'm not going to lie—I was terrified. My legs wouldn't stop shaking, and my heart felt like it was going to explode. This kid had no reason not to like me, but the color of my skin gave him all the reason he needed to hate me.

The closer it got to the end of class, the more nervous I became.

I wasn't a violent kid, and this would be my very first physical fight.

"I'll be waiting for you after class," he kept taunting, over and over.

Finally, the bell rang, and the bully bolted out of the classroom, positioning himself at the bottom of the six-flight staircase, waiting for me.

I didn't know what to do. All I could think about was how bad this beating might be. My options felt limited, but I made my decision.

I leapt off the flight of stairs and landed directly on top of him. Yes, I did a perfect swan dive onto the bully. His glasses flew off his face, and I immediately started punching him as hard as I could. Before long, a few teachers broke up the fight and hauled us both to the principal's office.

While sitting there, the bully was crying uncontrollably. Meanwhile, I felt an incredible sense of pride for standing up for myself and putting him in his place. I'd stood up to a radical bully, and it felt amazing.

We both received a two-week suspension. When I returned to art class, my Jewish teacher gave me a subtle wink, and I became a hero in the eyes of my classmates.

As for the bully, he was transferred to a different class. I saw him occasionally during lunch with his group of cronies. They would stare, whisper, and point at me, but they never dared to approach or mess with me again.

This experience taught me valuable lessons as a kid:

1. **Respect isn't earned by being a pushover.**
2. **You have to stand up for yourself when it matters.**
3. **Never go looking for trouble, but when someone brings trouble to you, be prepared to solve the problem.**

Personal Timeline of 1973

Younger brother Foster Sylvers from the family singing group **The Sylvers** made waves on the music scene with his debut hit single, *Misdemeanor*. The catchy tune quickly became a favorite, and watching him perform on shows like **Soul Train** was an unforgettable experience.

(You can find it on YouTube: Foster Sylvers - "Misdemeanor" on Soul Train.)

In the early **1970s**, desegregation was reshaping schools and neighborhoods, forcing us to interact and learn about each other in ways we hadn't before. At first, tensions were high, and the differences between us often led to arguments and fights. But something incredible happened—through these shared experiences, bonds began to form.

I vividly recall how, after that brawl I had in school, everything seemed to shift. Relationships evolved, and many of the white students who had once been hostile became some of my closest friends. We played sports together, laughed together, and even visited each other's homes. It didn't matter if you were from a family with money or if you came from humble beginnings.

Desegregation, while challenging, pushed us to find common ground.

The **1970s** were undeniably a turbulent time, filled with visible hatred and societal unrest.

But for me, they were also a time of great discovery, love, and friendship.

The kindness and camaraderie I experienced in the midst of the chaos made those years truly special.

Looking back now, I realize how deeply these friendships impacted my life. They were a testament to how even in the most divided times, people can find connection and shared humanity.

The memories of my childhood friends and the adventures we shared are something I still hold close to my heart today.

The 70s were both terrible and terrific—a paradox that shaped me in unforgettable ways.

A Love That Knew No Boundaries

As I sit here, retracing the chapters of my childhood, a distant yet deeply personal memory floods my mind—a memory of innocence, first love, and a heartbreak I never quite recovered from as a child.

She was my very first girlfriend in the Smith Homes housing projects, and our relationship was our little secret. No one knew— not my parents, siblings, or even my friends. Her family didn't know about me either, and that secrecy made it feel like something precious, a fragile bond only we shared. She wasn't like any other girl I'd ever known. She wasn't delicate or afraid to get dirty; she wasn't the kind of girl who'd sit on the sidelines and watch the boys play. No, she was what we called a tomboy.

She climbed trees with us, scraped her knees, and dove into every game we played—football, baseball, basketball—you name it, she was right there, in the thick of it. She held her own with such determination and spirit that I couldn't help but admire her.

It wasn't just the way she moved, effortlessly keeping pace with the boys, but the way she made me feel.

It's hard to describe what love feels like when you're so young, barely old enough to understand the word itself. But I felt it. I loved her in the only way a child knows how—with purity, honesty, and a heart so full it felt like it might burst.

When I nervously asked her to be my girlfriend, she said yes. That single word made my world feel brighter, as if nothing else mattered. I could tell she was nervous, maybe even scared about the idea of us being more than friends, but she said yes.

And for a while, that was enough for me. We didn't need labels or anyone's approval; we just needed each other.

Then, one day, she was gone. Her family moved out of the projects without a word, without a trace. I can still feel the weight of that loss, even now, as if a piece of me was taken away and never returned.

I didn't get a chance to say goodbye, didn't get to ask her why or where she was going. One moment she was there, laughing and climbing trees, and the next, she was just… gone.

I was devastated. For days, I waited, hoping she'd come back, hoping it was just a mistake, that her absence was temporary. But deep down, I knew. Her family had packed up and left, likely one of the many families who couldn't stand living among us. And just like that, the first person who made my young heart flutter was ripped away from me.

Through all the racial tensions I experienced as a child, through all the hate and hostility, she stood out as a beacon of hope. My very first girlfriend in the Smith Homes housing projects was white. Even back then, I saw no color. To me, she wasn't a "white girl." She was just her—a girl who climbed trees, played ball, and made my heart feel things I didn't yet understand.

Her sudden departure changed me in ways I didn't realize at the time. It made me wary of getting too close, of letting myself feel too deeply. It introduced me to the pain of loss, a pain that wasn't just about her leaving, but about the realization that the world around us wouldn't let something as simple and pure as our friendship thrive.

Even now, as I write this, I wonder where she is, what kind of life she's living. I wonder if she ever thinks of me, of the days we spent climbing trees and playing Those childhood games.

Chapter 19

Christmas At The Wright's House

Remember that episode of A Charlie Brown Christmas? The one where Charlie Brown picked out that scrawny little Christmas tree, and it was so frail that it tipped over when he put an ornament on it? Well, our first Christmas in the Smith Homes housing projects felt a lot like that.

We brought over our old artificial tree from our previous home. It had missing limbs and bald spots, but instead of buying a new one, we made do. No matter how many strings of lights or ornaments we added, the tree still leaned awkwardly to one side. It was ugly, but it was ours. We decorated it with pride and were grateful for what we had.

Some Christmases were better than others. My mom always managed to save just enough to get each of us one gift we truly wanted. Other times, our presents came from the Salvation Army gift box—usually some new underwear, T-shirts, and socks. I remember one year when the girls received a couple of things, and us boys got a few items, but we had to share everything. It wasn't ideal, but we made it work.

What made our Christmases special wasn't the gifts but the sense of creativity and community instilled in us. I've never lived in any other housing projects, but I'd wager that Smith Homes had something unique: young mentors who taught us how to be resourceful and work for what we wanted. They showed us that we didn't need to rob or steal; there were honest ways to earn.

In the biting cold and fierce snowstorms of December, they taught us to bundle up, grab a shovel, and head into the middle-class neighborhoods to clear walkways and driveways. As Christmas approached, we'd go door-to-door in groups, singing Christmas carols and spreading cheer.

When we saved enough money, my siblings and I made the long, freezing trek to Grandland Shopping Center to buy gifts for each other and for our parents.

Every year, my dad received a brand-new pair of Hush Puppies shoes—his only Christmas wish.

My mom always wanted a housecoat and a new pair of slippers.

Those were their simple joys, and we did our best to fulfill them. Around the holidays, we tried to relieve my mom's stress so she could focus on preparing Christmas dinner. We were thoughtful kids, and it brought us closer as a family.

Even though we didn't get as much as we had back on Dumbarton Street, we were thankful. We appreciated being together in good health, with a roof over our heads and both parents at home. We knew other families were in worse situations, and that made us even more grateful for what we had.

Christmas was still my favorite holiday. The projects would transform into a quiet, serene winter wonderland. Snow blanketed the streets in crystal white, traffic disappeared, and the world felt peaceful. A few windows would glow with Christmas lights, while families stayed inside, cherishing the season. It was a time of togetherness and tranquility, even in the midst of struggle.

A few days after Christmas, the peace would give way to excitement. Kids paraded their new toys and presents around the block. Others made the trek to the Evergreen bridge, sledding down the Jefferies Freeway hills before this part freeway was completed. Those post-Christmas adventures brought the neighborhood alive again, with laughter and joy echoing through the streets.

At night, we had a daring tradition we called *Shagging*.

We would wait for cars to drive through the projects, grab onto their back bumpers, and slide down the icy streets until the end of the block. It was exhilarating and incredibly dangerous, but we were kids, and the thrill outweighed the risk.

Every year, someone in the neighborhood would string together three or four hoses and run hot water all day, creating a man-made skating rink in a vacant lot across the street from the projects. Once it froze over, we'd spend entire days ice skating.

It's hard to believe now, but I actually knew how to ice skate back then!

A Holiday Memory

As kids, we would save up as much money as we could throughout the year. With that hard-earned cash, my friends and I would catch the city bus downtown to watch the Thanksgiving / Christmas Parade. The excitement in the air was palpable as we stood among the crowds, sipping hot chocolate and watching the floats pass by.

When the parade ended, we'd make our way to nearby Cobo Hall for the indoor carnival. We spent hours riding the attractions, laughing and making memories that would last a lifetime. Those were some of the best moments of my childhood—simple joys that brought so much happiness.

Why Christmas Means So Much to Me Today

Every year, without fail, my wife asks me why I'm so joyful during the Christmas season and why I tend to overspend on gifts for the family. The truth is, it's not just about the presents—it's about the memories, the love, and the joy I want to pass down to my family.

Growing up, Christmas was magical but humble. We didn't have much, but my parents did everything they could to make the holidays special. Whether it was sharing a single toy between siblings, hanging decorations on a lopsided tree, or bundling up to sing Christmas carols for a few extra dollars, every moment was filled with gratitude and love.

Those simple traditions and sacrifices shaped me in ways I didn't fully understand as a child.

Back then, the joy of Christmas wasn't about material wealth; it was about being together, making the best of what we had, and cherishing the little things. Yet, I remember wishing I could give more—to my parents, to my siblings, to the people who worked so hard to make our lives better.

I promised myself that one day, if I ever had the means, I'd make Christmas everything it could be, not just for me but for my own family.

Now, as an adult, I have the privilege of being able to create the kind of Christmas I used to dream about. It's my way of honoring those humble beginnings and making sure my loved ones never feel like they're missing out.

When I see their faces light up as they open gifts or gather around the tree, it reminds me of the joy I felt in those small but meaningful moments of my childhood.

For me, Christmas isn't just a holiday—it's a chance to relive the love, laughter, and warmth of those simpler times. It's about creating a legacy of joy and generosity, making sure my family knows how much they mean to me, and showing them that no matter what life throws at us, we can always find a reason to celebrate each other.

So yes, I might overspend on gifts, but it's not just about the presents.

It's about making memories that my family will carry with them, just like I carry the memories of those lopsided Christmas trees and shared toys.

It's about ensuring that the spirit of Christmas—the love, the joy, and the togetherness—always lives on in my family.

Now that's my explanation on why I spend so much money. Mrs. Wright. Stop counting my pockets every year. (laughing)

Chapter 20

Some of the Games We Used to Play

The games we played as kids in the Smith Homes Housing Projects were unforgettable and deeply rooted in tradition. Many were passed down from one generation to the next, creating a unique bond between the past and present. Others turned the entire project into one massive playground, where kids of all ages could join in the fun.

Back then, there was never a dull moment. We didn't have cell phones, the internet, or gaming consoles like Nintendo 64. Instead, we used our imaginations and the world around us. On any given weekend morning, you could look outside your window and see little girls playing hopscotch, boys shooting marbles, or kids sitting on the sidewalk playing jacks.

Here are some of the iconic games we played in Smith Homes:
Four Squares

This game likely originated in the 1950s, but we had our own twist on it. Four players would stand in their respective squares, with the goal being to hit the ball into another player's square. If a player hit the ball out of bounds, onto the square's line, or missed the ball entirely, they were out. The last person standing in their square became the "king" or "queen." It was a simple yet competitive game that could keep us entertained for hours.

Hide and Go Get It

A bold variation of the classic Hide and Seek, this game added an exciting twist: the chance to sneak a kiss. Played mostly when it got dark, we'd hide behind bushes, in the grass on the playground, in alleyways, or even on top of the center building. It was thrilling, slightly mischievous, and definitely a favorite among us kids.

Center Tag

This was a favorite for the boys. Played around the Smith Homes office building (the center), the rules were simple: avoid getting tagged. But our version was more adventurous. We'd run around the building, dart between the two structures, or climb onto the roof that connected them.

Some of the braver kids would even jump off the roof to escape being tagged. Amazingly, no one ever broke a bone!

Red Light, Green Light

This timeless game was one of my personal favorites. The lead player would stand at a distance, with their back turned to the group. At the command "Green Light," players would move toward the lead. At "Red Light," everyone had to freeze. If anyone moved after the "Red Light" command, they were out or became the new lead player. The goal was to reach the lead player first. It was a game of focus, strategy, and quick reflexes that brought out everyone's competitive side.

Go-Stop

Go-Stop was another urban game we used to play in the projects. It was a combination of Hide and Seek and Red Light, Green Light. The lead player would stand at a distance with their back turned to the other players. At their command of "Go!" the pack of players would run onto the field. When the lead player shouted "Stop!" everyone had to freeze or find a hiding spot as quickly as possible. Once the lead player commanded "Go!" again, the players would run to new hiding places, trying to stay out of sight. Anyone found by the lead player had to help search for the remaining players. The last person found was declared the winner and became the new lead player.

Flag Football

Flag Football was another favorite game we played. Believed to have originated in the late 19th or early 20th century, it followed the same rules as American Football, except tackling was replaced with pulling a flag from the ball carrier's belt. It was so popular in the projects that we often moved our games from the Smith Homes fields to Stoepel Park down the street. After a while, we grew tired of pulling flags and joined the older kids in playing full-contact football back in the projects.

Duck Duck Goose was a classic game we played during our younger years, especially in gym class. A group of kids would form a circle on the grass or floor. The "goose" would walk around the circle, tapping each player on the head and calling them a "duck."

When the "goose" tapped someone and called them "goose," that player had to jump up and chase the original "goose" around the circle, trying to tag them before they could sit in the vacant spot.

If the original "goose" was tagged, they remained the "goose," but if they escaped, the new player took their place, and the game continued.

The Rise of Technology and the Decline of Outdoor Games By the late 70s and early 80s, handheld video games and classic board games started changing how kids spent their free time. Games like *Pac- Man*, *Space Invaders*, *Donkey Kong*, *Frogger*, and *Super Mario* took over living rooms. As technology advanced, games like *Tetris*, *Street Fighter*, *Hogan's Alley*, and *Metal Gear* became the new addiction, keeping kids indoors for hours.

Then came the technology revolution: the introduction of personal computers in 1981, digital cell phones in the early 90s, and the birth of social media. Platforms like Friendster (2002), MySpace (2003), Facebook (2006), Twitter and Instagram (2010), Snapchat (2011), and TikTok (2016) changed how people interacted and entertained themselves.

The End of an Era

As social media and video games became the center of attention, the vibrant outdoor games we once cherished slowly faded into memory. The carefree days of running around the Smith Homes

Housing Projects, playing *Go-Stop, Red Light, Green Light*, and *Duck Duck Goose*, became relics of a simpler time. These games were more than just a way to pass the time—they were the foundation of our childhood. They taught us creativity, cooperation, and how to build relationships face-to-face, without the distraction of screens or notifications.

The shift wasn't immediate, but it was inevitable. As more households embraced technology, video games and personal computers started replacing the need for outdoor play. The neighborhood streets and playgrounds that were once filled with laughter, running feet, and shouts of joy began to grow quieter.

Even the "daring" stunts we used to pull, like jumping off roofs during *Center Tag* or shagging behind cars on icy streets, started feeling like tales of a bygone era.

The new generation wasn't interested in these kinds of games anymore. The sense of community that these games fostered also started to dissolve.

Before the rise of cell phones and social media, we learned everything about one another by simply spending time together.

We shared our stories, fears, and dreams while passing the ball in *Four Square* or strategizing over who would be the last person standing in *Go-Stop*. Our games weren't just fun; they were the building blocks of lifelong friendships and trust.

But with the arrival of advanced technology, something changed. Kids became more drawn to the glow of their screens than the fresh air outside. Instead of gathering in the playground or on the field, they gathered in chat rooms or multiplayer video game lobbies. Instead of running home breathless after a game of tag, they stayed indoors, glued to their controllers. It wasn't just the games that disappeared—it was the face-to-face connections that came with them.

Even today, I can't help but feel a pang of nostalgia when I think about those days. We didn't need expensive equipment, Wi-Fi, or the latest smartphone to have fun. A ball, a stick, or even an empty lot was all we needed to create unforgettable memories. The projects weren't just a place where we lived—they were a world we built for ourselves, a world of adventure, laughter, and camaraderie.

Now, when I see children buried in their phones, oblivious to the world around them, I wonder if they'll ever know the joy of running barefoot through the grass, the thrill of being "it" in a game of tag, or the pride of making up their own rules for a game.

Will they ever know what it's like to create magic from nothing but their imaginations and the company of their friends?

The end of this era wasn't just about losing games—it was about losing a way of life.

It marked the transition from physical play to digital entertainment, from spontaneous creativity to programmed stimulation.

While technology has brought countless advancements and conveniences, it has also taken away some of the innocence and simplicity of childhood.

Still, I hold on to the memories of those days.

They remind me of who I was, where I came from, and the community that shaped me.

"Those games weren't just about having fun—they were about creating bonds, learning to navigate challenges, and building a sense of community. Even as technology crept in and changed the way we interacted, the values and lessons from those moments stuck with me. Little did I know, those experiences were preparing me for a world that would be just as unpredictable and challenging as any game we played. As I moved through life, those lessons stayed with me, shaping how I approached friendships, challenges, and the changing times."

Chapter 21

My Wonder Years

Definition of a – CRUSH
A crush is when you have feelings of admiration for someone. It's usually superficial and based on limited knowledge of that person. An informal feeling of love and affection for someone, often a person you know you cannot have a relationship with. In other words, like they say in the streets, you have no game.

As I entered middle school, history became my favorite subject. My second favorite? The study of girls.

There was one girl who stood out among the rest. She lived just three doors down from me. Quiet and reserved, she rarely socialized with anyone in the projects. There was something about her maturity and composure that made her seem wise beyond her years. Every day, I would watch her walk to and from school in her signature Chuck Taylor Converse sneakers, radiating confidence without saying a word.

Over time, I worked up the nerve to strike up conversations with her. I'd do little things to make her smile—crack jokes, carry her books, and walk her home from school. Every evening, just before she turned in for the night, I'd steal a kiss on her cheek, feeling like I was on top of the world. Eventually, I asked her to be my girlfriend. To my surprise, she said yes!

But reality hit hard. Our relationship lasted all of two weeks. She was just too mature for me, and I was too immature to match her level of seriousness. It was a tough lesson, but one I needed to learn: girls really do mature faster than boys.

Throughout middle school, I developed a pattern of short-lived relationships.

I was well-liked by the girls in Smith Homes, but my own immaturity made it impossible to maintain anything serious.

I went through crushes and flings like running water.

If a girl wasn't liked by others, was too silly, mean, or had a foul mouth, I just couldn't bring myself to stay interested. And there was another, unspoken rule: my mom had to like her.

If my mother didn't approve, the relationship was over before it even started.

One memory from 8th grade still makes me laugh. I was dating a girl who invited me and a few friends over for her birthday party in their basement. They had this old stove down there that her family wasn't using anymore. Her brother carried down her birthday cake and placed it on top of the stove. About ten minutes later, one of my friends pointed out mice scurrying up through the eyes of the stove, nibbling on the cake. Needless to say, that was the beginning of the end for that relationship.

There were, however, a few girls who left a lasting impression— not just on me but also on my mother. My mom adored my best friend's sister. She would light up seeing the two of us walking to school together. "You two make such a cute couple," she'd sign to me with a grin.

Another favorite of hers was a girl from the back-streeter's side of the projects. This girl won my mom over with her genuine personality and her effort to communicate with her through sign language. My mom would sign back, and my girlfriend would look to me to translate. It was the sweetest thing to see them bonding in their own way. When I lost that relationship, my mother was visibly upset with me for weeks. Years later, she would still bring her up. "Whatever happened to that girl with the pretty smile?" she'd ask.

The last girl to gain my mom's approval was my neighbor's best friend. That one was tough for me. I really liked her, but she broke my heart.

Those wonder years taught me a lot about relationships—how they're built and how easily they can be lost. While my crushes may not have lasted, each one shaped me in its own way.

She was a couple of years older, beautiful, way too sophisticated, and far too advanced for me. I couldn't keep that relationship either. And because of that, she set her sights on the much older teenagers in the projects.

Then I dated a girl whose father was also a devoted Muslim.

She was gorgeous and so mature for her age. We were an item for a while, but then we broke up, and she ended up dating my best friend. That hurt—not because she ended up with him but because her mother liked me so much. I felt like I had disappointed her by not being the one to stay with her daughter.

Warren G. Harding Middle School was known for its beautiful and mature girls as well. If you didn't know better, you'd think the girls were already attending their first or second year of high school already. I had a lot of crushes, though most didn't amount to much.

I can vividly remember a girl who lived just a few blocks away from school on Stout Street—a bombshell tomboy. She did everything with the boys, played everything with the boys, and was admired by all of them. She was never afraid to play dodgeball or football with us. Athletic and confident, she was always the first picked for every volleyball team. But beyond her athleticism, she was a well-rounded and beautiful person to be around. She had that magnetic quality that made everyone gravitate toward her.

I had a strong crush on this phenomenal girl, but I didn't dare share how I felt. I didn't want to risk ruining our friendship.

At that point, I'd had my share of failed relationships, and I didn't want her to become part of my "personal statistics."
I valued our friendship far more than my feelings.

There was another girl—a tall, stunning beauty who lived right outside the projects, just a couple of blocks away.

With long, jet-black hair cascading down her back, she was goddess-like to all of us boys in the neighborhood. She was a middle school phenomenon, both in looks and intelligence.

Easily one of the prettiest girls at Harding, she was impossible to ignore. I was just one of the many boys caught in her web of charm.

Every day, a group of us would walk home from school together, and I would find myself stealing glances at her, captivated by her elegance. But her beauty came with a price—jealous girls often targeted her for no reason other than her good looks. Many times, she had to run home to avoid fights.

Eventually, I decided to take a chance and risk it all.

One day, I confided in a friend about my crush on her. For hours, I went on about my feelings but admitted I was too scared to tell her. "If you really want her to know, you should just tell her," he said.

I hesitated.

"Man, if you don't tell her, she'll never know! Walk over to her house, knock on the door, and tell her how you feel. Then ask her to be your girlfriend."

It sounded like a bold but promising plan. Finally, I worked up the nerve to go to her house on Heyden Street.

I walked up the sidewalk slowly, heart pounding with every step. As I climbed onto her porch, I felt my courage wavering.

I knocked on the door, and she answered.

"Eric, what are you doing here? How did you know where I live?"

In that moment, it felt like I had swallowed a whole frog. My knees were practically knocking together.

I wanted to turn around and run, but I forced myself to stay.

"Um…hi," I stammered. "There's something I need to tell you."

Before I could say more, her sister ran to the door to see what was happening. Now, two pairs of curious eyes were fixed on me.

"I... I don't know if you've noticed, but I have a serious crush on you," I blurted out. They kept listening, their faces unreadable.

"All the things I wanted to say wouldn't come out," I admitted. So I kept it short and got straight to the point.

"Um... I came over here to ask: would you be my girlfriend?"

The two sisters looked at each other and started laughing hysterically. This attractive young girl slammed the door in my face, leaving me standing on her porch.

I was so embarrassed, so humiliated—I could still hear the two of them laughing inside the house as I walked away. I felt like a nobody. From that point on, I made it my mission to stay far away from her at school. I didn't want her to embarrass me in front of my friends or even glance my way.

I started questioning myself: *Why did she do me like that? What was so funny?*
Maybe I was too short for her. Maybe it was the fact that I lived in the projects and her family was middle class. Maybe she wasn't into boys just yet. Maybe she thought I was ugly. Or maybe I just wasn't her type.

Whatever the case, she crushed my soul that day. Looking back, I can't believe I tried to win over the heart of the prettiest girl in middle school, knowing my track record with cute girls. It took me a few years to master the art of building confidence and learning how to carry myself with a smooth persona. But once I figured it out, there was no stopping me.

Of course, I had to endure a few more heartbreaks before I became *that dude*. (Laughing)

And on a side note: I'm sure that little girl grew up to become a phenomenal woman.

Reflection: Lessons From Heartbreaks

Looking back, I realize that every crush, rejection, and fleeting relationship taught me something about myself. That moment on the porch, as humiliating as it felt, wasn't just about rejection—it was a lesson in courage. It took a lot for me to put myself out there, and even though it didn't end the way I hoped, it showed me the importance of taking risks.

As I grew older, I learned to channel those moments into confidence. I started focusing less on what I thought I lacked and more on what I brought to the table. Those early heartbreaks taught me that not everyone will see your worth immediately, but that doesn't make you any less valuable.

I also learned the importance of timing and compatibility. Sometimes, it's not about you—it's about where the other person is in their life. That realization gave me a new perspective, one that made rejection sting a little less and self-respect grow a little more.

By the time I mastered confidence and charm, I wasn't just chasing relationships to prove something; I was seeking connections that truly mattered.

Those wonder years taught me resilience, humility, and that no matter how awkward or painful a moment might seem, it's all part of the journey.

"Looking back, those crushes, heartbreaks, and fleeting moments of affection were more than just teenage emotions. They taught me about vulnerability, confidence, and the importance of valuing meaningful connections.

While I didn't always handle things perfectly, each experience shaped the man I was becoming. As the years passed, I would learn that relationships—whether with friends, family, or potential partners—would always be a cornerstone of my journey. But life wasn't just about finding love; it was also about discovering who I truly was, one lesson at a time."

After writing this chapter, my mind wandered back to middle school. One of my friends had a severe case of eczema on her hands, neck, and face. She was a genuinely sweet girl, but every day, she endured relentless teasing from the other kids. It broke my heart to see her suffer, and I decided to stand up for her. From that moment on, I made it my mission to protect her from their cruelty. If anyone messed with her, they had to deal with me. She appreciated the protection, and it strengthened our bond. Over time, she developed a crush on me, but I didn't see her in that way. To me, she was like a sister.

As we transitioned from middle school to high school, she began visiting the projects, asking for me. Sometimes, she'd follow me home, dropping hints about wanting something more than friendship. Yet, I couldn't picture a romantic relationship with her—not at that time.

She was persistent, though, and I became increasingly resistant, unsure of how to navigate her feelings.

Then, about a year later, she came to the projects again. But this time, something was different. The medication she was using had cleared her eczema completely.

She looked like a completely different person. She wore light makeup, dressed beautifully, and carried herself with a newfound confidence. It was clear she had put in extra effort just for me.

She looked stunning, and suddenly, I felt a little selfish in my actions but began to see her in a different light. For the first time, I allowed myself to imagine the possibility of us being more than friends.

But I waited too late.

One day, tragedy struck. Allegedly, someone attempted to steal her family's car from their driveway. As the thief tried to escape, she and her mother came to the door.

The thief fired shots in their direction.

Allegedly her mother was grazed by a bullet, but the ricochet struck my beautiful friend, ending her life.

It was all over the news. I couldn't bring myself to attend her funeral. The thought of seeing her like that was too much to bear. Even now, over 40 years later, the pain of losing her feels as fresh as it did that day. I think about how I protected her in school from the senseless cruelty she faced, but when it truly mattered, I wasn't there to shield her from a stray bullet.

She was such a kind and beautiful soul. The world was better with her in it.

(Tears fill my eyes every time I think about this moment in time.)

That was my beautiful friend

Moral of the Story: Life is unpredictable, and every moment we share with those we care about matters more than we realize. Protecting someone from life's small cruelties is meaningful, but we must also cherish and express our feelings fully while we have the chance. Regret is a heavy burden, so never wait too long to show appreciation, love, or kindness to someone who holds a special place in your heart. Their presence may not last forever, but the impact of your connection can endure beyond a lifetime.

Chapter 22

Project Mentors

There are certain people in life who leave a mark on your soul, shaping who you become and guiding you through uncertain times. For me, these were the young men of the Smith Homes Projects. Though I cannot mention their names due to not having their permission, they know who they are. They were more than mentors—they were my brothers, and their guidance had a profound impact on my life. Wherever they may be now, I simply want to say:

Thank you.

*I also want to express my deepest gratitude to the incredible mothers of the Smith Homes Projects. **Y. J., V.G.** and **B.M.** You three were the glue that kept us all on the straight and narrow. For the two mothers who are no longer with us, may you continue to rest peacefully. You are never forgotten. To **V.G.** and **B.M.** I will always love you. Thank you for everything.*

As I mentioned earlier, these young men were more than just role models; they were protectors and guides. They taught us by example, showing us that hard work and community meant more than falling into the traps of the streets. They put money in their pockets by working seasonal jobs in nearby neighborhoods, never resorting to selling controlled substances or street drugs—at least, not to our knowledge. We watched their every move and imitated what we saw, striving to follow the positive example they set for us.

Through the mid-1970s and into the early 1980s, these mentors threw the most memorable parties at our project center and rental office, events we affectionately called **"The Center Parties."**

Boy, were they fun! I can still hear the records spinning, filling the room with music that became the soundtrack of my childhood:

- **"Watching You"** by Slave
- **"One Nation Under a Groove"** and **"Flash Light"** by Parliament Funkadelic
- **"Shame"** by Evelyn "Champaign" King
- **"I Love Music"** by the O'Jays
- **"Float On"** by Detroit's own Floaters
- **"Rock Steady"** by Aretha Franklin
- **"I'll Be Around"** by The Spinners
- **"Thin Line Between Love and Hate"** by The Persuaders
- **"Fire"** by The Ohio Players
- **"Zoom"** by The Commodores
- **"Funkin' for Jamaica"** by Tom Browne
- **"Let's Start the Dance"** by Bohannon
- **"Ring My Bell"** by Anita Ward

And of course, **"Get Off"** by Foxy—just hearing this music takes me back to those hot summer nights.

When the lights went off at the center parties, it was our chance to kiss and slow dance with our favorite girls. I still laugh remembering the small closet off to the side where some kids would sneak off to make out in secret. (Yes, that happened!)

The mentors didn't just throw parties; they gave us opportunities to grow. Cooking classes were held for kids at the center, and they organized movie nights and even summertime pajama parties. For those, we'd grab whatever we could—blankets, pillows, or a mat to sleep on.

Some of us didn't have much, so we made do with just a pillow we secretly sneaked out of the house.

Lying on the hard floor with friends, talking and laughing through the night, was all we needed to feel like we were part of something special.

When it came to sports, the big boys never excluded anyone. Whether it was football, basketball, or baseball, they made sure everyone had a chance to play. Personally, I loved playing football among friends, but when it came to the big leagues with the older kids, I stayed out of it. I wasn't a fan of getting hit hard—I'd seen too many young guys taken out of commission after rough tackles.

Broken arms, broken legs—oh yeah! The big boys showed us firsthand what getting hit hard felt like. But no matter what they did, we wanted to do it too. They were our heroes, our role models, and we followed their lead in everything, even if it meant a few bumps and bruises along the way.

Late at night, you could hear them singing and crooning under the streetlights. Their harmonies were magnetic, drawing the younger kids like me and my friends. Inspired, we formed our own little group and tried our best to mimic their sound. To our surprise, we didn't sound half bad!

We also watched how they interacted with girls, taking mental notes and copying their moves until we developed our own style for "pulling the honeys." It was a kind of unspoken education, learning the art of confidence and charm from the older generation.

One of our mentors had big dreams for his daughter and the neighborhood girls. Using the idea of a talent search, he set out to create his own all-girl singing group. Every weekend, he'd set up a mic, speakers, and a mic stand in his front yard and hold auditions.

It was quite the spectacle to see his daughter and the others trying their best to synchronize their dance moves and sing in harmony.

While some of us laughed at their efforts, we couldn't deny their determination and spirit. Another mentor took us on life-changing camping trips as part of the **Masai Club**, an organization named after the African word for "warrior." I vividly remember one trip to the Lexington campgrounds.

My mom had bought me a brand-new pair of khaki shorts for the occasion, and for some reason, I decided to stash a can of Vienna sausages in my pocket before heading out.

As I wrestled with a friend while waiting to load into the van, he flipped me onto the ground, landing on top of me. The can burst open in my pocket, and the oil soaked into my new shorts. The smell of Vienna sausage oil clung to me the entire trip. When I got home, my mom was furious. She whipped me for ruining the shorts, hitting me on my arms, legs, and back. At that moment, I realized I was getting too big for regular butt whippings. (Laughing)

There was a time when a best friend disrespected my dad after he told him to get out of the yard. Everyone gathered around to see what would happen. Fueled by anger and adrenaline, I circled him and landed a few jabs to his face before throwing a right cross that busted his lip. A mentor quickly intervened, breaking up the fight. "Hey, hey, hey. That's enough—you two, break it up!" he said.

Later, the mentor pulled me aside and asked, "Where did you learn to throw a jab like that?" I proudly told him, "I watched a lot of boxing with my dad."

He smiled and said I had natural talent, suggesting I join a boxing gym to hone my skills. That one comment filled me with pride and confidence.

The following week, my friend and I joined the Crowell Recreational Center after school. On my first day, the trainer paired me with an experienced boxer to test my skills. We danced around the ring until he landed a combination that hit me on the unpadded top of my headgear, knocking me out cold.

Despite the rough start, I kept coming back to practice, even when my friend quit after three weeks. The mentors in the projects weren't the only ones who shaped me. I was fortunate to have mentors within my own family—uncles, aunts, and cousins—all of whom helped guide me into manhood.

But I've often wondered what happened to the generation that came after us. Every Black generation navigates life differently, shaped by the opportunities—or lack thereof—available in their time. Despite these differences, we all share the same cherished memories of growing up in Smith Homes.

We played sports and neighborhood games together. We rode our bikes through the streets, went to school together, and even got into fights, only to reconcile the next day. We were rowdy, mischievous, and full of life. Those were the wonder years—years that shaped us into the people we are today.

We all swam in the swim-mobile when it came around in the summer.We also swam at Rouge Park, ran through the water gushing out of fire hydrants, shared and traded food from the center lunch program, and worked our summer jobs together.

Halloween was no different—we went trick-or-treating together. We did so many things together. We became one huge family in the Smith Homes Projects. But something happened to the kids who grew up behind us.

Not all of them, but some. Maybe the mentors didn't connect with them the way they connected with us.

Drugs began infiltrating our communities, and kids were faced with two choices: stay far away and continue on a favorable path, or use the opportunity to make fast money as young dealers. For some, the lure of that second choice was too easy to embrace.

I'm not saying none of my generation made that choice—because I know some who did—but in my family, it was up to me, as the big brother, to make absolutely, positively sure no one in my family followed that path. If I wasn't out there selling drugs, they wouldn't be either.

I said we were poor, not desperate.

I made it my personal responsibility to be the head knocker of the family. No one was going to die from drugs, get strung out, or do time in prison for them.

No one was going to disappoint or embarrass my mother like that. I did my best to know my siblings' whereabouts and what they were up to at all times.

That's not to say some of those kids who initially chose the fast-money route didn't eventually turn their lives around and do amazing things. Many of us in the projects went on to have wonderful careers.

The War on Drugs

What I couldn't stand was hearing people on television talk about the "War on Drugs" while programs in our neighborhoods were being cut left and right.

The swim-mobile and bookmobile stopped coming around, leaving kids with nothing productive to do. Jobs were scarce for parents, and in **1982**, the minimum wage was just **$3.35** an hour.

After the Vietnam War, our own government turned a blind eye to the growing problems in urban communities. Crack cocaine made it easier to fill prisons with people like us.

Drugs tore families apart. Fathers left at alarming rates, mothers turned to prostitution to support their habits, and children were left to fend for themselves. Some of those kids felt they had no choice but to move up the ranks and become young kingpins.

By the early '80s, you had buyers addicted to drugs and dealers addicted to money. Crack turned people into monsters—whether they were using or selling. This wasn't just an epidemic; this was chemical warfare.

Even the police weren't immune to the corruption. Some were paid off by dealers to allow them to operate in their territories.

Imagine the authorities making a drug bust, confiscating all the drugs and cash, then splitting the cash among themselves and reselling the drugs back onto the streets. This wasn't a conspiracy theory—this was the Blue Wall of Silence.

Rising Violence

Murders in Detroit skyrocketed. Drug dealers became targets for rival dealers. Shootouts became a horrifyingly common occurrence in our neighborhoods. Friends and family members were overdosing and dying.

Drugs didn't just devastate individuals—they destroyed entire communities. And as I reflect on those days, it still breaks my heart to think of all the lives lost and futures stolen by addiction and violence.

"As I grew older, I realized that the lessons I learned from those mentors in the projects were priceless. They gave us more than just guidance; they gave us hope, discipline, and a sense of community.

These values would stay with me and shape the way I navigated life's challenges. Yet, while mentors provided wisdom, my peers brought adventure. Together, we found ways to turn every moment into a story worth telling, and some of those moments are etched in my memory forever."

Detroit's Own Style: 70's and 80's Fashion Back When I Was A Kid

Growing up in Detroit during the 70s and 80s, fashion wasn't just about clothes—it was about making a statement. The style reflected who you were, what you stood for, and where you were from. And let me tell you, Detroit had its own unmistakable flair. Our city was a melting pot of creativity, blending classic trends with a bold, street-smart edge.

Here's a list of iconic Detroit fashion staples that defined my childhood:

1. **Jingle Boots** – If you didn't hear the jingle, you weren't walking right.
2. **Karate Shoes** – Lightweight, sleek, and perfect for kids on the move.

3. **Jelly Shoes** – Popular with the girls, these colorful, see-through sandals made every outfit pop.

4. **Swedish Knit Dress Pants** – A must-have for a sharp, clean look.

5. **Silk, Roland Dress Shirts with Long Collars** – The ultimate in smooth style.

6. **Horse Whip Key Chains** – Dangling from belt loops, these were as much an accessory as a statement piece.

7. **Big Belt Buckles That Spelled Your Whole Name** – Nothing said bold like a custom buckle in silver or brass.

8. **Triple F.A.T. Goose Winter Coats** – Stylish and warm for those brutal Detroit winters.

9. **Pro Ked Sneakers** – A classic on the basketball court and the playground.

10. **Converse All-Stars (Chucks) Sneakers** – Timeless and versatile.

11. **Beepers** – The early status symbol for anyone wanting to stay "connected."

12. **Bell Bottoms** – Wide-legged and groovy, perfect for the dance floor.

13. **Cross Colours Clothing** – A vibrant, Afrocentric style statement of the late '80s.

14. **Bossalini Hats** – Topped off every sharp outfit with class.

15. **Big Hair and Afros** – Hair was power, and bigger was always better.

16. **Jump Suits** – The one-piece wonder of comfort and style.

17. **Kangol Hats** – A nod to hip-hop culture before it even had a name.

18. **Stack Hill Shoes** – Elevated style with a bit of height.

19. **Glass Heel Shoes** – Unique and unforgettable, these were a bold fashion statement.

20. **Boom Boxes** – Music was portable, and the bigger the better.

21. **Walkman Cassette Players** – For those who wanted to take their music on the go.
22. **Fanny Packs** – Functional and trendy, worn around the waist with pride.
23. **Apple Hats** – A touch of classic charm.
24. **Adidas Shell Toe Sneakers** – Paired with fat laces, they were a staple in hip-hop fashion.
25. **Knitted Neckties** – A quirky yet stylish addition to formal wear.
26. **Large Rope Chain Necklaces and Big Hoop Earrings** – Accessories that screamed personality and status.
27. **Jerry Curls and Shags** – Hair trends that defined an era.
28. **Air Jordan Sneakers** – The 1985, 1986, and 1988 editions were game-changers.
29. **Dashikis** – A celebration of African heritage and pride.
30. **Circle Flip-Up Shade Sunglasses** – For those who loved a unique, futuristic look.
31. **Wallets with Chains** – Practical and stylish, often paired with biker vibes.
32. **British Knights Sneakers** – Flashy and bold, they were a hit in the streets.
33. **Buster Brown Dress Shoes** – The classic choice for Sunday best.
34. **S.S. Kresge Plastic Bottom Tennis Shoes** – Affordable and ubiquitous, yet memorable. (Cheap and tore easily)

Personal Timeline of 1973

It's impossible to talk about this era without mentioning the birth of hip-hop music. While it started in New York, its influence quickly reached Detroit, blending with our city's own creative flair. Hip-hop wasn't just about the beats—it was about the culture, the attitude, and most importantly, the fashion.

(New York's Dapper Dan Fashions paved the way, but let's not forget that we Detroiters have always been trendsetters in our own right.)

Whether it was the way we wore our Kangol hats tilted to the side or paired our Adidas shell toes with Detroit swagger, we took the essence of hip-hop and made it our own. The streets of Detroit became a runway, and each block was a fashion show.

The 70s and 80s were more than just decades—they were the backdrop of my childhood, painted with the vivid hues of community, culture, and unforgettable style. Detroit's fashion wasn't just about looking good; it was about feeling proud of who you were and where you came from.

Never forget, we are trend setters. Always have been. It's just who we are.

Chapter 23

Hitting A Rough Patch

Don't get me wrong—I wasn't too bad of a kid, but there were times when I veered off the straight and narrow. I hit a rough patch a few times and did some things I'm not proud of. My mom never knew about most of it. If she had found out, she probably would've just thrown up her hands and told my dad to handle me.

Here's a list of a few things that come to mind:

I remember one time I was heading home from the grocery store, just about to enter the projects, when I saw a girl cleaning out her garage. I asked if she needed help, and she said yes. "Can you move these boxes for me? They're too heavy for me to lift." I happily helped her organize the garage, and that's when I spotted this sweet boom box sitting on one of the shelves.

"Whose boom box is that?" I asked. "I don't have much money, but would you sell it to me?"

She replied, "No, it's my dad's, and I don't think he wants to get rid of it."

I couldn't stop thinking about that boom box. Twenty minutes later, I asked her again, "Are you sure your dad doesn't want to sell it?"

"No! I think he wants to keep it," she replied. "But I can go inside and ask him if you like."

The moment she walked into the house, I unplugged the boom box, snatched it off the shelf, and ran straight to the projects with it. When I got home, my dad asked me where I got it. I lied and said, "One of my friends bought a new one and gave this one to me." He didn't ask any more questions, but I never walked that route to the grocery store again.

Another time, my sweet tooth got the best of me. I was a Hostess Twinkies and apple pie lover back then.

I had an old winter coat with a huge hole in the pocket that tunneled around to the back of the coat. I'd go to the store for my mom, grab a shopping cart, and casually stroll down the snack aisle. I'd stuff as many cakes as I could into my pocket and push them to the back of my coat. Then I'd continue shopping for my mom's groceries like nothing was amiss.

I never walked out of the store with a bulging front pocket—just a suspiciously large-looking back! (laughing)

To be honest, I lost count of how many times I used that coat to sneak something out of Cunningham Drugs or S.S. Kresge at Grandland Shopping Center on Fenkell Avenue.

In elementary school, my mischievous side started to show again. I became a bit of a class clown. One day, just before the lunch bell, my music teacher had us all lined up single file to leave the room. There was a two-sided chalkboard on a wooden stand that swiveled. As I walked by, I "accidentally" kicked it, and it crashed to the floor.

When the teacher asked the class what happened, the other students ratted me out immediately. She sent me to the principal's office, and I got suspended.

My dad asked why I was in trouble, and I spun this elaborate lie. I told him, "The music teacher doesn't like me. She's had it out for me since day one and lied, saying I knocked over her chalkboard when it wasn't me!"

That lie lit a fire under my dad. He took my mom and me to the school and stormed into the principal's office.

When my music teacher arrived, my dad cursed her and the principal out so badly that it became embarrassing for everyone involved. Sitting there, I felt terrible for causing such a ruckus.

My bold-faced lie steamrolled into an atomic bomb within my dad. He said that if they didn't allow me to come back to school the next day, they would have to see him again. The very next day, they allowed me to return, but I couldn't step foot in her music class ever again. Looking back, I should have apologized and told my dad the truth. I should've come clean and apologized to my teacher and the principal as well.

Incidentally, that was the one and only time my dad came out in support of me.

He never came out to watch me play basketball, and even though we both loved boxing and watched it on television together, he never came out to watch me box. He wasn't there to cheer me on when I received my second-place volleyball trophy. Not even for the play I wrote and starred in. We lost the talent contest to a kid who played the trumpet, but we were the talk of the whole school.

Even when I entered my very first essay contest, he replaced the $5 award I lost, but he never came out and sat in the auditorium to watch me. Cursing everyone out in the principal's office was the only time he came out in support of me.

But getting back to my rough streak: every year on Devil's Night, we would go out on Evergreen Road and throw eggs at cars, then run back into the projects to hide when the vehicles stopped and the drivers and passengers chased us.

Soon, we got the idea of throwing eggs at whoever walked out of the store across the street. The store owner finally came out to tell us to stop throwing eggs at his customers. So we took a whole bunch of eggs and threw them at him.

One time, me and a few friends were walking through the neighborhood on Devil's Night. One of my friends decided to pick up a Big Wheel parked on the sidewalk and threw it through someone's picture window.

We all laughed and ran back to the projects for safety. I wasn't the one who caused all that damage—I was just guilty by association.

135

We also used to snatch Halloween bags from other kids. The projects were always our safe zone. No one would be foolish enough to take the chance of coming after us. Their safety would be in serious jeopardy.

I was also known for climbing in and out of windows to make out with girls. I was a great window climber back in those days. (laughing)

Stoepel Park had a trail of bushes almost surrounding the whole park. In between the bushes was a dirt bike trail.

Not to mention any names but I have had some kissing and touching with girls from the projects a few times under those same bushes. (laughing)

One time when I was walking home from a 7-Eleven store on Fenkell Avenue and Evergreen road. I was on my way to the projects when I saw this young woman unloading groceries out of the trunk of her car. This woman kept staring at me as I walked closer. I asked if she knew me. No!

But can you help me bring my groceries in the house, she asked.

I helped bring her last bag in her kitchen and instead of giving me a few dollars for helping her she thanked me then proceeded to kiss me on the lips. This was an attractive, young woman. Mid twenties I guessed. At that point she had me really curious to why she would do such a thing.

She unfastened a few buttons on her blouse, took my hand and led me upstairs to her bedroom.

Now she didn't ask how old I was. In fact, I don't think she even cared. She could also tell I was a bit nervous, which made her giggle and laugh at times. She thought my shyness was pretty funny.

To make a long story short, we laid in her bed and started kissing when suddenly we heard keys and the door opening downstairs.

She told me her husband was home and she hid me inside a closet for a whole 3 hours until he fell asleep, Hell, I heard every conversation and everything they did, sitting in that dark closet.

She was finally able to sneak me downstairs and back out their home.

Talking about a close call.

That big dude would've kicked my ass. Looking back, I wouldn't have known what to do with her in that bed anyway. I would've failed all expectations. But that didn't stop me from taking a lot of chances as a kid.

I remember one time my siblings and I had gone Christmas shopping at the Grandland Shopping Center on Fenkell Avenue. It was a winter day with no snow on the ground yet. For some reason, my brother and I decided to play "Froggy" in between moving traffic. I would wait until the cars were just close enough, then dart out between them, crossing the two-way street. My brother followed my lead, doing the exact same thing.

Now, at this point, we just knew our sisters would never attempt such a reckless feat. Suddenly, to our surprise, one of my sisters decided to try her luck. She darted out into the busy street but didn't make it. A car structed her.

She was rushed to a nearby hospital, leaving the rest of us to come home and explain to our parents why she didn't return with us.

"Hey! Where is your sister?" my dad curiously asked as soon as we walked in.

Since I was the oldest, it fell on me to break the news.

It took me a while to form the words and explain the situation.

"She's in the hospital," I finally muttered.

"Why? What happened?" he asked, persistently pressing for answers.

After I explained how and why she got hit by the car, my brother and I got the beating of our lives. I got the worst of it since I was the oldest and responsible for my siblings' well-being. That beating felt like it lasted forever. To top it all off, I didn't get any Christmas gifts from my parents that year.

As I got older, I grew out of being a bad kid. In my group of friends, I was the one often talking them out of doing something stupid. Sometimes they called me a punk, but deep down, they knew I was right. Many times, I saved them from getting into serious trouble.

I became good at talking people out of bad decisions. I always used logic, and most of the time, it worked. My rough streak was short-lived, and I found my way back to the right path.

Personally, I could have easily gone down a darker road.

I could've taken advantage of senior citizens, broken into homes and cars, committed armed robbery, or worse.

I could've sold drugs to someone's mom, dad, sister, or brother, contributing to the devastating crack epidemic that destroyed so many lives.

But I chose not to sell that tormenting poison. I chose to be a leader, not a follower. I chose not to embarrass my mother—that was always the most important thing to me.

My mother had already endured so much in life, and I refused to add to her pain. She carried me for nine months, brought me into this world, nurtured me, and made sacrifices every day to take care of me.

Ending up in prison would've been the ultimate slap in her face. Her love and sacrifices shaped my decisions, and I'm forever grateful that I chose to honor her by staying on the right path.

That was my mindset in those early days.

"Although I hit a rough patch during those years, they became lessons disguised as missteps. Life in the projects was a constant balancing act—teetering between what could go wrong and what we could make right. It was in those moments of chaos that I began to understand resilience and the value of choices. Little did I know, the next chapter in my life would hold opportunities to shape my identity, including my unexpected journey into basketball."

Moral of the Story: Life is a series of choices, and those choices shape who we become. Even in the face of temptation, hardship, or pressure, we have the power to choose a path that honors the sacrifices of those who love us.

Growing up, it's easy to fall into traps set by your environment, but real strength comes from rising above those challenges. My story is a testament to the importance of responsibility, self-awareness, and integrity.

While youthful mistakes may happen, it's the lessons learned and the decisions made afterward that define character. Choosing to reject the easy but destructive path in favor of a righteous one isn't always simple, but it's worth it.

Above all, this chapter is a reminder to honor those who have poured their love, energy, and sacrifice into our lives. For me, it was my mother's unwavering support and resilience that inspired him to stay on the right path.

By choosing to protect her dignity and make her proud, he found the strength to avoid becoming a statistic and to lead by example for his siblings.

The lesson here is clear: choose to lead, not follow. Choose to uplift, not destroy. And most importantly, choose to live in a way that reflects gratitude and respect for the people who have sacrificed so much for you. When you stand for something greater than yourself, you leave behind a legacy of strength and hope that inspires others to do the same.

Chapter 24

The Last Stand Against The Klan (*Mid-1975*)

It was the mid-70s, and for the most part, people seemed to be getting along quite well—blacks and whites alike. Gone were the days of being chased home, spat on, or constantly fighting with one another. The "N-word" was heard far less frequently, and my old enemies had become my friends. Soul and Pop music dominated the airwaves—stations like WDRQ and WCHB kept the vibe alive—and disco brought a sense of unity, making life feel a little easier for everyone.

Back then, my biggest worries were making sure I didn't miss the next yard party and deciding which polyester pants, stacked shoes, and silk shirt I'd wear that night. Yard parties were everything. The music would guide you to someone's backyard, where you'd blend into the crowd without a care for whether you knew the homeowners. The more, the merrier.

In those days, violence wasn't a concern. No one was worried about guns or drive-bys. Fights, when they happened, were bare-knuckled and over as soon as they began, often about some girl. For the most part, though, we partied the night away, enjoying life to its fullest. Even after-school parties were full of joy, interrupted only occasionally by rival school kids trying to disrupt the fun.

The mid-70s were about big Afros, iconic music, wild dancing, vibrant fashion, and unforgettable times. Racism felt like it was fading into the background, and we all shared a love for the same music and culture. The 70s were a decade of unity, at least on the surface.

But even amidst the good times, our community had one last major hurdle to face:

The Ku Klux Klan

Growing up, I'd heard horrifying stories about the Klan—a secret society of domestic terrorists spreading terror across the South and even into northern states.

Their long history of violence included cross burnings, property destruction, lynchings, voter intimidation, and countless murders. They propagated their hateful ideology to assert the so-called superiority of their race over others.

I was told that they wore white robes and hoods to hide their identities, but sometimes, they didn't bother hiding at all. They infiltrated police forces, held positions as judges, and could even be the neighbor living next door—or worse, one of your friend's parents. It was a chilling thought: anyone could be a Klansman.

By the mid-70s, we were just beginning to coexist peacefully, but the shadow of hate still lingered. The two hot summer days of 1975 that followed were a stark reminder that racism hadn't gone away.

Word spread quickly in the projects: the Klan was planning a rally within two days. They had set up shop in a vacant store right next to the library on Burt Road and Fenkell Avenue.

You couldn't miss the place. They hung stuffed monkeys by their necks in the windows as a grotesque display of their hate. When I first heard what was happening, I rushed to tell my mother. She asked me not to go to the rally, afraid that something could happen to me, and she didn't want me getting hurt. But defiance got the better of me. The rally was supposed to start at 1 p.m. the next day, and despite my mother's pleas, I secretly joined others from the projects to bear witness to what we all believed could be a historic moment.

As we approached the massive crowd lining both sides of the street, the heavy presence of law enforcement became clear. Police officers were stationed to keep people away from the old storefront where the Klan had set up shop.

141

Yet, in that moment, a powerful sight emerged: blacks, whites, the middle class, and the poor—all walks of life standing together, united, shouting, **"Go back to where you came from! We don't want you here!"**

For the first time, I witnessed true unity and alliance against racial hatred. It was an indescribable feeling—anger, solidarity, and pride all rolled into one.

It's hard to put into words what that day meant to me.

The Klan eventually began their march down Fenkell. The old storefront door opened, and one by one, hooded members filed out, standing defiantly in the middle of the street.

With hate-filled flags raised high, they began their march down Fenkell Avenue. From where we stood, on a rooftop just up the street, we could see them advancing.

The tension in the crowd was electric, and when the Klan reached us, we unleashed. Bottles, rocks, stones—anything we could find became a weapon against their hate. For me, every throw was personal:

- A rock for my ancestors who endured unspeakable horrors.
- A bottle for my great-grandparents and their sacrifices.
- A stone for my parents, especially my father, who had endured more than his share of injustice.
- A rock for Emmett Till, Dr. King, Malcolm X, Medgar Evers, and all the martyrs of the civil rights movement.
- I flung bottles for the lives lost in the 1967 Detroit Rebellion and hurled them for future generations who might face similar struggles.

As the Klan tried to press forward, their march turned into a retreat. Wounded and bloodied, they stumbled back into their rented office, but the crowd's fury was far from extinguished.

Police were slow to respond, giving us time to disperse before they could catch anyone.

A couple of hours later, the Klan tried to regroup and continue their march, but the sheer number of people still gathered made it impossible. By the next morning, the stuffed monkeys and hate-filled symbols were gone from the windows. The Klan packed up their belongings and vanished, never to return to our side of town.

When I returned home, my mother gave me a look—a knowing, silent glance that said she suspected where I'd been. But she never asked, and I never told. It remained unspoken between us.

That day remains one of the proudest moments of my life. We stood together—blacks and whites—united against the Klan and their hatred.

"That day in **1975** was more than just a stand against hatred; it was a moment of unity that proved strength lies in collective resolve. It left an indelible mark on my childhood, reminding me that courage and solidarity can ignite change, even in the face of fear. As Detroit continued to change, so did my experiences growing up in the Smith Homes Housing Projects. What followed were memories filled with music, laughter, and the unmistakable rhythm of a city that never stopped dancing."

Of course, this didn't mean racism in our neighborhood vanished overnight. Far from it. But for one powerful moment in **1975**, we proved that when people stand together, even the deepest hate can be pushed back into the shadows.

In 1975, we still had a long way to go and a much taller mountain to climb.

But as I remember it, that event proved one powerful thing: we could stand together against hatred whenever we wanted to or needed to. The unity I saw during that time gave me hope.

What I didn't realize then was that, in the years to come, some people would attempt to turn back the clock to a time when equality was a distant dream.

Even more disheartening, my own people would fall victim to the devastation brought on by drugs and systemic oppression.

143

Crack cocaine infiltrated our communities, and brainwashing led us to turn on each other in violent and destructive ways. The government had a hand in pouring drugs into our neighborhoods and then had the audacity to declare a "war on drugs," handing out disproportionately severe prison sentences to Black and Brown people. **Isn't that some shit.**

So many other significant things happened in **1975**. Disco and soul music dominated the charts, bringing vibrant rhythm to our lives. Detroit's iconic dance show, *The Scene,* debuted on television, showcasing our style and moves.

The Vietnam War officially ended, a momentous occasion that brought relief and heartbreak for so many families. The movie *Jaws* premiered, captivating audiences in nearby theaters. Patty Hearst made headlines when she appeared on the FBI's Most Wanted list. Kodak introduced the first digital camera, marking a technological leap that no one at the time fully understood.

Closer to home, the yard parties carried on, filled with music, dancing, and laughter.

My own popularity was slowly growing among my peers, something I hadn't quite expected but enjoyed.

This was the beginning of one amazing childhood in the Smith Homes Housing Projects. It was also the start of understanding the resilience, strength, and courage our community displayed in the face of racial division. Despite the struggles, we found joy, unity, and determination to keep moving forward. **That is a lesson I carry with me to this day.**

Something else happened in **1975**, one of the most iconic events in sports history unfolded: Ali vs. Frazier III, famously known as "The Thrilla in Manila."

This legendary boxing match took place on October 1, **1975**, in the sweltering heat of the Araneta Coliseum in Quezon City, Philippines. It was the third and final encounter between two of the greatest heavyweights of all time, Muhammad Ali and Joe Frazier, and it cemented their rivalry as one of the most intense and storied in sports history.

Ali and Frazier had split their previous two fights. Their first bout, "The Fight of the Century," in **1971** saw Frazier hand Ali his first professional defeat. Ali would avenge this loss in their **1974** rematch. By the time they met for their third bout, the stakes were sky-high, not just for the heavyweight title but for their legacies.

The "Thrilla in Manila" was a brutal, grueling contest that pushed both fighters to their physical and mental limits.

Ali later described it as "the closest thing to dying that I know." The fight lasted 14 punishing rounds in the oppressive tropical heat, with both men trading fierce blows that showcased their willpower and skill.

Ali's strategy was to exploit his superior speed and mobility, while Frazier relentlessly pressed forward, landing devastating hooks to the body and head. The fight saw incredible moments of courage and resilience from both men.

Ali's sharp jabs and combinations found their mark, but Frazier's relentless pressure and punishing body shots kept the fight competitive.

By the 14th round, Frazier's face was swollen, and his vision was nearly gone, while Ali, though ahead on points, was utterly exhausted.

Frazier's trainer, Eddie Futch, made the decision to stop the fight before the 15th round, saying, "Sit down, son.
Nobody will ever forget what you did here today." It was a merciful decision that preserved Frazier's dignity and health.

Ali emerged victorious, but it was a hollow triumph in many ways. In the aftermath, he admitted that Frazier's relentless assault had pushed him to the brink of collapse.

He even called Frazier the toughest opponent he had ever faced, saying, "He brought out the best in me." For those of us growing up in the projects, the Ali-Frazier trilogy was more than just boxing—it was a symbol of strength, resilience, and overcoming the odds. Muhammad Ali represented a larger- than-life figure, embodying the courage to stand up for what you believe in, while Frazier epitomized relentless determination and grit.

I remember the older guys in the neighborhood replaying the fight in their minds, discussing every jab, hook, and counter-punch. For weeks, it seemed like the entire world was talking about the Thrilla in Manila.

The fight didn't just make history; it left an indelible mark on all of us who watched, teaching us lessons about perseverance, respect, and the human spirit.

Ali was the greatest and will always be the greatest

Chapter 25

How I Met My 3rd, 4th, and 5th Best Friends
(The Ghetto Avengers)

My second friend brought over this kid he wanted to introduce me to. His large family had just moved into the projects. After a few conversations, I asked him how many brothers and sisters he had. He replied, "I have two brothers and five sisters. Two of my sisters are a set of twins."

The kid I was introduced to was already blessed with natural athleticism. It was like he came out of the womb with strength, fitness, speed, and agility. He could play any sport and be automatically good at it. By the time I saw him at age fourteen, he was already built with toned muscles. For some reason, we instantly clicked. He was also funny and would say the craziest things. We became so tight that we were like blood brothers. If you saw him, you saw me, and vice versa. In fact, other kids in school used to ask if we were related. Sports were what we all had in common, but he was better at most of them. I was also like a third son to his mother. If my family was looking for me, they knew exactly where to find me—at his house.

Another thing he was good at? Getting the prettiest girls. He just seemed to have that charm, and girls would cling to him like Saran Wrap. But as tight as we were, our friendship would be tested more than once.

The same young girl I was infatuated with—the one who laughed at me and slammed her door in my face? Yeah, her. They ended up having a few classes together. From the start, they didn't like each other at all. When we all walked home from school, they would talk about each other and let it be known how much they despised each other. He would try to hurt her feelings by calling her "Olive Oyl," and in return, she would call him a "monkey."

Personally, I was fine with him not liking the same girl I liked.

This went on for weeks until one day, their nagging each other turned into a little flirting. I didn't like what I was witnessing at all. Deep down inside, I was really getting pissed off. But he was my best friend, and she was the girl I admired since 8th grade. My emotions were caught in the middle of them both.

Now, everything he joked about made her laugh, and each giggle I heard from her made me even more jealous. It's a good thing nothing ever developed between the two, but throughout our adult years, I had to hear her name over and over again. Every blue moon, I still do.

Looking back, I realize how selfish and childish I was to think that an attractive girl with a cute chin dimple liking my best friend could tarnish a lifelong brotherhood.

Now, let me explain how my 4th friendship developed.

Me and a buddy were having a conversation in my yard when he mentioned that a new family had just moved across from him.

While talking about the new neighbors, we saw a young boy in his yard chasing a squirrel around a tree. We decided to go over and introduce ourselves.

"You're never going to catch that squirrel," my friend told him. "So, you just moved in? Welcome to the projects. How many brothers and sisters do you have?"

He responded by saying he had one sister and two brothers.

In mid-conversation, his sister came outside and paraded in front of us. She was much taller than any of us, had a sweet mocha skin complexion, and I could instantly tell she had a beautifully magnetic personality. We made a few seconds of eye contact before she stepped back inside.

She was an extreme pleasure to look at, and because of her height, I was immediately attracted to her.

I asked the kid who she was. "Oh, that's my sister," he told me.

I quickly changed the subject and asked him if he would like to hang out with us. We gave him the tour of the projects, showed him where the nearest store was up the street, and from that day on, we all became friends.

I quickly found out that he was incredibly book-smart in school. Wearing those glasses made him look even smarter. It didn't matter what the subject was—he passed his classes with flying colors. Out of the four of us, he was the most impressive, especially when it came to mathematics.

One evening, I was invited over for dinner—one of the few times I couldn't resist his mother's outstanding southern cooking.

His sister was sitting on their couch, braiding their little brother's hair. Once again, we made that brief eye contact, and this time, she gave me a small, acknowledging smile.

After washing my hands, his mother made my dinner plate. The food looked so good, I couldn't wait to dig in.

"This food is delicious," I said.

"Well, thank you," she replied graciously.

"Make sure we're locked up before you all turn in for the night," his mom told her kids before heading to bed.

Shortly after, his two brothers also went upstairs. The only ones left watching TV were my friend, his sister, and me. By now, it was 2 am. During a commercial break, my friend ran upstairs to use the restroom. I took the opportunity to tell his sister, jokingly yet nervously, that when she went to bed, I was going to join her.

To my surprise, she told me she'd be wide awake and waiting for me. I asked if she was serious, and she said yes. A few minutes later, she went upstairs to bed, leaving me and her brother in the living room.

By 3 am., my friend said, "Hey man, I'm going to bed. If you want to spend the night, you can sleep down here on the couch. I'll see you in the morning."

I took him up on the offer. The house was now completely still and quiet. My mind was racing. I contemplated whether I should quietly walk upstairs. But then I thought, I've got to be crazy. My best friend or his mother could catch us doing whatever.

The idea was tempting, but I'm so glad I didn't pursue his sister. Who knows? My best friend could be my brother-in-law right now. (Laughing)

And boy, oh boy, did I have a thing for taller girls back then.

So there you have it—four of the closest friends that ever walked Crescent Drive. There were many groups of tight-knit friends in the projects, but if there was such a thing as a Smith Homes Hall of Fame, our small group would definitely be included.

I compared us to comic book heroes, *The Avengers*: different personalities, but each of us possessing a superpower or two.

Let me explain (laughing).

As I said earlier, the first person I ever met was the kid in my art class. Over the years, we became the best of friends. He was incredibly humorous, and the girls loved it. If he made a girl laugh, she was all in afterward. Even his own laugh would make you crack up.

Out of the four of us, he and I had the most in common when it came to creativity. We had the best drawings, paintings, jewelry, and ceramics in our art classes. We even took some art studies at The Detroit Art Institute together.

We once created a funny skit in a school play that had the whole auditorium laughing. So, I'd say his superpower was his mental creativity, artistry and comedy. This dude was funny.

The second friend was a sports fanatic—a hard worker, highly athletic, and very well respected by his peers. He also had a great sense of humor. And boy, was he comedic.

He could say something so funny it would make you cry while laughing.

He was responsible for helping me get my first real cooking job.

This awkward dude had no rhythm at all and couldn't dance a lick, but that never seemed to bother him. He kept on dancing anyway, and we cheered him on every time. He was kind, generous, and considerate, and the girls adored him for those qualities.

I think his superpower was philosophy. We had countless personal and private conversations in those early years. He would talk about why life was the way it was, why certain things happened for a reason. He had a way of making you think, and whatever he told you always seemed to make perfect sense.

So yes, even as a young boy, he was a philosopher. I believe that was his superpower, along with comedy and sports.

Now, as I said before, my third friend was someone I believed was naturally blessed with abilities and talent. He was respected by his peers and had a great sense of humor as well.

One thing we had in common was how competitive we both were.

Looking back at our childhood, I can't remember ever having a single argument with him. For years, most people thought we were brothers, and we just played along with it.

We were so tight that sometimes the other two friends would jokingly hint that we were doing things and going places without them. But that was never the case—things just happened that way.

In his family, he was the definition of a big brother in every sense of the term. His family loved him and proudly bragged about everything he did. I admired that about his family dynamic.

This kid could get the prettiest girls without even trying.

If he decided she was the one, he loved her deeply and intensely. But if he lost interest, he would simply move on, leaving her in the past. Most of the time, she would fall by the wayside.

So, I guess his superpowers were mesmerizing the girls, excelling at sports, and comedy.

Now, I had plenty of arguments with my fourth friend.

That was only because we were both headstrong, and one of us always had to be right.

But I never saw anything wrong with that. Both of our opinions often made sense—it just depended on how others looked at them.

Remember, he was the one who was book smart, while at that time, I was street smart. And trust me, there's a difference.

If I'm not mistaken, He was the first of us to get his own vehicle.

I can remember the very first thing we did was drive up and down Woodard avenue yelling out the window at all the street walking prostitutes.

That was our past time fun. See back in those days, they were decent looking women, not all crack piped out like they are now. A street walker could be waiting at a bus stop carrying a briefcase and nicely dressed in business attire. A city bus could approach her five straight times and she would never step on it. But if a car pulled up for sexual services, she wouldn't waste any time getting in the passenger seat.

One night we all were in his car, making the trip down Woodward avenue. This time my friend drove closer to a sexually infested, apartment building.

"How much for all of us, my friend asked a street walker?" "Well,

It depends on what you want," she says.

He then decided to speak for all of us in the car. "We all want oral," he told the lady.

"Park on the side of this building and follow me up the back staircase," she instructed.

I tried to tell everyone this was a bad idea and that she might be setting us up to get robbed or hurt.

"Either stop being so scary or wait for us in the car," one of my friends told me.

I didn't want to be the only one sitting in the car in a dark alley parking lot, so I went up the stairs also.

"You all have a seat. It's forty dollars for ten minutes of head. Does everyone have their money ready?" the prostitute asked.

We all said yes.

"Let me slip on something comfortable," the prostitute told us. "I'll be right back."

While she's away to maybe slip on something revealing, I panicked and told everyone that we're being setup.

Finally in the last minute everyone agreed with me.

At the same time, we all decided to make a run for the door, back down the stairs and to my friend's car.

We quickly sped off, laughing hysterically all the way home. That was daring, fun and a little unsafe for all of us to experience.

We never tried that again and that was the end of our street walker past time fun.

Best friend number four also had a different approach to talking to girls than best friend number three.

He was sort of an intellectual. A smooth talker. Very confident and persuasive.

If he had an interest in a young girl, he would sweet talk her until she thought he was the best thing since slice bread or her panties finally fell off.

So yeah, he had a super power also. The gift of gab and a extra large brain.

Now let's talk about my superpowers. (laughing)

When it came to sports, I was average. In baseball, I could catch but sucked at pitching and batting. In the game of football, I could run, dodge, catch, and throw, but I was a terrible tackler and always afraid to get hit. When it came to soccer, I was okay. I even had my own little league soccer team at one time.

When I decided to box, I had natural, raw talent. In track and field, I wasn't fast, but I was a phenomenal distance runner.

I can remember when we all joined the Y.B.A. (Youth Basketball Association). I was terrible at first. I couldn't dribble, pass, or shoot, and I was dropped from the team. But in this sport, I became an unstoppable force, thanks to some help from a family member. Oh! I forgot to mention—she was female. I'll finally let the cat out of the bag and share the hidden secret about why I was so good at playing this game I loved so much in the next chapter.

Anyways, I was also the type of kid who never got into physical altercations with anyone. Not that I was afraid to fight back, but I knew I could use sophistication and talk myself out of a brawl.

But make no mistake—I was a hothead. If you made me angry and backed me into a corner, I had no choice but to pull out my raw boxing skills and whoop that ass.

Most times, though, I didn't feel it was necessary to ball up my fist and scrap. I simply wasn't the violent type and never wanted to be. I was the peacemaker. I also had no intention of fighting any of my best friends either.

Well, there was one time when I had no choice—I had to defend my father, brother, and our property. But other than that, I believed best friends didn't fight each other.

Now, we may have had strong disagreements and not spoken to each other for a couple of days, but throwing blows was a no-no—for me, anyways.

Around fourteen or fifteen years old, I was just starting to mature and also began talking my friends out of getting into any possible trouble.

Whenever my friends thought of doing something reckless, I would give them a strong, valid reason not to do it. Yes, I was the one who made you think before you did something stupid. So, I think my superpowers were the power of reason, artistry and eventually, the game of basketball.

As far as the girls, I finally overcame my battles with very short relationships.

The young girls I knew liked to be charmed, and I began to understand that. They needed to feel important. They had to know they were number one. I quickly learned this from watching my older mentors. So, once again, I used the power of reason, and I too developed the gift of gab.

I was sweet and thoughtful. And although I had very little money —or no money at all—kindness and originality made up for it.

Getting the baddies or the sophisticated, pretty girls rose to a whole new level. Soon, I would start dating tenth, eleventh, and twelfth graders. Maybe I had more than just two superpowers. (laughing)

After a few years of the four of us being together, we added another friend to our group. This kid was a little different.

Sometimes, he was considered a loner, meaning at times he stayed to himself, hung out with us, or hung out with other people.

But we considered him a friend of ours anyway.

All I know is this skinny kid could play some basketball, and that's what a few of us had in common.

I really don't remember how he was with the girls. His superpower? We really didn't know. Basketball?

Put us all together, and allegedly we were the good kids of the projects. Parents would see our group and want their kids to hang out with us. I strongly felt at the time that parents trusted us and loved each and every one of us.

And I'm absolutely sure my close friends' parents loved me. Each one treated me like their own son. So, besides my own mother, I had three other mothers taking care of me.

"Friendship in the projects wasn't just about hanging out or sharing laughs—it was about building a family outside of your own. These bonds strengthened us, carried us through challenges, and shaped our sense of loyalty. But life in the Smith Homes wasn't just about camaraderie; it was also a training ground for resilience.

And sometimes, the lessons in strength came from the most unexpected places, like a makeshift basketball court under the summer sun."

A Jefferies Projects Memory

I remember dating this young girl who lived in the Jefferies Projects. She was the cousin of a girl who lived in the Smith Homes Housing Projects. A very sweet and beautiful girl who could dance her butt off—that's one of the many things I liked about her. She would visit her cousin, and the following weekend, I would take the city bus to visit her.

That's how we both managed to see each other every week.

One night after a visit, she walked me from her home to a nearby bus stop, which was maybe three or four blocks away. Once we got to the stop, I gave her a kiss as we said our usual goodbye.

As she started her way back to her apartment building, five boys ran across the street and approached me.

"Say man, do you live in the Jefferies?" one of the guys asked. I

answered, "No, I don't."

Another kid began to check my pockets. "Hey man, you got any money on you?"

I pushed him off while one tried to sucker punch me in the face. As I tried to back away from the guys, I heard a soft voice in the background.

"Hey! What are you all doing?"

All five boys suddenly stopped in their tracks.

"Is this your boyfriend or something?" one of the guys asked.

"Yes, that's my boyfriend. Leave him alone," she said firmly.

The five boys apologized and backed off. My girlfriend saw the danger I was in and ran back to save me from being robbed and getting my ass beat to a pulp that night. She waited with me until my bus arrived and made sure I boarded safely.

As she started walking back toward her apartment, she waved and blew a kiss at me before the bus pulled off.

Can you imagine what would have happened if I told those hood rats I was from the Smith Homes Projects?

I would have gotten a full-blown beat down.

I never forgot what she did that night. She was a beautiful and amazing young girl and well-known in her community.

Maybe because she had brothers. I don't remember if she did.

Unfortunately, we couldn't continue seeing each other just on the weekends. It began to be an inconvenience for the both of us, and we mutually agreed to end the relationship. We did, however, remain friends.

Moral of the Story: True kindness and loyalty often come in unexpected moments. In a world that sometimes feels divided, the ability to stand up and protect someone, even when it's risky, is a true act of bravery. My girlfriend's quick thinking and fearless intervention saved me that night just two blocks away from the Jefferies Projects. It's a testament to the strength of genuine connections, even at a young age.

This experience taught me the value of having someone in your corner who truly cares for your well-being, no matter the circumstances.

It also served as a reminder that while the world can be full of challenges and dangers, there are still people willing to rise above it and show compassion and courage.

Sometimes, it's the people we least expect who make the biggest impact on our lives. Though our relationship didn't last, her actions left a lasting mark on my heart. True courage is not about physical strength—it's about standing up for what's right, even when the odds aren't in your favor.

Chapter 26

My Secret Summer Boot Camp
No One Ever Knew About

After school ended for the summer, my dad used to always pack everyone up and drop us off at my grandmother's house. Every day, we would help with designated chores on her farm. Some summers, it would be just me and my brother. Other summers, it would be just me. Collecting eggs from the chickens, feeding the goats, milking the cows, pumping well water all day, picking berries so she could make her delicious homemade pies, and shucking corn were daily tasks for me, my siblings, and all my cousins.

My grandmother had an old shed, carport, or garage—something like that. I can't quite remember. It had been torn down, leaving only the cement foundation. My aunt had turned it into a half-sized basketball court.

"After you're done with your chores, I'm going to show you how to shoot a basketball," she told me. She brought out this huge piggy bank full of pennies and placed it on the court.

"Okay, before we begin, here are the rules: For every shot you make, I'm going to give you five pennies. This will be your spending money every week while you're here for the summer. I'm not just going to give you money—you have to earn it. Now watch how I shoot this basketball."

She showed me how to arc the ball properly when shooting. What she didn't know was how terrible I was at playing basketball.

"Now it's your turn. Shoot the ball." I made an attempt, but she slapped the ball in mid-air.

"Now dribble the darn ball away from me and shoot it in the basket," she instructed.

I tried again, but once more, she slapped the ball out of the air. This time, I had to fetch it from my grandmother's rocky driveway.

We stayed on that court for an entire hour, and I still hadn't made a single basket. Not a single penny landed in my pocket.

After a while, she snatched her basketball, picked up her piggy bank, and walked into the house without saying a word to me.

I was devastated and so humiliated that I started to cry.

I thought there was a very real possibility that I'd go home at the end of the summer with no pennies saved up. I kept thinking, *I'm never going to be able to shoot over my aunt's head.*

The next day, after finishing my chores, she called me over to the court again.

"Today, I'm going to teach you how to dribble a basketball," she said. For twenty minutes, she made me dribble around the court. Then, she took the ball and showed me how to dribble it between my legs.

"Now, I'm going to try and take the ball away from you," she said.

As I dribbled with my back to her, I tried to make my way toward the basket, but she easily snatched the ball from me.

"Try it again," she said. "This time, don't look at the ball while you're dribbling. Know the spot you want to shoot from. If you don't want to shoot from a distance, you can always do a layup."

She took the ball from me 10 to 20 times in a row before finally packing everything up and leaving me on the court again. Still, with no pennies in my pocket, I felt so damn frustrated.

The next day, she called me over once more. By this point, I felt like I was being taken advantage of and didn't want to touch a basketball ever again.

But as she pulled out the piggy bank, I couldn't take my eyes off all those pennies.

I quickly changed my mind.

I started dribbling as she stood with her arms wide open. I got as close as I could to the basket and quickly pulled up for a jumper. The ball circled the rim and, surprisingly, dropped in.

She smiled, quietly walked over to the piggy bank, and handed me five pennies. "Do it again," she said, "but this time, drive for a layup." I followed her instructions.

The ball hit the backboard and went in again. She gave me five more pennies, but this time, I think she let me make that basket. It didn't matter—those two baskets I made in a row felt encouraging, and for the first time, I was proud of myself. That night, I found a tin can to put my pennies in.

The following afternoon, I saw her on the court again. She didn't have to call me over because I already knew what time it was.

"Today, I'm going to teach you how to be a defender. You try and stop me from making a basket."

I thought this would be impossible, considering she was much bigger and taller than I was. I tried defending, but she kept bumping me closer to the basket. At one point, I fell, and she told me to get my butt up.

"You need to learn how to move around and steal the ball," she said.

Once again, I did exactly what she told me to do. I took the ball, shot, missed, got the rebound, and shot again.

To my surprise, the ball went in. I collected five more cents. This went on every day.

By the end of the summer, I had collected a whopping $2.45.

It wasn't much, but I began to enjoy this game called basketball. I still remember my aunt giving me an extra twenty-dollar bill before my dad picked me up to go back home to Detroit.

"I want you to know, you gave a good effort, and you deserve this," she said.

Twenty dollars was a lot of money for a kid back in those days.

For two or three summers straight, my auntie made good use of that cement court and took me through what I called her grueling basketball boot camp. I learned the proper way of shooting, passing, defending, and dribbling. I even developed speed, longevity, and stamina.

I took those skills and became the one to beat among my friends. No exaggeration—if I played ten games of 21 among friends and peers, I would win at least six out of the ten games, sometimes more. I simply never got tired, and I had all the skills. My friends gave me the nickname *Super Sonic EW* before it was later changed to *Ezee* (for getting the easy buckets).

As I got older, I played with the college kids coming home from school in Farmington Hills before tearing ligaments in both heels at the same time. Boy oh boy! Were those games exciting. Later in life, I continued to have physical trouble as both knees lost cartilage from playing on concrete courts all those many years.

Now, it's possible that my brother went through that same rigorous boot camp. He became an even better ballplayer than I was. His shot was so smooth and so hard to block.

You couldn't stop him from coming through the hole—no matter what you did, he would glide through anyway. And his jumper shot was amazing.

I remember a few times when my cousins came over to visit us.

The very first thing they wanted to do was play on the project basketball court. We'd play four-on-four: me, my brother, and my two cousins. We were pretty good and terrorized the whole court. Together, us farm/city boys were some phenomenal street ball players.

Now, if you want to blame all those butt whippings I dished out as a teenager for all those years, you'd have to blame my auntie for showing me the fundamentals of this game we love to call basketball.

Sorry, fellas. If you're reading this, the cat is finally out of the bag.
(laughing)

"That basketball court, my aunt's persistence, and those long summer days weren't just about learning how to shoot hoops— they were lessons in patience, determination, and perseverance. Those summers shaped more than my skills; they shaped my character. But beyond the farm and the projects, Detroit itself was a classroom, and some of its lessons came from unexpected places, like the thrill—and terror—of a rollercoaster ride at Edgewater Park."

From   To
Super Sonic   MR. EZee
E.W.

Another Auntie Memory

(Detroit's Edgewater Park)

When my dad no longer drove a vehicle, my aunt used to pick us up from the projects and take us places. Whether it was fishing, Boblo Island, the old Edgewater Amusement Park on Detroit's West Seven Mile near Grand River Avenue, or the drive-in, she always made sure we had something exciting to do.

I even remember one of the movies she took us to see—*Westworld* (1973, starring Yul Brynner).

One particular time, she picked up me and my sister to go to Edgewater Park. This is where my lifelong fear of roller coasters began. I went on a mini roller coaster ride with my aunt, which at the time was called *The Wild Mouse*. Most Detroiters my age should remember this ride. The tracks were metal, but the entire structure was made of wood.

I sat next to my aunt as the ride operator pulled the safety bar down over our waists. The car started to move slowly up the hill. We finally reached the top, but to our horror, we realized the safety bar hadn't locked down properly.

As the car rushed down the track, the bar lifted forward. My aunt reacted quickly—she pushed me under the front dashboard of the car, held me to the floor with her feet, and used her arms to brace the back of the seat for dear life. We went through the entire ride like that, her strength and quick thinking keeping me safe.

That was my first—and last—time ever riding a roller coaster. That childhood experience traumatized me for life.

I also remember the time we entered the fun house to see "the smallest human in the world." From a distance, we kept seeing the top of someone's head running around inside a large box.

My aunt and I thought whoever it was had black, curly hair. We gave the man our tickets and, as we got closer, we finally saw what was really inside the box—it was a black poodle!

How did they ever get away with that? (laughing)

164

Chapter 27

A Letter To Mother (Part One)

"Grief never ends... but it changes. It's a passage. Not a place to stay. Grief is not a sign of weakness or a lack of faith. It is the price of love."

– Queen Elizabeth I

I'm adding this chapter because I want everyone to know the type of person my mother was. I can't physically see you anymore unless it's in a picture or in my dreams. But I can still feel your presence around me. I know you're closely watching me as I write these memoirs. Some of the short stories in this book might shock you, and others might make you laugh hysterically. I miss your laughter. I miss everything about you.

Your strength and courage were unmatched. I can no longer see you, but I hold the memories of you close to my heart. It was amazing being your firstborn son. You did an outstanding job taking care of me when I was a child. You protected me, taught me right from wrong, and showed me how to be strong while navigating this strange thing called life.

You were mild-mannered, but we could always tell your mood by the expressions on your face. You had a gentle soul. Besides the occasional argument with Dad, I never saw you in a dispute with anyone else. You were well-liked and so easy to get along with.

I remember our walks to D&C Supermarket. That was our private time to talk about people, current events, and what was happening in our lives. We rode the city bus everywhere together. That was our time too—visiting the old Hudson's building downtown, Woolworth's, and Kresge.

We'd often stop to catch the latest Bruce Lee movie before heading home. Sometimes, we'd have lunch at the old Flaming Embers restaurant on Grand Circus Park. Those moments were special.

You couldn't hear the words to a song or the music being played, but you could feel the beat through the floor if the television or radio was loud enough.

Remember how we'd dance in the middle of the living room together?

You were so good to the people I surrounded myself with. They loved you too, Mrs. Wright. Your kindness touched everyone you met.

Your brothers, sisters, and in-laws spoiled you every chance they got. I used to love watching how they treated you with so much love and respect. It was clear where you got your sweetness from —you were definitely your parents' daughter.

Every so often, I look at pictures from your younger years. Ma, you were absolutely beautiful. You were also incredibly strong. You beat cancer and lived life as though you had never faced such a challenge.

You were an amazing, gentle soul, but also a fighter in so many ways. I truly believe no one could say a bad thing about you because, while you were here with us, you were nothing but loving and kind.

Ma, do me one favor. Can you say hi to my grandparents for me, please?

"Writing this letter felt like a way to keep my mother close, to honor her memory, and to remind myself of the love and lessons she left behind.

But life, even in grief, continued to move forward, filled with moments that both challenged and inspired me. From personal achievements to shared experiences, each memory carried her influence.

Chapter 28

The Dance Show That Came On
At 6 O'clock 5 Days A Week (1975)

Okay! Do you remember one of the longest-running dance shows called **Soul Train**? It ran from October **1971** to March **2006**. Well, Detroit had a popular dance show of its own. The dance show was called **The Scene**. It ran for 12 years, from **1975** to **1987**.

The show blew up in its first-year debut, and I wanted to get on this show so bad. I was a dancing fool back in those days, and I knew I would fit right in. Every time I hear the song *I Love Music* by The O'Jays or *The Jam* by Larry Graham and Graham Central Station, it reminds me of this incredible show of the mid-70s.

The show was taped at the first and only Black-owned studios of WGPR in downtown Detroit on East Jefferson. Back in those days, the show aired on Channel 62. No matter where you were coming from or what you were doing, you made sure you were in front of your TV, updating yourself on the latest urban dances and laughing at the silliest commercials.

At 6 p.m., the streets of the Smith Homes Housing Projects would be empty for one whole hour.

Personally, I think the best years for this television show were between **1975** and **1979**. This is only my opinion.

Teens were doing some serious dancing back then. After watching this dance show on television, we couldn't wait to show off our new dance moves at the next Smith Home Center party or the after-school dances.

Also, back in those days, there was a lot of gang-banging, drug trafficking, gun violence, and extortion across the city.

I can still remember some of the names of these Detroit gangs of yesteryear: the **Fenkell Avenuers**, the **Seven Mile Killers**, the **Latin Kings**, the **B.K.s (Black Killers)**, the **Chene Gang**, **the Bishops**, the **Smurfs**, the **Schoolcraft Boys**, the **Gangster Disciple**s, and the **Sconies**. Later, there were **Y.B.I. (Young Boys Incorporated)**, the **Pony Down Boys,** the **Best Friends**, and the **Black Mafia Family**.

One Detroit gang was also known for their foot working dance moves: the **Errol Flynns.**

In my personal opinion, this was the best Detroit dance era ever. Between **1975** and **1978**, I always made sure I was home, watching these gangland dance steps on *The Scene dance show on television station W.G.P.R.*.

I also used to watch these gang members on the streets or at yard parties doing their thing, throwing their gang-colored handkerchiefs in the air. These moves were so *gangster* to me. I loved dancing like these street thugs and was pretty good at copying their footwork. I knew I was a good dancer, and I owned it.

If you want a glimpse of this style, I recommend watching a YouTube clip of this dance. Just search for *The Errol Flynn*.

The dancers on *The Scene* seemed to change a bit over the next few years. They started getting more creative with their moves and incorporating their whole bodies.

This marked the next great era of Detroit dance.

It was during this time that iconic dances like Detroit's own **Schoolcraft, The Cabbage Patch, The Smurf, The Wop, The** *Reebok*, and *The Prep* started spreading through the urban parts of the city.

The next dance era came in the mid-to-late 80s, bringing dances

like The Running Man, The Roger Rabbit, The Kid 'N' Play, The Robo Cop, The Biz Markie, The Tom and Jerry,

The Fly Girls, The Bart Simpson, and The Running Man.

My best friend's sister wanted to appear on the show, and we had planned to go together, but we changed our minds at the last minute.

After that, the dream of being on *The Scene* never resurfaced.

It's sad to admit, but wanting to be on the show was one thing—having the courage to actually go for tryouts was another.

By then, the dancers were making drastic changes to their styles, and in my opinion, they weren't doing the same dances we were doing at home, at parties, in clubs, or in our neighborhoods.

Forgive me if I sound biased, but it felt like something was shifting. The clothing and music were also evolving, with a new Detroit sound being invented: *Techno*.

Around this time, another street dance was born—the famous *Detroit Jit*. While I was smoother at doing the *Errol Flynn* in the mid-70s, the *Jit* of the late 80s required much quicker footwork, physical creativity, skill, and perfect timing to match the beat of the music.

The Scene aired its last episode in **1987** but was followed by a spin-off called **The New Dance Show.** This show continued in Detroit from **1988** to **1994**, eventually moving its taping to Highland Park, where it ran from **1994** to **1996**.

So tell me—does anyone from Detroit, who was a 60s, 70s, or early 80s baby, remember the words that was said at the very beginning of every *Scene show*? " The host would asked, "what's the name of this town?" Everyone in the studio would say,

"Geek town". At the very end of every show *he would say,* "Sugar is sugar, salt is salt, if you didn't get off, it isn't our fault".

On a Side Note:

As a child, I often practiced my dance moves while dancing with my mother. She couldn't hear what the music sounded like, but she could feel the strong beats vibrating through the floor beneath her feet. That's one of my favorite memories—dancing together, feeling the rhythm in a way only we could.

The History of Detroit's Errol Flynn Gang

The **Errol Flynn Gang** was one of Detroit's most infamous street gangs during the **1970s** and **80s**. Unlike many other gangs of the era that were focused solely on crime and turf wars, the Errol Flynn Gang stood out for their unique style and culture, which left a lasting impact on Detroit's identity, particularly in dance and fashion.

The group took its name from the Hollywood actor Errol Flynn, known for his charismatic persona, debonair style, and adventurous roles.

The gang adopted a similar flair, embodying flashiness, confidence, and an almost theatrical swagger.

They were recognized not only for their street presence but also for their dance moves, which became a signature element of their identity.

Their signature dance, which was a smooth and rhythmic footwork routine, gained legendary status and became known as *"The Errol Flynn."*

Fashion and Style

The Errol Flynns were as much about style as they were about toughness. They became known for their sharp, flashy attire, including:

- **Tailored suits** paired with high-end accessories.
- **Wide-brimmed hats** that exuded a sense of sophistication.
- **Flamboyant shoes**, including alligator-skin designs and other exotic styles.

Their emphasis on fashion set them apart from other gangs, and they became trendsetters in the Detroit streets.

Their style was a statement of confidence and pride, reflecting their belief that they were superior to others.

Dance and Cultural Impact

One of the most defining elements of the Errol Flynn Gang was their association with dance. Their namesake dance move, *The Errol Flynn*, became synonymous with their image. It involved intricate footwork that required both skill and rhythm.

The move was performed at house parties, yard parties, and Detroit's iconic dance show, *The Scene*, cementing their place in Detroit's cultural history.

Their dance wasn't just a form of expression; it was a way to assert dominance and mark their presence. It became so popular that even those who had no affiliation with the gang adopted the dance. For many, performing *The Errol Flynn* was about showing off their own style and flair, independent of gang ties.

Criminal Reputation

Despite their cultural contributions, the Errol Flynn Gang was still a street gang, and they engaged in criminal activities typical of the era. They were involved in:

- **Extortion** in Detroit neighborhoods.
- **Robberies** to fund their flashy lifestyle.
- **Drug trafficking**, which became increasingly prevalent in the city during the 80s.

They built a reputation for being dangerous and unpredictable, but they also commanded respect for their style and presence.

Legacy

The Errol Flynn Gang left an indelible mark on Detroit's history. While their criminal activities faded with time, their cultural contributions, particularly in dance and fashion, continue to be remembered.

The Errol Flynn dance is still celebrated and referenced in Detroit's music and cultural conversations.

Their story is a testament to how a gang could influence not just the streets but also the cultural fabric of a city.

For those interested in seeing this history come alive, YouTube clips of *The Errol Flynn* dance showcase the unique footwork and charisma that made this gang iconic. Their legacy remains a fascinating blend of danger, style, and Detroit's enduring creativity.

Chapter 29

Warren G. Harding's 1976 Middle School Volleyball Championship

We were unstoppable—the team to beat. We didn't realize another team was coming for us, determined to take our first-place trophy. Up until then, we were crushing every opponent we faced. How could we not? Our team was made up of athletic powerhouses: me, best friend number two, and best friend number three. We also had the tomboy from Stout Street on our side, along with a few other classmates from the projects who were solid players.

We operated like a fine-tuned engine, with just one problem: we had one player who wasn't athletic at all. He was overweight, couldn't jump, and, no matter how hard he tried, couldn't hit the ball over the net. Instead of chasing the ball, he'd just stand there and let it drop onto the gym floor.

For the purpose of this story, let's call him Jerry.

Every time we scored points and the rotation shifted, we'd tense up. Whenever a fly ball came Jerry's way, one of us would dive in front of him, hit a pass to a teammate, or spike the ball over the net. We had to use this strategy in every game we played. Our gym teacher constantly reminded us not to be selfish and to let Jerry play his part, but we knew better. If we wanted to win, we had to keep the ball away from him.

Jerry had a twin brother who was just as nonathletic. We had already beaten his brother's team earlier in the week. Neither of them were much of a threat on the court.

Meanwhile, another team was rising in the ranks. This team was full of students who were bussed to our school from Detroit's Mettetal Middle School.

174

They were good, but we knew we were better.

All we had to do was play our high-energy game and prove we were the best team at Warren G. Harding Middle School.

Before long, it all came down to us and them in the championship game. It was our exciting, project-born team versus the bragging, trash- talking bus students from Mettetal.

Our gym teacher flipped a coin to decide who would serve first. We won the toss. My best friends stood ready at the front of the net, with our tomboy teammate from Stout Street not far behind them. The game began.

The ball flew back and forth as both teams fiercely spiked it over the net. Jerry stood there, uninvolved, while the rest of us scrambled to keep the ball in play. We dove for every inbound ball, determined to maintain our lead.

Finally, we built up a solid lead. The other gym teacher called a timeout for the losing team. They huddled on the sideline, strategizing. When they returned to the court, they had a new plan: "Hit the ball to Jerry."

Their server sent the ball directly to Jerry. It smacked him square in the chest. "Put both hands together and hit the ball!" a teammate yelled at him. The server hit the ball to him again. This time, Jerry made contact, but the ball sailed out of bounds.

The game became much closer. Jerry rotated to the middle of the floor, and the other team spiked the ball right in front of him.

At this point, the score was tied at twenty. With the game on the line, the championship would be decided by whichever team could win by two points.

The other team continued targeting Jerry, determined to exploit our weak spot. Meanwhile, we scrambled to step in front of him, tripping over one another in our desperation to keep the ball alive.

The gym echoed with the sound of shoes squeaking and players shouting.

The score edged to twenty-one to twenty in favor of the other team, and they were serving. The ball sailed over the net, and we managed to return it. We braced ourselves, assuming they would aim for Jerry again. In a moment of panic, most of us moved toward him, trying to shield him.

But instead of targeting Jerry, the other team lightly tipped the ball into one of the back corners where no one was positioned. It landed just in bounds.

We lost the championship.

The other team erupted in celebration, laughing and teasing us for the final mistake. I stood there in disbelief, my heart sinking. We had been so close. I couldn't help but feel crushed—not just for myself, but for our team and for the pride of the Smith Home Housing Projects.

I was tired of coming in second place. It felt like every time I reached for something great, it slipped just out of my grasp.

The gym teachers began unpacking the trophies and lining them up on the gym floor. The first-place trophies were tall and gleaming, adorned in beautiful blue and silver. The second-place trophies were tiny, almost laughable in comparison. When I saw the difference, I couldn't hold back my emotions. I ran to the boys' restroom and broke down in tears.

To me, this loss was about more than just a game. It was about proving something—to myself, to my friends, to the community. I wanted this victory for all of us.

When I finally emerged from the restroom, my eyes still red and puffy, I saw Jerry standing alone.

Tears were streaming down his face. In that moment, I realized how much he was hurting. He wasn't just crying because we lost; he was crying because he felt like he had let us down. He was likely battling feelings of inadequacy, not just on the court but maybe even at home.

Suddenly, my frustration and anger toward him melted away.

Even though we didn't win, Jerry was still part of our team. We had made it this far together, and that mattered more than the outcome of the game.

I walked over to my gym teacher and asked to take Jerry's trophy. Then, I turned to Jerry and presented it to him myself. "You deserve to have this as well," I told him.

The rest of the team quickly gathered around. We hugged Jerry, tears flowing freely from all of us. In that moment, the loss didn't seem so significant anymore.

In the end, I realized I hadn't truly lost. I had gained something far more valuable: Jerry's friendship and the bond we all shared as teammates.

"That championship may not have ended in victory for our team, but it gave us something far more lasting—lessons in resilience, camaraderie, and the value of lifting each other up even in defeat. Life continued to teach us these lessons, not just on the volleyball court, but in unexpected moments of kindness and courage.

Moral of the Story: True victory isn't always measured by trophies or accolades; it's measured by the connections we make, the empathy we show, and the bonds we strengthen along the way.

In moments of defeat, we have the opportunity to lift each other up, to show kindness, and to recognize that everyone carries unseen burdens. This experience taught me that while winning feels incredible, the real prize is in the friendships and memories we build together.

Supporting and valuing one another, even when the outcome isn't what we hoped for, is the ultimate triumph. It's not about who scores the most points or earns the biggest trophy—it's about how we treat one another when it matters most.

Personal Timeline 1976 – 1977

In **1976**, Stevie Wonder's *Songs in the Key of Life* came out, a double album with a 45' tucked inside. When one of my best friend's sisters bought it, it felt like the whole block got a copy. We would gather around, listening and dancing to the album for hours, sometimes until the early morning. The music was like magic, bringing everyone together. Every house in the projects seemed to have Stevie's voice playing on repeat. Sure, there were other hits from that year—L.T.D.'s **"Back in Love Again"**, The Emotions' **"Best of My Love"**, and Marvin Gaye's **"Got to Give it Up"**, just to name a few. But nothing captured our attention and emotions like Stevie Wonder's masterpiece.

Then, in the sweltering summer of **1977**, Earth Wind & Fire released *All 'N All*.

The album introduced us to yet another level of creativity in music. Songs like **"Fantasy"**, **"Love's Holiday"**, and **"Be Ever Wonderful"** weren't just music—they were experiences. For me and my best friends, this album sparked something unexpected: we discovered we could sing.

We became a popular trio in the projects.

The girls loved it when we sang, and our harmonies got tighter with every song we practiced.

We sang everything from Detroit's own Dramatics and Enchantment to The Floaters, The Whispers, and of course, The Spinners.

Our favorite was the Coca-Cola commercial theme from **1977** (*"Coke Adds Life"*)—we nailed it every time.

Looking back, I sometimes wish we had pursued music more seriously. With professional training, maybe we could have gone far. But knowing the cutthroat nature of the music business, perhaps it was better we didn't. At the time, it wasn't about fame or fortune—it was about connecting, creating, and finding joy in the moment.

The Legacy of The Spinners

The Spinners, originally from Detroit's Herman Gardens Housing Projects, started their journey as The Domingos in the **1950s**. They later changed their name to The Detroit Spinners and, eventually, simply The Spinners. Their rise to fame wasn't instant. Like many artists of their time, they faced challenges, including label struggles and lineup changes.

But their perseverance led to timeless hits like "I'll Be Around", "Could It Be I'm Falling in Love", and "One of a Kind (Love Affair)".

Their smooth harmonies and relatable lyrics made them icons, not just in Detroit but across the world. They weren't just a music group—they were storytellers who captured the struggles, hopes, and joys of everyday life.

For me, The Spinners symbolized the power of resilience.

They came from humble beginnings, just like us, and showed that greatness was possible. Every time their songs played, it felt like a piece of Detroit's soul was shining through.

Their journey wasn't just about music; it was about breaking barriers and inspiring generations. Listening to them gave us hope. It reminded us that no matter where we started, with enough determination, we could achieve something extraordinary.

Even today, when I hear The Spinners, it's not just their music I admire. It's their story—their journey from **Herman Gardens Projects** to the world stage. Their legacy is a reminder that Detroit isn't just a city of challenges; it's a city of champions.

Chapter 30

Big Fat Woman
(A School Play Me And A Friend Wrote Together)

I feel love and joy in my heart recounting this memory in **1977**. By now, I was used to getting in front of classrooms and reciting what I wrote. But writing and putting together a school play was a bit challenging, considering I had to get other friends and classmates interested in the project. Within a few weeks, a school talent show would take place in our auditorium. It was our last year attending Warren G. Harding Middle School, and our class had to go out with a bang.

At that time, a singer by the name of Joe Tex had a song out called *"Ain't Gonna Bump No More (With No Big Fat Woman)."* I wanted our play to be based on this particular song. The play revolved around a happening disco club. Everybody was socializing, dancing, and having a great time—except for one person. She was a pretty hefty woman sitting all by her lonesome, with no one attempting to ask her to dance.

Suddenly, a guy notices the woman and feels bad that she's not enjoying herself. He decides to take her by the hand and invites her to the dance floor. That's where our hilarious skit gets a little crazy.

Now keep in mind, it's **1977**, and the popular dance at that time was called "the bump."

My character was the guy who asked the big woman to dance. Friend number one played the big woman. He borrowed one of his mother's wigs and stuffed his dress full of pillows to make himself look fat. My friends and classmates played the patrons of the club. And yes, even my new friend Jerry from the volleyball team was included in this funny skit.

The record player was behind the curtains, the stage was set, and everyone knew their places. The auditorium, filled with students, teachers, and parents, buzzed with anticipation.

The record started to play, and everyone began dancing with each other as if they were in an actual club. While dancing with a girl, I excused myself to approach the lonely woman sitting in the corner. I invited her to join the disco boogie along with everyone else on the dance floor.

I took this hilariously dressed "woman" by the hand—played by my buddy—and we began to do the bump. She pretended to be so excited that she bumped me hard, and I tripped and fell all over the stage, knocking down tables and chairs. I think I even fell off the stage onto the main auditorium floor.

The whole place erupted in laughter. Teachers were crying in the aisleways because they were laughing so hard.

I climbed back onto the stage, determined to continue the dance. My friend bumped me into other dancers, and when I fell again, Jerry ran over and picked me up off the floor. Finally, my pillow-stuffed, wig-wearing friend bumped me one last time—so hard that his wig flew off.

The sound of laughter grew even louder, continuing throughout the entire auditorium. In the end, we received a long standing ovation from everyone, including the principal.

We were confident we had won the talent show, hands down. Everyone had played their parts perfectly, and once again, we aimed for another 1st-place trophy.

As the show concluded, all the participants were called onto the stage while the judges turned in their scorecards. The principal had the task of announcing the winners of the show.

Ladies and gentlemen, we have our first-place winner in our annual talent show. But first, I will start by announcing our 3rd-place winner.

Third place went to a ballet dancer, and second place was awarded to two brothers who played the trumpet. Yes, they were good, but we knew we had stolen the show. As we waited in anticipation, a lot of us were still hopeful about being named the stars of the evening. But my friend and I weren't worried. We just knew we had this in the bag.

"And for your winner of this evening's talent show…"

The whole auditorium went silent. I could feel my heart pounding inside my chest. I was also feeling a bit lightheaded. I thought about all the times I had been a class clown and how it often got me into trouble back at Angell Elementary School. I hoped my antics would finally pay off in a good way this time.

"And the winner is…"

I saw my classmates and close friends holding each other's hands, anxiously awaiting the announcement. The principal finally called out the winner, and it was…a little Korean girl who played the violin.

We were devastated. We felt robbed. It was clear from the murmurs in the crowd that many of the students, teachers, and parents didn't agree with the judges' decision. I couldn't believe we hadn't even placed in the talent show. Some of us started to cry as we walked off the stage.

But I wasn't going to cry this time. By now, I was starting to get used to feeling like a failure. Still, you couldn't say my heart wasn't broken. We worked so hard on this project, and I couldn't shake the feeling that the judging panel had been a little biased.

The next day, a few teachers got together and held a meeting during lunch break in the teacher's lounge. From what I heard, they discussed what had happened at the talent show. They came to us later and asked if we would perform our skit again in front of the whole school for the kids who missed it the first time.

We reluctantly agreed, but I had a plan. If I was going to step on stage and do this again, I was going to make it even funnier this time.

The next afternoon, we filed onto the stage again. As Joe Tex's *"Ain't Gonna Bump No More (With No Big Fat Woman)"* started playing, the curtains rose, and we recreated our disco club scene.

This time, when I walked over to the lonely "lady" sitting by herself and asked her for a dance, I pulled her onto the dance floor by her dress. The audience roared with laughter as we started doing the bump. But instead of being knocked around like last time, I began bumping and knocking her all over the stage.

"Hey man, calm down! You're being a bit rough," my friend whispered, trying to stay in character. His wig slid sideways and then popped off his head again, causing the entire auditorium to erupt in laughter.

"Hey man, chill!" he whispered again as I pulled on his dress. Suddenly, the front of it ripped, and all the pillows he had stuffed inside came tumbling out onto the stage.

We were even funnier than the first time. The laughter echoed from the balcony all the way to the front of the stage. When we finished our skit, we received another standing ovation and became the talk of the school for the rest of the year.

That was the last time I wanted to make people laugh in a school setting. No more clowning around. As I looked back on this experience, I realized it was time to grow up and take life more seriously.

I was starting to notice the social issues around me and felt the need to face them head-on. My awareness and consciousness were beginning to awaken.

Moral of the Story: Sometimes life will not reward your efforts in the way you expect. You may feel overlooked or even unfairly judged, but the true reward often comes in the joy and connection you create along the way. In this case, our skit may not have won a trophy, but it gave us the chance to bring happiness and laughter to so many people. And that, in itself, was a victory worth celebrating.

Another Harding Middle School Memory

Incidentally, the student who won the talent show was in a few of my classes. She was a very quiet girl but one of the smartest in our entire school. Whenever it was time to receive report cards, she consistently earned straight A's in every class.

One time, she received a B in one of her classes. The look on her face was filled with horror. Her eyes brimmed with tears when we asked what was wrong.

"I can't go home today," she said.

When some of us asked why, she explained that her parents would beat her if she came home with a grade lower than an A. This was the first time she held a conversation with any of us for more than five minutes.

When the bell rang to release us for the day, she stayed seated and cried even harder.

"I was born here, but my parents are from Korea and will not accept this grade on my report card. They will say I didn't try hard enough. They won't stand for failure. I can go home, but I also have nowhere else to go.

They will beat and embarrass me in front of my siblings."

I couldn't believe what I was hearing. We were all confused but kept trying to console her. Each one of us explained that getting a B wasn't a bad grade, but nothing we said seemed to comfort her. She was physically shaking, terrified.

"You don't understand," she said. "My parents are very strict, and they expect nothing less from me or my brothers and sisters."

"Would you like some of us to walk home with you?" one girl suggested.

She nodded yes to the kind offer. "We will walk with you in solidarity and make sure nothing happens to you. Now calm down; it's going to be okay."

A few girls from class rallied around her and walked her home.

At that moment, I remember thinking, *Man, I wish my parents were on top of my school grades like that.* Every time they looked at my report card, they would close it, set it down somewhere, shake their heads in dismay, and keep moving without saying a single word to me.

When I was a small child, I used to get whippings for bringing home bad grades. But as I got older, they didn't seem to care as much. Not participating in any school events or sports I was involved in didn't help my cause either.

Maybe it was their handicap that stopped them from being involved with my schooling. Maybe it was my fault for not asking them to come see me perform on stage or watch me play sports.

Maybe they had more important things to worry about—like how they would pay the next bill, clothe us, or feed us with the little money they had. Maybe they just didn't have the time.

Whatever the case, it sure would have felt great to see my parents proud of me in an audience-type setting.

When it came to accomplishments, I was on my own.

Reflecting on moments like this taught me how different everyone's experiences could be, even in the same school, sitting in the same classrooms.

Some of us longed for the kind of strict guidance our classmate had, while others couldn't imagine the pressure and fear she lived with daily. It was a stark reminder that each of us carried invisible struggles, shaped by the expectations and challenges of our families and backgrounds.

As I moved forward, I began to realize that understanding and supporting each other could bridge those differences. It was moments like this that pushed me to start thinking about the bigger picture—how our experiences shape us and how important it is to look out for one another, even in the smallest of ways.

Chapter 31

A Man's Journey Through the Wisdom of Women

You know, there's one thing my dad used to always say:
"A woman can never teach you how to be a man."
Throughout my childhood, I kept hearing these words.

My dad never even talked to me about the birds and the bees. A grown woman outside the home taught me everything sexually I needed to know. I was just a fifteen-year-old kid, and she was a primed thirty-two-year-old woman. But besides that, women never seem to get the credit when it comes to boys turning into young men.

The more I experienced as a child and the older I got, the more I found my dad's statement to be somewhat false. Would you say this to a boy whose dad is not present in his life, and he only has his mom to rely on? No, I don't think so.

Fortunately, I lived in a two-parent home, but I've learned so many things from strong and confident women throughout my life— things that taught me how to be a better man.

I learned a lot from my very own mother. Even though she couldn't always express herself through words, her actions spoke volumes. If she saw me act incorrectly with any of my girlfriends, she would get super pissed off and give me a certain look that let me know she didn't approve of my disrespectful or reckless conduct.

If a girl left the house angry or sad, my mom would intervene and ask, *"What's wrong with her? What caused her to leave like that?"* If it turned out to be something I did, she would make me go after her and apologize. She never taught me to be disrespectful toward any female, and that *look* she gave me was all it took for me to straighten up.

I also get my mental strength from my mother.

Watching her overcome cancer gave me the strength to overcome challenges in my own life. Her willpower was truly amazing to witness, and it left a lasting impression on me.

Even though they probably thought I wasn't paying attention, I learned so much from my strong-willed sisters. I watched their struggles and how they empowered themselves to overcome adversity.

There have been so many women who have influenced and played a major part in my life. I come from a long line of powerful women—my sisters, grandmothers, aunties, and cousins. I watched and learned from them all.

Yes, I learned many things from my dad, uncles, and other male figures, but I learned just as much, if not more, about life from women. They were the ones I spent most of my time with as a small child.

I mentioned one of my aunties earlier in the book. She never had children of her own, but I was her child. She taught me so many things that shaped me into a better man as I got older.

Another auntie, who looked so much like my mother, was also like a second mom to me. She was loving and mild-mannered, but make no mistake—she would put you in a child's place if you got out of line. I never got on her bad side, and I knew she loved me like I was one of her own sons.

She doesn't know this, but she was the one who musically influenced me. I used to spend weekends with her and my cousins. At night, when she told us to take our baths and turn in for bed, she would light candles and play her amazing album collection.

The beautiful art form of music would smoothly find its way into our rooms, even when the bedroom door was closed for the night.

Just like someone reading a bedtime story, the rich sounds of smooth jazz and soulful R&B would eventually lull us to sleep.

I remember hearing artists like Brenda Russell, Nancy Wilson, Phoebe Snow, Minnie Riperton, Roberta Flack, Nick Ashford and Valerie Simpson, Patti Austin, Angela Bofill, Dionne Warwick, Luther Vandross, Deniece Williams, and Phyllis Hyman, just to name a few. I would closely listen to the lyrics of these love songs, and they became my musical blueprint for how to treat and respect a female at an early age. These records would later influence me to become a DJ in my adult years.

I was so in tune with music that I could predict the next big hit on an album. Seventy percent of the time, I was absolutely correct. Man! They don't make musical artists like that anymore.

I had another aunt who I have fond memories of. She also treated me like her son. Every time I hear a Marvin Gaye or Al Green song, it reminds me of the times I spent with her. She would play those songs over and over.

I remember how she used to take long walks from the apartment and back. While walking with her, we would have conversations about different topics. I guess those were the times she could clear her thoughts. Even though I was pretty young, I learned a lot through those conversations. She was also so much fun to be around. Continue resting in peace, Auntie. I bet you've got all the angels laughing hysterically.

My other aunts—oh, how I admired them. I watched them protect their dignity and proudly display their beauty, glamour, grace, hard work, and dedication. They set the standard for the kind of future girlfriends I wanted.

It's true when they say to be careful of what you say and do because a child is always watching.

As a child, I was hungry for information. I was a watcher, dissecting everything adults did and said.

I learned so much about life from the women around me.

The two biggest influences in my life were my two grandmothers. Nobody—and I mean *nobody*—had a bigger effect on my life than these two women. I had the best of both worlds with them, and they shaped me into the person I am today.

As I reflect on the profound impact the women in my life have had, I realize that their influence goes far beyond what words can express. They taught me lessons in resilience, kindness, strength, and love. Through their actions and guidance, I became the man I am today.

But with all the gratitude I feel, there's still a lingering pain—a sense of loss that never truly fades. As I look back on these memories, I'm reminded of the love and wisdom they left behind and the void their absence has created.

And so, with this chapter, I turn the page, holding their lessons close as I share the next part of my journey—a story of remembrance, faith, and the unshakable bond between a mother and her son.

But I've got a bone to pick with you, Lord, when it comes to the two most important women in my life.

Chapter 32

A Letter to God

(A Private Conversation)

Dear God,

I was so blessed as a child, but I didn't always realize just how blessed I was. I had two of the greatest women a boy could ever have in his life—my two grandmothers. They gave me the best of both worlds and completed me. I am who I am today because of these two extraordinary women. They were the greatest I have ever known. But, God, I have a bone to pick with you.

I'm writing this letter to tell you how I felt about their leaving this earth without me. I understand that we all must eventually leave this world, but you took my first grandmother when I needed her the most. That loss changed me forever. She's your angel now, but she was my angel while she was here with me. She was a beautiful person with a gentle soul, and I cherished every moment I spent with her.

Dear God, I have to ask:
Why do I still cry, and why do I still feel this pain?

You could've waited until I fully understood death. You knew I wasn't ready at that time.

Lord, you must understand that I still feel anger sometimes, even when I know it was your will to take her. You must understand that while I was growing into manhood, I still needed her in my life. Lord, I know I sound selfish, but you have to see that this was bad timing. You didn't prepare me for this, and I took her passing very, very hard.

Watching her as a child taught me so much. I'm a giving person, and I actually care about others. I'd like to think I got that from her. She taught me faith, love, and compassion. She loved my granddad with everything in her. Because of her, I witnessed the proper way to love someone.

Dear God, I miss my grandmother so much.

I miss waking up to the sound of gospel music filling the house, signaling it was time for breakfast. I miss the time we spent listening to Martha Jean "The Queen" on the little radio she kept on top of the refrigerator. I miss waking up to Sammy Davis Jr.'s "Hello Detroit" playing in the background.

I miss her world-famous peach cobbler and strawberry cake—nothing I've ever tasted comes close. I miss that spare bedroom with the most comfortable bed I've ever laid on. As a kid, I always thought that room was meant just for me.

I remember the time I ran away from home. I ran straight to her, and she welcomed me with open, loving arms. I laid in that warm, comforting bed until my parents came to get me. I didn't want to leave. I wanted to stay with her forever.

A few Sundays, she took me to church with her. I loved how everyone greeted her like she was royalty. My grandmother was special—she was my heartbeat, my joy, my everything.

But, Lord, I must admit, you upset me when you took the one person I loved most in this world. Her passing changed me for the worse. For a while, I felt lost.

I lashed out at others who still had their grandparents. I picked fights and arguments. I quit going to worship. I started smoking cigarettes for a couple of years. While I had been a social beer drinker, I turned to hard liquor to dull my pain. That's also when I tried marijuana for the first time.

No one knew I was falling apart.

I kept it all hidden and never sought help.

I never even shared this with my mom, who was also dealing with the loss of her mother.

After two or three years, I finally pulled myself back together. I knew my grandmother wouldn't want this for me.

Lord, I hope you've forgiven me for being angry and so selfish. Please understand—she was my world.

Lord, I would also like to talk to you about my other grandmother. She was an extraordinary, spiritual, and loving person. She's the one who taught me strength, hard work, and dedication. As a child, I spent many summers with her, and those were some of the most amazing times of my life.

She owned a huge farm, and I got the chance to pick berries, help feed the livestock, and go fishing with her. I also had the joy of watching her cook incredible southern dishes. Watching her work tirelessly on her farm inspired me to work hard for everything I ever wanted to accomplish.

Now, I wasn't very good at feeding her animals. In fact, I was terrified of them. When it was time to prepare a chicken for dinner, I would watch her grab a few by the head and spin them until their necks broke. Then, she'd throw the heads and bodies to the ground, where the bodies would still jump all over the place. This later created a mental phobia for me—I can't stand seeing dead animals. To this day, seeing one lying in the street sends me into a panic.

I can also remember the large family gatherings she hosted for Thanksgiving and Christmas. The little boy in the picture on this book's cover? That photo was taken at one of those gatherings. I remember congregating around her large dinner table, holding hands with my grandmother, parents, uncles, aunts, cousins, and siblings. Each of us would recite a Bible verse as part of the prayer before eating.

When it was my turn, I always said the same verse: "Jesus wept," the shortest verse in the Bible. One year, she asked me if I knew any other Bible verses, and everyone burst into laughter. Looking back, I'm so glad I had the chance to make her laugh.

My grandmother was such a strong and independent woman. She raised 12 children all by herself.

One morning, one of my uncles played a prank on me and my brother. He wrote out a ridiculous breakfast wish list: bacon, sausage, waffles, pancakes, hash browns, omelets, scrambled eggs, toast with butter and jelly, fresh fruit, cereal, grits, or oatmeal.

He handed her the note, and after reading it, she yelled at us to take our butts outside. Later, when she realized it was a prank, she laughed. That memory of her laughter is one I hold dear to my heart.

She lived a long, full life, but Lord, there's something that still bothers me. I can't blame you for this—it was my own mistake. Lord, I knew I had my own mind, but why didn't you instill in me the importance of asking these questions?

I missed a golden opportunity to sit down and truly get to know her. I wanted to learn so much about her past, but for some reason, I was afraid to ask.

What was her childhood like? What was the world like when she was young? What was my grandfather like? What were her parents like? What did she endure during segregation and the civil rights era? Why didn't I know she used to be a schoolteacher?

My favorite subject was history, and I know she was rich in knowledge, but I was too afraid to ask. I had so many questions, but now she's gone, and I feel like such a fool for not having those conversations with her.

Lord, it hurts to know there are no second chances. I blew it.

What Happens When the Family Tree is Interrupted

(Lord, This Is Just My Personal Opinion)

My grandparents had the highest branches on our family tree, and I always believed that grandmothers, a long with my grandfather, were the essential glue in keeping families together.

Here's what I mean.

When you visited your grandparents, it wasn't just about spending time with them—you also got to see aunts, uncles, and cousins. As children, you had the chance to play with your cousins, walk to the store together, and share ice cream. You treated each other as though you were blood brothers and sisters. Your aunts and uncles wanted to catch up with you and were genuinely interested in what was going on in your life.

I can still picture myself sitting down with my grandfather, watching a televised Detroit Tigers game. Everyone in the family seemed to have missed you, and they welcomed you with the biggest hugs.

One grandmother welcomed me for whole summers, showering me with love and care. My other grandmother was a bus ride away, and I'd spend summers at her house too. These were some of the best memories of my life. I thrived under their love and affection, and it felt like everything was right in the world when I was with them. That's the glue I'm talking about—the kind of love that keeps a family together.

You get addicted to that divine love.

But then the inevitable happens.
You lose the top of the family tree—your grandmother. The person you adored your entire life. The person you held closest to your heart is now gone.

It's the third season, and slowly, the rest of the leaves on the tree begin to change colors and fall to the ground. Each leaf represents a family member.

When the Glue Begins to Dissolve

Adulthood takes over, and everything becomes unglued.

There's no one there to stop the once-beautiful family tree from dying. Family members begin to drift apart.

Reunions stop. Facebook messages fade away. Phone calls to check in with each other become nonexistent.

Families expand, but second and third cousins grow up without ever meeting each other. Aunts and uncles stop catching up. Visiting each other becomes a thing of the past.

Birthdays are missed, and holiday gatherings become unheard of.

I remember a time when I told a family story about meeting a girl in a club I was interested in. After a long conversation, I found out she was my first cousin.

For years, that story was funny—a way to laugh at an odd coincidence. But now? It's not funny. It's shameful.
We can't blame anyone but ourselves for this separation.

A Wider Issue

Lord, I know I'm guilty of these acts of separation.

I also understand that this isn't just a Wright family issue. It's a Black family issue.

Time and time again, I hear the same story in other Black families. Once the grandparents are no longer there, the family begins to crack and come apart.

But even as I reflect on the loss of the strong women who held my family together, I realize that their lessons and love are still alive in me. The legacy they left behind has shaped my values, my strength, and my ability to navigate life.

As I move forward, I carry their spirit with me, especially in the way I choose to honor my family, my roots, and the journey we've all shared.

Their love was the foundation, but what happens when the next generation is left to build upon it? Let me tell you how I've tried to preserve what they left behind and how I continue to pass on their legacy

It's the third season. The top of the family tree is gone, and soon the rest of the leaves will change colors and fall to the ground. Each leaf represents a family member.

– Eric Wright

"It's hard to find a new norm when you lose someone you love."

– Comedian Deon Cole

Side Note:

This was the hardest short chapter for me to write. It took a whole month to complete, and I cried every single day. To my grandparents, thank you so much for being in my life.

R.L.W. and F.M.W.
And I miss my Grandfather J.W. As well

Reflecting on the Journey So Far

Chapters 16–32: Building Bridges Between Laughter and Loss

As we reflect on chapters 16–32, the tapestry of memories becomes even richer, blending moments of humor, discovery, and heartfelt reflection. Each chapter invites the reader deeper into a world shaped by friendships, family bonds, and the ever-present backdrop of Detroit's vibrant and challenging environment.

Themes and Moments That Stand Out:

- **Friendship and Brotherhood:** From the formation of "The Ghetto Avengers" to the school volleyball championship, these chapters celebrate the loyalty and camaraderie that define lifelong friendships.

- **Resilience Through Loss:** Honest letters to God and heartfelt tributes to beloved grandparents explore the pain of loss and the profound lessons drawn from grief.

- **Cultural Reflections:** The golden era of Detroit's music and dance scene—from "The Scene" to the rise of the Detroit Jit—offers a nostalgic look at the soundtrack and rhythm of the times.

- **Life Lessons From Strong Women:** Moving tributes to the women who shaped the narrator's life highlight the strength, wisdom, and influence of mothers, aunts, and grandmothers.

- **Humor and Joy Amid Hardship:** From hilarious school plays to memories of summer boot camps on a makeshift basketball court, these chapters balance moments of levity with deeper reflections.

A Message for the Reader:

These chapters remind us that life is a mosaic of highs and lows, victories and defeats, laughter and tears. The stories of this section invite us to cherish the connections that shape us, reflect on the lessons we learn from those who came before us, and find joy even in the face of adversity.

As we move forward to the final chapters of this memoir, let us carry with us the enduring spirit of resilience, the warmth of shared memories, and the hope that the future always holds the promise of new beginnings.

Lets proceed with this Journey from childhood to young adulthood.

Chapter 33

King Of Detroit
(The Man Who Moved Detroit Forward)

You can say what you want about this man—claim he was part of corruption, not friendly to the media, had a mouth with no filter, or rode around in an official limo with bulletproof windows. Some say he was part of Detroit's decline.

I personally think his critics were resistant and spreading lies just to get media attention. He ran Detroit with an iron fist, accepted no nonsense, and didn't tolerate racism from the media. If he was so bad, why did he serve five terms as the city's first Black mayor? He was in office for 20 years before retiring, taking a city in ruins from the 1967 rebellion and turning it into a competitive city again. Yes, he was part of the rebuilding. He was also a **Tuskegee Airman** and the first to implement a youth summer jobs program that changed lives.

During his administration, he financially saved my family, as well as many others in the Smith Home Housing Projects. After the school year ended, many of us signed up for his program and went to work. My siblings and I could relieve some pressure on our mother by buying our own school clothes and contributing to the household. Often, we gave her money to get something she wanted for herself.

Finally, my mother had a little less stress, thanks to the man I used to call the **"King of Detroit."**

My First Summer Job

My first summer job was as a reading tutor at the Brightmoor Community Center, right across the street from my middle school.

I took pride in teaching kids how to read, some of whom came from the projects.

One boy, in particular, was stubborn at first because he didn't want me to know how bad he struggled. But by the end of the summer, he had made progress. He wasn't an expert, but we formed a bond, and he appreciated my efforts. He's no longer with us now.

Rest in peace.

My Second Summer Job

My second job was as a camp counselor. Every day, we boarded a bus at the Brightmoor Community Center and took kids to Kensington Metro Park.

Our first assignment was to teach them how to make fishing poles from fallen tree branches. Afterward, we were instructed to wrap the string around the pole and secure the hooks to avoid accidents.

Unfortunately, I didn't secure my hook properly. While riding the bus back, my hook snagged a little girl's finger. A senior counselor had to remove it as she screamed in pain.

When we arrived back at the center, the girl's mother was waiting. She cursed me out, calling me every name you could imagine. I felt terrible—not just for being careless but for causing that little girl pain. That summer taught me a lesson I'll never forget.

My Third Summer Job

In my third summer, I worked as a Junior Counselor at Detroit's Vetal Elementary School. These kids were tough.

Some wouldn't listen, others had anger or self-esteem issues, and some dealt with serious struggles at home. Every day was a challenge, but it taught me patience and resilience.

My third summer job was unique.

My role was to have personal and private conversations with students who were sent to the principal's office for bad behavior or had to stay after school.

It was tough in the beginning, but I had to make these kids understand that I wasn't much older than they were—and that I probably lived in their shoes at one point.

I was already pretty good at getting kids to understand right from wrong, and convincing them that acting out in school wasn't the way to go. Once again, I found myself using my superpower. (Laughing) Some of these kids just needed someone to talk to, and honestly, this job felt perfect for me. I only wished it wasn't just a summer job. I loved it. I truly felt like I made a difference in some of their lives—or at least, I hope I did.

The Last Summer Job

My final summer job wasn't nearly as inspiring—it was downright nasty. My best friends and I worked for a Detroit waste management company near the Southfield Freeway, just before the Joy Road exit.

None of us had cars yet, so every morning at 7:15 a.m., we hopped on our bikes and rode to a bakery on Schoolcraft Road. There, we ordered our favorite apple fritters before heading to work by 8 a.m.

Our tasks included spraying down garbage trucks, cleaning break rooms and bathrooms, sweeping and mopping truck garages, and organizing office spaces.

It was a terrible job, to say the least, but the good feeling of bringing home a paycheck made it bearable. Thankfully, it was my last summer job before landing my first year-round position. I'll tell you about that one later.

A Family Effort

My siblings were also able to work in the summer jobs program. First, my sister joined, then my brother, and eventually my two youngest sisters. At one point, all of us were working these jobs simultaneously.

For my mother, this meant fewer worries about school clothes, groceries, or utility bills. It was a relief to see her sit back a bit and enjoy some peace of mind.

It was also amazing to witness so many kids in the projects working summer jobs. You could spot who had the newest sweatsuits, the latest sneakers, or the freshest silk shirts and Swedish knits. Many of us took our hard-earned money to Northland Mall and shopped for ourselves, a newfound independence that we cherished.

Some of us performed so well in these jobs that they turned into full-time, year-round positions because employers needed reliable workers.

The Legacy of the King of Detroit

All of this was made possible by the King of Detroit and his administration.

He added the youth to the workforce every summer, giving us something productive to do and keeping us out of trouble.

But that wasn't all.

His accomplishments went beyond the summer jobs program:

- He convened gang leaders to reduce gang violence in Detroit.
- He created the "No Devil's Night" initiative to keep the city safe.
- He put more Black men and women on the police force.
- He integrated City Hall.
- He launched the Montreux-Detroit International Jazz Festival.
- He introduced the International Grand Prix to Downtown Detroit.
- The Renaissance Center, the Riverfront Apartments, and the Medical Center were all built during his administration.
- He oversaw the construction of the Downtown People Mover.

A Flawed But Great Leader

Did the King of Detroit have his faults? Of course. But don't they all? His shortcomings don't overshadow the great memories he created for me and countless others.

In my mind, this was a great man. He single-handedly gave me my first opportunities to be part of Detroit's workforce and, in doing so, shaped my path forward.

Reflecting on the King of Detroit and his profound impact on my life, it's clear that his leadership extended beyond politics—it touched the lives of ordinary people in extraordinary ways. His programs gave us a sense of purpose, pride, and independence during our formative years.

As we move forward, I can't help but think about the power of opportunity and the lasting influence of those who pave the way for others. While no leader is without flaws, it's their ability to inspire and uplift that leaves an indelible mark on generations to come.

The next chapter explores another pivotal moment in my journey, reminding us of the lessons learned from community, resilience, and the figures who shaped our lives.

Chapter 34

An Old Man's Story

I'll never forget this for as long as I live. As a teen, I remember walking up to Sonny's restaurant on Evergreen Road and Schoolcraft for some quick cheeseburger sliders. The only people in the place were myself, an old man, and the short-order cook. I decided to sit at the counter, three seats down from the old man.

"What can I get you, young man?" asked the cook.

I placed my order: "Can I get a cheeseburger combo and make my drink a Coke, please?"

The scruffy old man leaned over and said, "Today's my 89th birthday."

I congratulated him and said, "I hope you have a lot of great memories."

He thanked me, smiled, and continued his meal. Then he leaned over again and whispered, "There are way too many things I wish I could forget."

I replied, "Don't worry. If you make it to 100 years old, I'm pretty sure you'll have a handful of regrets."

At that point, I didn't know why I said something like that. It sounded harsh coming from me. The man was at a burger joint all by himself celebrating his birthday, and that was all I could think of saying. I quickly apologized.

"Sorry about that. My words came out wrong."

He stared at me with the strangest look on his face. "You have no idea, young man," he said.

He continued, telling me that back in the day, he used to be a Detroit firefighter in the mid-1930s and early 1940s.

"That's a very prestigious job to have," I told the old man.

He responded, "Yeah, it should be."

"The '30s and '40s were a very different time in every way possible. You know that, right?"

"Oh yeah, I bet," I replied.

He said, "Back then, I was a very different man. Who knew we'd get to where we are today in society? And I'd be feeling this way about the decisions I made in those times."

Curiously, I sat there wanting to know what terrible decisions he had made in his life. Did he leave his family? Did he commit murder? Did he spend most of his life in prison? Something told me that whatever it was, it was horrible.

Right before a long pause, he looked at me and whispered, "Back then, it was common for firefighters who looked like me to leave people who looked like you in burning houses, buildings, and terrible situations, just to say we couldn't get to them."

He said that, more times than he'd like to admit, he heard Black people and little Black children screaming in burning buildings, houses, apartments, stores, and cars, and he deliberately pretended not to hear them.

"The last time I did it," he continued, "I made eye contact with a baby in a burning building. I went in to save the child, but I turned my head and deliberately didn't."

He said that was the last time he did it, and he quit being a firefighter that year. He added, "The nightmares haven't stopped. I still haven't forgiven myself, and the guilt of those horrid memories eats away at me every single day."

I can remember my meal being placed in front of me. I couldn't even eat it—I was in so much shock.

When it came to firefighters, I never thought of them in this way.

Like when it came to police officers, lawyers, and judges, I knew they didn't give a fuck about us—especially police officers.

They were the enforcers of a system that didn't value our lives, and growing up in Detroit, this was a truth we all knew too well.

But for some reason, it never occurred to me that firefighters could harbor the same hatred. Firefighters, in my mind, were supposed to be heroes—the ones who ran into burning buildings, no questions asked, to save lives. The ones kids looked up to, dreaming of wearing those helmets and sliding down poles. Yet, sitting in Sonny's Restaurant that day, my perception of heroism was shattered.

From my ancestors to my great-grandparents, to my grandparents, to my parents, and now to me—the cycle of hate and systemic oppression seemed never-ending. The weight of generations of pain fell on me as I sat there, hearing this old man's confession. Almost everyone in power, at one point or another, had a hand in deliberately making our lives harder, stripping away our dignity, and trying to erase our humanity. It wasn't just the police, the lawyers, or the judges. Now, it seemed, even those tasked with saving lives carried the same darkness in their hearts.

I was shaking uncontrollably. My body couldn't handle the anger and betrayal I felt. After I managed to calm down, I thought about everything the old man had told me. His story wasn't just horrifying—it was haunting. I couldn't help but wonder: Why me? Why did he choose me to unburden himself? Was it guilt? Was he seeking forgiveness from someone he felt represented the people he had wronged? How many others had he told this story to, or was I the first? Had he ever sought redemption in the eyes of God? And, more than anything, how could someone be so heartless?

These questions spiraled in my mind, but none of them brought me comfort. Instead, they opened a broader wound: Why is there so much hate in the world for us?

What did we ever do to deserve this? I couldn't answer that question then, and honestly, I still can't.

What I struggled with most was the image of him—this man who once held the power to save lives—pretending to help while knowingly turning his back on innocent people.

The thought of him walking into a burning building, seeing a child crying for help, and choosing to leave them to die because of the color of their skin—it was unbearable.

I lost my appetite. The smell of the burger I had ordered now made me nauseous. I couldn't sit there any longer, listening to this madness. I felt sick to my stomach, physically and emotionally. Without taking a single bite, I paid for my meal and left it untouched on the table.

As I walked out of Sonny's Restaurant, the world seemed different. The air felt heavier, the streets colder. I wasn't the same young man who had walked in for a quick bite to eat. I left that place wiser, more aware of the evils lurking in the world.

I walked home in silence, replaying the man's words in my mind. I thought about my own life and the responsibilities I now carried. The man's confession wasn't just a glimpse into a darker past—it was a warning, a reminder of how easily the world can forget our humanity.

That day, I made a promise to myself: I wouldn't let this world define me or take away my faith in who I was. I was born for a reason, and I came to understand that my life was a gift—not to be squandered, but to be protected and nurtured. I became the caretaker of my own life, and in doing so, I found a strength I didn't know I had.

Looking back now, I realize that encounter wasn't just a coincidence. Maybe it was meant to teach me something, to push me to see beyond the surface, to face the ugly truths of the world so I could rise above them.

Whatever it was, I'll never forget that old man's story—for as long as I live. Walking home that day, my mind raced with thoughts of justice, morality, and the weight of history.

That old man's story was more than just a confession—it was a mirror reflecting the scars of a world that had failed so many. But even in the darkness of his tale, I found a glimmer of purpose. If the past was filled with hate and pain, I knew I had to play my part in creating a better future.

Little did I know, the lessons I had just learned would shape how I viewed the world and my role in it from that moment on.

Moral of the Story: Hate, when left unchecked, not only destroys the lives of those it is aimed at but also corrodes the soul of the one who harbors it. We all carry burdens and regrets, but it's never too late to confront them and seek redemption. The old man's confession is a reminder that even the darkest truths can spark the light of change. It's up to each of us to break the cycle of prejudice and to ensure that our actions today build a more just and compassionate tomorrow.

Chapter 35

A Different Kind of Lesson

This was before I knew anything about love, relationships, or the complexities of adulthood. It was long before my crushes, jealousies, or sneaking out to meet girlfriends in secret. Back then, I was just a kid—curious about girls but still figuring out the world. This story is one I've carried for years, tucked away in the corners of my memory. It's about a woman whose actions walked a dangerous line, but at the time, I never said a word.

At sixteen, I made a mistake that fractured my relationship with my mom. It was one she couldn't forgive. She packed my bags, set them on the porch, and told me I had to leave. With no plan and nowhere to go, I was taken in by a woman I'd known from my past. She offered me a roof over my head in exchange for helping with her kids. At first, it seemed like a blessing—a safe space and a second chance.

But living in her home came with its own rules, expectations, and complications. She had a firm grip on my life, one that lasted for several years. She was possessive, sometimes jealous, and her interest in me went beyond what I understood at the time. While I stayed, I became a willing participant in her world, and looking back, I now see how deeply complicated those years were.

The Much-Kept Secret

A family had moved into the Smith Home Projects, and to my surprise, I already knew the now divorced mother and father from years earlier when we lived on Dumbarton Street. The parents had been our Sunday school teachers—kind, loving, and deeply involved in the church. But things had changed. The mom and dad were divorced now, and she was raising her kids alone.

Her kids quickly grew attached to me, calling me their honorary big brother.

I didn't mind; I enjoyed spending time with them, and they filled a void I hadn't realized was there.

Their mom worked second shift, and she struggled to balance her schedule with childcare. One day, I offered to stay with the kids after school to help out.

When she came home that evening and saw the kids tucked into bed, she seemed relieved. "Thank you," she said. "They haven't been this peaceful in a long time." After a pause, she added, "Would you be interested in watching them on weekends? I can pay you fifty dollars a week."

To a sixteen-year-old with no real income, it sounded like a great deal. Fifty dollars a week was more than I'd ever had to my name, and the kids were easy to care for. It felt like a win-win.

I enjoyed being around her kids; in fact, it didn't feel like a job at all. The fifty dollars a week she paid me was just an added bonus. I agreed to babysit them on weekends, and over time, I grew to cherish my role as their big brother.

We spent our evenings playing in the front yard, tackling chores together, diving into board games, and watching cartoons. Their mother was pleased with how clean the house stayed, often thanking me for teaching her kids life skills and keeping them safe. One time, she even gave me a kiss on the cheek to show her gratitude. At the time, I didn't think much of it—just a gesture of appreciation.

A Shift in Dynamics

Over time, our dynamic began to change. She started asking more personal questions, probing into my thoughts and experiences in ways I didn't fully understand.

I brushed it off, assuming she was simply curious. Yet, I noticed subtle shifts—gestures and words that felt more complex than a simple gratitude for my help.

One evening, after a long day, I fell asleep on the couch.

When she returned home, she suggested I rest in her bed, insisting I leave my dirty clothes behind to keep her sheets clean.

It felt unusual, but I didn't overthink it and complied.

These moments, while initially innocent in appearance, slowly developed into a dynamic I now see as an imbalance of power and understanding. As a very young teenager, I was unsure of how to interpret these experiences or what they truly meant.

The Move

She had finally made it out of the projects, leaving behind the noise, the chaos, and the constant struggle that seemed to hover over every day. After spending months crashing on my friend's couch, got in a cycle of uncertainty, I made the decision to move in with her. There was a sense of relief in having a place to call home again, A quiet space away from the hard streets.

Initially, I focused on taking care of her kids. I embraced the role of their big brother, spending evenings helping them with homework, playing games, and ensuring the house was tidy before their mother returned from work. She often expressed gratitude, sometimes with small gestures that seemed heartfelt. At the time, I saw her appreciation as nothing more than kindness.

That Changed. Eventually, we became more intertwined with the late night games and like a kid in a candy store, I wanted to tell all my close buddies what was going on between her and I, but I fought the temptation and continued keeping my mouth shut. I told no one as I became physically addicted and wanted to learn more about the female anatomy. I did nothing to hinder that. I didn't end it and I let her do whatever she wanted to and I basically did whatever she asked.

This chapter is not meant to cast blame or to dwell on regret. Instead, it's a reflection on a pivotal moment that shaped my understanding of relationships and personal agency. It serves as a reminder of the importance of healthy boundaries, especially when trust is placed in someone else's hands.

It taught me that not every act of kindness comes without strings, and not every safe place is truly secure. Learning to recognize the difference between genuine care and hidden expectations become a crucial part of growth.

Moral of the Story

Some lessons come wrapped in complexities that take years to untangle. As a young person, you may not always recognize when boundaries are crossed, but reflection reveals the truths you couldn't see before. It's a reminder to nurture healthy relationships, respect others' boundaries, and advocate for yourself, even in difficult situations.

This chapter is more than a story—it's a step toward understanding how the events of our past can shape who we are today. It's a reminder that even in moments of confusion and challenge, there are lessons to be learned, if we're willing to reflect and grow.

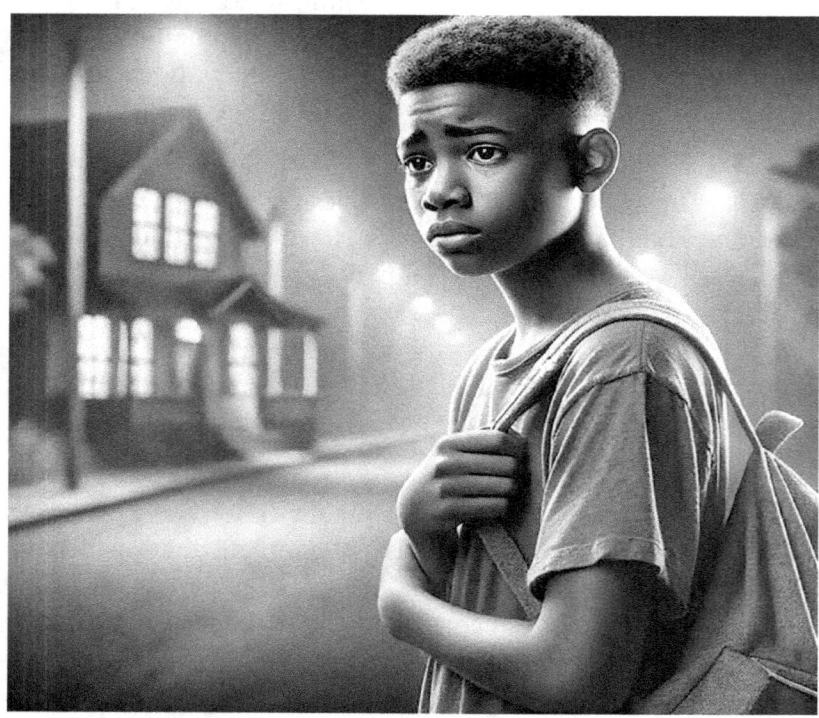

Chapter 36

Finally Finding My Own Lane

One of my closest friends landed his first year-round job in the newly built Renaissance Center in downtown Detroit. He was hired and trained as a full-time cook. One day, he told me that the job was looking for a nighttime dishwasher and encouraged me to apply. The next day, I took the bus with him to work, applied for the position, and got a call back the very next day. I was thrilled—this was no summer gig, but a real, steady job. At $10.75 an hour, it was a good wage for a kid back then.

I washed dishes for just a week before someone called off sick, leaving the kitchen short-staffed. The lead cook asked if I'd be willing to step in, and that was the beginning of a new chapter. My time as a dishwasher was short-lived.

At first, the work was challenging, but it gave me something to focus on. I was able to attend school during the day and work evenings five days a week. I threw myself into learning everything I could: how to handle knives properly, use slicer machines, operate ovens, stoves, and fryers, read tickets, and prepare dishes to exact specifications. I also learned to label, date, and rotate produce and meats properly—key steps to prevent anyone from getting sick.

Working in a kitchen came with its hazards, too. I learned to be vigilant about sharp objects, harsh chemicals, and slippery floors. Cleanliness was another lesson drilled into me—it was essential for safety and professionalism.

This was my first real job, and I worked hard to keep it. I was always on time, never late, and I never called off. I quickly realized that a good work ethic and dependability set me apart. My work clothes were always clean and neatly pressed. I avoided drama and earned the respect of my coworkers.

Before long, I became one of the go-to people in the kitchen whenever a manager or server needed something.

I picked things up quickly and had natural, creative abilities in the kitchen. My first job kept me busy and off the streets, and I found that I was genuinely good at this cooking thing. It felt like I had finally found my own lane. Years later, this would become my career. But before that, I'd have to navigate the ups and downs of the food industry.

Learning the Realities of the Business

As a newcomer to the restaurant industry, I discovered that the profession had both its rewards and its challenges. I read once that being a chef was the second most stressful job, just below being an air traffic controller. Long hours, strenuous work, and the constant pressure to prepare meals quickly took their toll on many.

I saw firsthand how this stress led to accidents, addiction, and sometimes even worse. I made it a point to steer clear of the pitfalls I witnessed, staying focused and cautious.

One day, the lead cook became entangled in a messy affair with the lead waitress. She eventually broke things off with her long-term boyfriend, and he didn't take the news well. One night, after the restaurant had closed, the front gate was pulled halfway down when a man slid under it and entered with a handgun.

He found his ex in the back, wiping down tables. "If I can't have you, no one else will," he yelled.

The man waved his gun wildly as he chased the waitress through the dining room. She darted around tables, eventually slipping under the half-pulled gate and into the tower hallways of the Renaissance Center. He followed her briefly but couldn't catch her. Thankfully, she wasn't hurt, and no shots were fired.

The man fled into the Renaissance Center parking lot, but the police apprehended him shortly after.

The incident was terrifying. It could have ended much worse, and we were all shaken by how close we had come to being in harm's way.

Soon after, both the lead cook and the waitress transferred to another location at Eastland Mall in Harper Woods, leaving a void in our kitchen.

I was promoted to lead cook in his place. While I was proud to take on this new role, it wasn't long before I began witnessing the toll this job took on people. The restaurant industry exposed me to the personal struggles and mental battles of those working in it.

A Tragic Turn

One coworker I remember vividly was a waiter—a friendly and likable guy who was clearly under immense pressure. He was behind on child support payments for his young daughter, and the child's mother made it her mission to remind him of it.

Every Friday night, she would show up at the restaurant, demanding to know how much money he had made that week. She would berate him in front of staff, threatening that he'd never see his daughter again until he caught up on payments.

Instead of bringing their daughter to see her father, she would throw pictures of the child at him.

"Here," she'd say, "this is the closest you'll ever get to her. Catch up on your payments, and maybe I'll let you see her."

Her public shaming didn't stop there. She would call him names, question his manhood, and make wild accusations. "I caught you in bed with another man," she'd yell.

The other staff would laugh at his expense, fueling her tirades. Even the restaurant manager, busy counting cash in his office, remained unaware of what was happening in the dining room.

Her harassment escalated.

Fridays turned into Saturdays, and before long, she was coming to the restaurant four times a week. On some visits, she even brought her brothers to intimidate him. They waited outside, threatening to harm him when his shift ended.

Despite the abuse, he remained focused on trying to support his daughter. He asked the manager for additional shifts, working seven days a week.

He also picked up another job, working under the table and giving every spare dollar to the child's mother.

No matter how hard he worked, he couldn't catch up. The court raised his payments, and visitation rulings were ignored. His paychecks were garnished to the point where he could barely survive. The stress was unbearable, and he began to unravel.

A Heartbreaking Discovery

One day, he simply stopped coming to work. No one heard from him—not the manager, his coworkers, or even his family. A week passed, and the silence grew unsettling.

On a Monday morning, the sanitation crew arrived to empty the dumpsters behind the Renaissance Center. As the driver lifted one of the bins, he noticed a body lying behind it. Stepping out of the truck, he walked over to investigate and saw a handgun nearby.

The authorities were called, and when they arrived, they confirmed what everyone feared: the waiter had taken his own life. He was just 22 years old.

That little girl lost her father, and the memory of what happened stayed with me for years. What a tragedy.

I remembered being so devastated and the thought of this young man shooting and taking himself out stayed with me for years.

Now I have full control of the kitchen so I was responsible for the hiring and firing of the kitchen staff.

One time I hired this guy who was like Dr. Jekyll in public but in private he became Mr, Hyde. He was an older gentleman who gave me no problems and did everything I asked him to do. I was very happy to have him on board.

I say this because most times I would hire a cook and they would turn out to be the wrong person for the position, simply because the person couldn't except authority coming from a teenager.
Believe me, I had a lot of assholes who refused to work under me. Every day this man had to be off the clock and be home by 3pm so that his girlfriend could leave him with her 2 kids and make it to work by 4pm. One day after leaving him with the children, a terrible thing happened. After sending them off to bed and making sure they were asleep, he would grab a cloth and some record, vinyl cleaner. He poured the liquid into the cloth and went back into the kids bedroom. He would then put the cloth over the little girls face to completely knock her out. He preceded to sexually molest her. When he was finished, he walked over to the little boy's bed and did the same thing to him. The little girl was able to wake up on her own. Her little brother never made it. He died from inhaling too much of the vinyl cleaner. In a panic, he called his girlfriend to tell her something was wrong with her son. When she got home, she immediately saw her child motionless with no response to anything she tried to do. reviving him was a lost cause. That's when the authorities were finally called. After a intense investigation, the cloth and the cleaner was found still in the apartment and under the kitchen sink.

The autopsy showed that the little boy died from asphyxiation and inhaling too much of the toxic and dangerous chemical. Child protection services was called in after discovering that both children were continuously molested. So, this wasn't the first time he committed this crime. Authorities put the whole story together and a warrant was made out for this cook's arrest.

After the chain of events, I went into a mental depression.

I played what happened to those kids over and over in my head.

How could someone be so evil to do this to children. I also felt I was too young to be in charge of the hiring and firing of cooks and didn't want that to be my responsibility any longer. I sat down in a meeting and management agreed that I was way too young, too inexperienced and not ready for that type of responsibility. So all interviews, hiring and firing of the kitchen staff returned back to the manager and his assistant.

Yes! I may have been too young to deal with other people's social problems but after high school, I would later be promoted to kitchen manager, assistant manager, then finally promoted to manager and transferred to my own restaurant to run in Oakland County Michigan. All by the ripe young age of 22. I would be one of the youngest to do so in the company. Like I said earlier, I finally found my own lane, but I would have to witness these crazy moments while also having these surprising experiences in the restaurant business. Here's just a few more of these crazy moments, but believe me, I can go on and on with never ending stories about the restaurant business. I once worked with a guy who use to come to work dressed sharp as a tack. He was one of our front desk host. His job was to greet the customers, sit the guest down at a table and give them their menus. He was also the cashier. A really nice guy who got a long with everyone.

Here's just a few more of these crazy moments, but believe me, I can go on and on with never-ending stories about the restaurant business.

I once worked with a guy who used to come to work dressed sharp as a tack. He was one of our front desk hosts. His job was to greet customers, seat guests at their tables, and hand them menus. He was also the cashier. A really nice guy who got along with everyone.

He seemed to have it all together.
He was also openly gay, which didn't bother anyone.

He was such a fun and charismatic person to be around that it was simply a part of who he was. Besides, he was a valued member of our restaurant family.

Before changing into his work clothes, this guy would arrive so impeccably coordinated—from his shoes and socks to his brimmed hats. Even on his off days, he would stop by the restaurant for lunch, showing off his latest boxed-shoulder suit jackets or bright, flamboyant zoot suits. His favorite color to wear was often pink.

People would frequently ask him where he shopped for his outfits, but he never revealed his sources.

I guess he didn't want anyone copying his style. He was the man when it came to fashion coordination. Soon, I found myself wanting the kind of attention he got, but I knew I'd have to step up my wardrobe game to get it.

At first, I didn't really care much about how I looked in clothes. That changed when he was hired. After that, dressing well started to matter to me—especially when it came to impressing young ladies. He made me realize that no woman wants to go out with a guy who looks like he doesn't take care of himself. He set an example for me to follow.

Then one day, he got really sick. A few weeks later, he stopped showing up for work altogether. We eventually learned that he had been in the hospital for some time.

He was the very first person I personally knew to be diagnosed with HIV. Tragically, he passed away from complications related to AIDS.

I still remember how devastated we all felt when the news reached us. In his memory, we closed the restaurant early that day. It's because of this young man that I developed such a love for suits and nice shoes.

He inspired me to create my own unique style of fashion. During a training session at another restaurant, I witnessed another unsettling event. There was a dishwasher who had a habit of being late or calling off altogether. On one particular day, he tested the patience of the new assistant manager by showing up tardy on her shift yet again. She'd had enough and fired him on the spot.

Visibly upset, he stormed out and went next door to a nearby restaurant, where a friend of his worked. He vented to his friend about what had just happened and mentioned that he planned to return later that night to rob the place.

After his conversation, he left the mall.

Four or five hours later, he returned. He jumped over a short dining room wall, hurried past the remaining closing employees, and made his way upstairs to the manager's office.

Startling the assistant manager, he pulled a sharp knife from his pocket and held it near her throat, threatening her to give him everything in the safe. The terrified woman complied, taking all the cash and placing it into a bank bag.

After taking the bag, he noticed some duct tape and a pair of scissors on her desk.

Spotting another door in the office that led to the furnace room, he dragged her by her hair, forced her to the floor, and taped her wrists to a nearby pole.

Then, in an act of cruelty, he began slapping her before using the scissors to cut off her long, jet-black hair. She was of Indian nationality, and her hair nearly reached her feet. He left her there, bound to the pole with her hair scattered beside her on the floor. After closing the furnace room door, he ran downstairs and disappeared out the back door with all the cash.

Downstairs, my coworkers and I—three employees in total— heard nothing. Not a single sound of the commotion happening upstairs.

Somehow, the assistant manager managed to free herself from the tape.

She crawled out of the furnace room and ran down the stairs, screaming for help.

"We've been robbed!" she yelled, her voice shaking. She was hysterical, clearly in a state of physical and emotional shock.

Police were called to the scene, and the violent events that had taken place went under thorough investigation. Two to three weeks later, one of the waitresses received a mysterious phone number on her pager.

Curious, she called the number back using the restaurant's phone at the hostess station. A man on the other end asked, "Are you still selling that washing machine? I'm still interested in buying it."

She replied, "Sure, when would you like to pick it up?" "How about next Monday around noon?" he suggested.

She told him she was in the middle of waiting on a table and would call him back with her address to arrange the pickup.

After the call, the waitress contacted authorities to inform them that the man who had robbed the restaurant was planning to stop by her house to pick up a washing machine. That following Monday, the man arrived at her home as promised, but instead of leaving with a washing machine, he left in handcuffs. The police were ready and waiting for him.

Another frightening robbery occurred in our restaurant one night.

"Okay, ladies and gentlemen, nobody try anything stupid. This is what you call a robbery!" shouted one of the three armed men who burst into the restaurant. "Get in the office, line up facing the wall with your arms up in the air. Do it now, and no one will get hurt!"

The gunman turned to the manager. "Are you the manager?" he barked.

"Yes, I am," the manager replied.

"Good! Leave the safe open and give me all the money in it!"

The manager began loading the cash into bank bags as instructed. Suddenly, one of the dishwashers turned around defiantly and said, "Do what you gotta do. I got somewhere I need to be."

One of the gunmen immediately pressed the barrel of the gun to the dishwasher's head. "Shut the fuck up, fat boy, and turn your ass back around!" he ordered. The dishwasher, now trembling, nervously complied and resumed his position against the wall.

After grabbing the money bags, the robbers ran out of the restaurant.

The manager told everyone to stay put, saying he had already called the police and planned to follow the robbers to see where they went.

What none of us knew at the time was that our store manager was actually in on the heist. He had never called the police.

The manager never returned to work after that night. He vanished without a word.

A couple of weeks later, authorities received an anonymous tip about his whereabouts. It turned out he had taken his share of the stolen money and planned a trip to the Kentucky Derby. While placing a bet, the police nabbed him, immediately cuffed him, and escorted him back to face justice.

As I mentioned earlier, I quickly learned that a kitchen is a very dangerous place to work if you're not careful.

One day, a cook noticed a bucket in the freezer that was half full. Unaware of what was inside, he decided to fill the rest of it with hot grease. What he didn't know was that there was an aerosol can hidden in the middle of the frozen grease.

As the boiling liquid reached the can, it exploded, shooting straight through the ceiling.

If the cook had been looking into the bucket at that moment, he could've lost his entire face. The explosion was so loud that it sent paying customers fleeing from the restaurant. While the cook escaped unharmed, the restaurant lost a lot of unpaid orders that day.

Back in the day, health inspectors often paid close attention to the kickboards around the bottom of kitchen walls. Cleaning those areas showed an effort to maintain hygiene under counters and around equipment.

With an inspection coming up, it was my responsibility as the kitchen supervisor to ensure we passed. After closing one night, I asked one of my cooks to clean the kickboards behind the grill.

He decided to get a bucket of hot, soapy water, a spray bottle of degreaser, and a few towels. On all fours, he crawled under the grill to clean it. Unfortunately, he forgot to turn the grill off, and his Jheri Curls caught on fire. As he yelled for help, I immediately ran into the kitchen, grabbed his ankles, and pulled him out from under the grill. Using his wet towels, I patted his head until the flames were completely out.

Another time, I asked a cook to pull all the hood vents in the kitchen so they could be cleaned. I made sure we did this every week, spraying them down with degreaser and running them through the dish machine. But that day, she was in a hurry—she had somewhere to be after finishing her task.

For some reason, she decided to place two metal sheet trays on the warm, flat-top grill. She then brought out a short ladder, stepping on the trays to reach the vents.

One false move, and she was in serious danger.

She had two choices at this point: fall into the fryers next to her or slip onto the hard, concrete floor. She managed to pull one vent, bending over to set it down safely. She pulled the next one and set it down as well. When she went to pull the third vent, it was stuck. She tugged and tugged until the metal sheet trays slid out from under her feet.

She fell and hit her face on the edge of the flat-top grill, losing all her front top and bottom teeth. The woman was in her mid-sixties. She had no business standing on metal trays on top of a grill in the first place. That was the end of her time with us—she never returned to the kitchen. It was a devastating loss because she had been one of my best cooks.

The restaurant kept its plates and bowls warm by placing them in a low-temperature oven. One day, I came to the line to start sautéing my pasta orders. I opened the oven door to grab a bowl when a huge flame shot out at me, burning all the hair on my arms and scorching my mustache clean off my face.

It turned out that the pilot light hadn't been lit while the gas had been on for part of the afternoon. The gas fumes built up inside the oven and reacted with the flames on the grill, creating an explosive reaction. After that incident, I looked very different—with blonde eyebrows and no mustache.

In those early years, I had so much doubt about staying in this business. I witnessed pain, struggle, agony, and mishandling through the experiences of others.

There were times I wanted to quit, finish school, and go in a completely different direction.

Instead, I stayed focused, holding onto hope that management and cooking would pay off in the future.

I was just a teenager, but I had already lived through so many adult experiences.

One of my best friends got his first full-time job and pulled me up with him, giving me the same opportunity. Once I got into management, I did the same—I pulled another one of our friends up.

That's the way it should be: when the opportunity presents itself, find a way to pull each other up.

Rest in peace, my buddy K.O. You were responsible for getting me my first full-time job, and I'll never forget that.

This chapter marks a turning point in my life—a realization of what it means to navigate the complexities of work, relationships, and responsibility while holding onto hope for a better future.

Every story, from moments of triumph to shocking incidents, taught me valuable lessons that shaped my resilience and determination.

As I move forward, the experiences I've shared here serve as a reminder that growth often comes from unexpected challenges. What lies ahead is a continuation of that journey—one filled with even more stories, lessons, and the unwavering belief that we can always find our own lane, no matter how chaotic the road may seem.

Chapter 37

MAMA'S SALMON BURGERS AND CROQUETTES

My mother wasn't a great cook. In fact, compared to my grandmothers, who were masters in the kitchen, she was mediocre in her skills. But that never stopped her from trying her best. She had an uncanny ability to make something out of nothing. In the early project days, when money was tight, she worked culinary magic with what little we had—government block cheese, flour, corn grits, and Spam. To this day, I marvel at how she turned these humble ingredients into meals that brought us comfort.

My mother had a favorite ingredient: salmon. Saturdays were her salmon days, a routine we all came to love. She'd whip up patties with ease, filling the house with their savory aroma. This was her warm-up for Sunday's big dinner, which she poured her heart into preparing. We had it all—baked salmon, sautéed salmon, salmon burgers, and my personal favorite, salmon croquettes.

Back then, salmon wasn't the luxury item it is today. It was cheap and accessible, a staple of our meals. We ate it so often that I memorized her recipe without even trying. Watching her cook was like watching an artist at work. She had a rhythm, a flow, and no matter what she made, it always tasted good.

In her memory, I decided to honor her creativity by introducing her salmon burger recipe at my place of work. At first, it was just a special item, something I'd run occasionally as a tribute. But it didn't take long before it became a hit. Customers loved it so much that it earned a permanent spot on the menu. For 25 years, it was one of our best sellers, and even now, it's still going strong.

Note: Others might argue about the origins of the salmon burger, but I know the truth. The Recipe came from somewhere, right?

The original recipe didn't come from some fancy chef—it came from my mother, who had the gift of making something extraordinary out of the simplest things.

Thanks, Mom, for your unknown contribution to the culinary world.

In Memory of My Mother: The Salmon Burger Recipe

This recipe is more than a set of instructions—it's a piece of my family's history. Every time I make it, I'm transported back to those Saturday mornings, sitting at the kitchen table, watching my mother work her magic.

1. **Dice:**

   - ½ yellow onion
   - ½ celery
   - ½ red pepper
   - Place them in a mixing bowl.

2. **Prepare the Salmon:**

   - Chop up 2 lbs of salmon and set it aside.

3. **Blend Seasoning:**

   - In a food processor, add:
   - A pinch of dried thyme, oregano, parsley
   - ½ tsp of crushed garlic
   - 1 tsp of salt and 1 tsp of pepper

4. **Blend the Salmon:**

   - Place the diced salmon in the food processor along with:
   - 2 egg whites
   - ¼ cup of heavy whipping cream
   - Lightly blend until slightly lumpy.

5. **Combine Ingredients:**

   - Add the blended salmon to the mixing bowl with the diced peppers, onions and celery.
   - Mix in **3 full cups of bread crumbs.**
   - Thoroughly combine all ingredients.

6. **Shape the Patties:**

- Form into 6-ounce burger patties or 3-ounce croquettes.

7. **Cook:**

- Add a little oil to a pan and fry both sides for 2 minutes.
- Finish cooking in the oven at **400°F** for 6 minutes.

8. **Optional Toppings:**

- Add a slice of cheese on top.
- Serve as a sandwich or enjoy as croquette appetizers.

This isn't just a recipe; it's a legacy. It's my way of keeping my mother's memory alive, one salmon burger at a time.

"We were poor, but we knew the power of family, faith, and hard work to turn struggle into strength."

– Michelle Obama

In Loving
Memory
of My Mother

Chapter 38

An Urban Ninth Grade Love Story

Ninth grade is always a challenge when entering a new school. You feel completely lost in the beginning, and the older students can see the freshman ways about you. Looking for your classes and finding your new locker felt like walking in the middle of a maze. Redford High felt so different from the previous middle school. The school was bigger, the subjects became a little harder, and the teachers were a little stricter. High school is also a place where you learn the beginning stages of sophistication, confidence, and adulthood.

It could also be the place where you find your first high school sweetheart.

My close friends and I never had a problem fitting in during our first year of high school. It's true that we were part of the newest class of freshmen and stood out. But we stood out for different reasons. In fact, we quickly became popular in school—not because of the sports programs or the school's academics, and not even because we were the coolest ninth graders to walk the halls. I think it was simply because of the way we dressed.

While most students came to school in wrinkled jeans, short pants that we used to call floods, graphic T-shirts, and worn tennis shoes, we came to class in nice Roland silk shirts, Swedish knit slacks, and Sibley's footwear. By this time, the young man at work I talked about in an earlier chapter had fully influenced the way I dressed, and I was ready to impress the flock of young girls roaming the hallways. And yes, we already knew the power of an iron. Each of us made sure our clothes were nicely pressed before walking out the house.

Not to say we didn't own tennis shoes, but the ones we wore had to be the latest style and always clean. The white laces were changed often. Thanks to the Salvation Army, our old man's suits and sweaters became a classic fit for us on Fridays.

Riding our bikes to the old Northland Mall every payday was also a plus. The girls loved our style of clothing, and we loved all the attention we were getting. My friends and I learned at a very early age that this was how you got the girls. You also had to smell good. Back in those days, British Sterling, Lagerfeld, Aramis, Nautica, and Halston were the colognes to wear.

This love story I'm about to tell begins with a nicely knitted sweater I was wearing.

Just five lockers away from me was this little girl. For name purposes, I will choose to call her Lynne in this story. Every day, this girl and some of her friends or classmates would gather in front of her locker, giggling and fooling around before heading to the next class. She was very cute, petite, and seemed a little calmer than her associates.

For whatever reason, I decided to zoom in and concentrate on this particular individual in the group of girls.

The following semester, we just so happened to have a social studies class together. I remember glancing at her from across the room. She would shyly isolate herself and try to stay focused on her books. Right away, I picked up on her innocence and her effort to not get herself involved with boys at that time. But I gradually became curious, and through my actions toward her, I made it known that I was very interested.

One day, while standing by our lockers, Lynne spoke to me for the very first time.

"I like your sweater," she said.

I wanted her to repeat what she said. "What was that?"

"I said, I like your sweater. It looks very nice on you."

But then again, you always come to school looking dapper."

While walking toward her, I asked, "What's your name?"

She laughed a bit and replied, "Now we're in the same social studies class, and you don't know my name yet? My name is Lynne, and I already know yours. I asked someone, just in case you try to kidnap me. You're the same guy that keeps staring at me in class like I'm a piece of meat or something."

I thought that was the most hilarious thing to say to someone. I nervously laughed her comment off and then asked if I could carry her stack of books to the next class. She said, "Sure." From that point on, I would always be a few minutes late to my classes because I found myself carrying her books to all of her classes every day.

Soon, a couple of my friends noticed. "Man, all these girls in this school, and you're already stuck on just one?" one of them asked. "Who is she anyway?"

I responded, "Her name is Lynne, and she's going to be my next girlfriend. Just watch and see."

I can remember telling my mother about my new friend at school. Mom would communicate with me through sign language.

"Another one?" she signed. "What happened to the last girl that lives just down the street?"

I explained that we were no longer together, but this new girl I'd met in school was very nice. My mother responded, "Son, I hope she treats you good, but I will miss your last girlfriend. She was really a pretty girl. You two should give it another try—see if you can work things out and get back together."

She really liked my last girlfriend. Mom thought that young girl was everything.

Truth be told, she was everything to me as well, but it would have been awfully hard to explain to my mom that one of my best friends was now her new boyfriend.

Sounds crazy but true.

"Thanks, Mother. That's not what I wanted to hear."

231

But anyway, getting back to this story...

A few weeks went by before I finally worked up the courage to ask Lynne to be my girlfriend. This frightened her a little. She wasn't sure if she could say yes. Instead, she told me she'd have to think about it. I found out later that she needed to have a serious discussion about me with her dad. After all, I would be her very first boyfriend ever.

She once told me the conversation with her dad went like this:

"Dad, can I talk to you for a minute?"

"Sure, hon. What's on your mind?"

"There's this really nice boy in school, and I think he likes me."

"How do you know he likes you?"

"Well, Dad, he carries my books and walks with me to every class. Recently, he asked me to be his girlfriend."

"And what did you say to him?"

"I didn't give him a definite answer. I told him that I would have to think about it."

"Well, can I ask you something?" "Yes, Dad."

"How do you feel about him?"

"He treats me like I'm special, and I also like him."

"Well, if he's a gentleman, treats you nice, and really likes you, give him a chance and see where it goes. Just be careful. I also would like to meet this young man and speak with him myself."

The following Monday, Lynne walked up to me at school.

"Hey, Eric, I want to ask you something. Remember the question you asked me, and I told you I had to think about it? Well, I want to say yes, but first, you would have to meet my dad. Do you have a problem with that?"

I told her I didn't, but deep down, I was a little nervous about meeting him. At that point, I had had many girlfriends, but this was the very first time I would have a sit-down talk with someone's dad about their daughter.

After school, I rode the bus with her home to meet her dad. "Don't be so nervous; my dad's cool," she told me.
As she entered her home, I attempted to stay outside. She laughed.

"Why are you still standing on the porch? Boy, come in the house."

Lynne laughed even harder.

"Dad, this is Eric. Eric, this is my dad."

"It's nice that we could finally meet," he said. "I've heard so much about you."

As we reached out to shake hands, he firmly gripped my hand.

"Have a seat," he told me. "You know, I love my daughter, and I'm responsible for her well-being. No boy—and I mean no boy—is going to break my daughter's heart. If you do, you will surely hear from me, and I won't be as nice. Do you understand what I'm saying?"

I quickly responded, "Yes, sir."

"My daughter really likes you, so you continue to be good to her. Understand?"

"Yes, sir."

"And one other thing. I work afternoons and won't be here by the time you two get out of school. You're more than welcome to come over and spend just a couple of hours with her, but be on your best behavior with my daughter. Do you understand?"

"Yes, sir."

I almost swallowed my tongue; I was so terrified.

"I don't want any fooling around with my daughter in here, if you know what I mean."

I understood every bit of what he meant. No sex.

After the serious talk with her dad, Lynne finally decided to say yes to being my girlfriend. In fact, the next day, she took everything out of her locker and moved her belongings into mine. I guess that action made everything official. I stopped calling her Lynne and gave her a new nickname. Her new name was **Baby Love**.

Such a perfect name for her. She was my little baby, and I definitely loved her. Because of the understanding and trust I had with her father, I also became his daughter's protector. I kept her away from everything I thought was bad for her. I continued carrying her books so she wouldn't have to, I made sure she was on time for each class, and I consistently rode the city bus home with her to ensure she safely got into her house. Then, I walked a few blocks to my bus stop and took another bus home. I did this every single day.

Baby Love was being cared for, and I considered her to be my responsibility as well. She had two male figures looking after her.

We were a great couple in high school. We did everything together, and wherever I appeared, she was right there with me—and vice versa. She became the new Miss Everything to me.

She was sweet, innocent, and smart, with a good sense of humor, while at the same time, she was extremely shy, especially when it came to kissing and touching each other.

We were the total opposite of one another. She was beauty, and I was her beast. I was kind of hoodish and street smart, while she was housebound by choice and book smart. That's what made our relationship unique. We didn't seem like we belonged together, but we were the perfect fit for each other.

I vividly remember one time riding home with her, one of those occasions when I decided to keep her company for a while before making my way home. We sat on the couch to watch a little bit of television when, suddenly, my young hormones started to race.

Hoping she wasn't paying close attention, I slowly put my arm around her.

She quickly removed herself and went into the kitchen to whip up a couple of sandwiches for us. Once she returned and sat back on the couch, I slowly placed my hand on her lap. Again, she removed herself and went into the bathroom.

When she came back, I tried to French kiss her. The kiss lasted a little longer than I expected when, suddenly, she stopped us before anything else could happen. She was overly cautious, but I also sensed something different about her.

After a few more intimate attempts, I began to recognize this distant behavior. Her detachment brought back memories of what happened to me as a small child on Dumbarton Street. My feelings about her lack of involvement were exactly right, but I didn't learn why she kept leaving me alone on the couch until years later.

I quickly stopped my hormonal pursuit and returned to protecting the innocence and newness about her. Besides, her dad came to mind again, and I wasn't going to be the one to betray his trust.

Out of respect for Lynne and without getting into pacific details, she told me about an incident that happened with her and some neighbor's that lived directly across the street.

This broke my heart.

You know, when you're young and in your discovery stages of life, you don't always know how to handle certain situations. By the end of ninth grade, I started noticing some things I didn't like about my relationship with Lynne. But I never attempted to do anything about saving it either.

We were too good to each other, but there were some evil forces trying to work in between us. I just let things happen when I shouldn't have. I should have spoken up. But you don't always know these things when you're young. One thing's for sure: you get to learn from your mistakes.

Or better yet, the projects in me should've taken over, and I should've whooped some ass and taken some names later. Instead, I continued playing the nice guy.

Lynne had a best friend who would always come around our locker or in between classes at odd times. He would see us together but never acknowledge me. I always graciously returned the favor. From the beginning, I had a lack of trust for him. To me, it always seemed like he wanted more than just friendship.

Before I came along, he and Lynne were like hanging buddies and talked on the phone all day. After I came into the picture, it became very hard for him to keep her attention. The jealousy became more apparent every day. I always felt that he was planning something to break us apart, and that plan came in the form of something I didn't have yet—an automobile.

It took me until the tenth grade to even get my driver's license.

Now remember, we rode the bus home together, and I made sure she was safe every day.

But the wedge between us began when her friend started bringing her to school and taking her home.

"Are we riding the bus together today?" I would ask.

"No, my friend said he was driving me home," she would reply.

In time, this made me very angry, but I said nothing. On the outside, I kept my cool, but on the inside, I was fuming.

There were times after school when her friend would show up and ask if she was ready to go. Lynne would give me a kiss goodbye and walk off with him. I could clearly see the shady smirk on his face. This infuriated me, and again, I said nothing. I never put a stop to this, and I never discussed how I felt.

My friends began to ask what was going on and why we weren't riding home together anymore. Classmates started asking questions, and rumors began to swirl around school.

Finally, I couldn't hold back the embarrassment. Our relationship was ending, and I didn't know who to blame.
Do I blame myself for letting this go on for so long?
Do I blame myself for not sharing my feelings with Lynne?

Do I blame myself for not putting my foot in her friend's butt?

Do I blame Lynne for not recognizing how wrong this was? Or do I blame her for not realizing that this was a game her friend was playing between us? I was so pissed off that I wanted to get even. I wanted her to know how I felt.

I never verbally told her that we were no longer together. It would have been too painful for me to tell her. Instead, I took all her belongings out of my locker and placed them on the floor in front of hers.

She asked, "Are we breaking up?" I never answered. I admit, it was very painful to see her cry in front of her friends and classmates. Privately, I even cried.

She had just bought her red and gray school sweater with a patch that said **Baby Love** on it.

But by then, I was parading around school with her new nemesis. Boy, this breakup sounds very childish, but that's exactly what we were—kids just trying to figure things out. The new relationship didn't last long. She talked too much. In fact, she talked my head off. I was only with her to teach Lynne a small lesson: to be a little more considerate of other people's feelings and to be aware of what people's evil intentions are. But how would she know if I never expressed my feelings?

I also had to learn a valuable lesson: if I don't agree with something, speak up and don't keep my feelings inside. Whenever something is troubling me, I need to let it out and let it be known.

Lynne never had the opportunity to meet my mother. If she had, my mom would have loved her like a daughter and talked us out of ever breaking up. I could even see my mother trying to teach Lynne sign language so they could communicate with each other a little better.

Looking back, I really didn't handle the situation the right way.

I let my anger get the best of me, which allowed me to think irrationally. I used to blame Lynne for what happened to us when, in reality, it was my fault for not expressing how I felt about her friend taking her home every day. I believe she would have made it all better with the right adjustments.

I remember this as being a very painful breakup. Something had to finally change. I decided to take a page out of the girls' playbook. The young girls were going after guys who were a couple of years older.

So, with much success, I went after the older female students. By mid-ninth grade, I only dated girls who were in the eleventh and twelfth grades. Looking back, I realize I handled the situation completely wrong. I let my emotions take over, allowing anger to dictate my actions. Instead of confronting Lynne about her friend and expressing how it made me feel, I stayed silent. My silence not only created distance between us but also allowed jealousy and frustration to grow.

In the end, I blamed Lynne for not recognizing how wrong the situation was, but the truth is, I never gave her the chance to make things right. I didn't communicate my feelings or let her know how much it hurt me to see her leave with him every day. If I had spoken up, she might have understood, and we could have worked through it. This breakup taught me an important lesson about relationships and life in general. If something bothers you, speak up. Don't keep your feelings bottled inside, thinking they'll go away on their own. Communication is key to understanding and resolving conflicts.

As kids, we're often just trying to figure things out, making mistakes along the way. But it's those mistakes that help us grow and learn.

At the time, I thought moving on to someone else was the solution.

I started dating older girls, thinking they would be more mature or less complicated.

But in reality, the issue wasn't with Lynne or even her friend—it was with me. I had to learn how to handle my emotions, communicate my feelings, and take responsibility for my part in what happened.

The moral of the story? Relationships require honesty, communication, and trust. Without those things, misunderstandings and jealousy can tear even the strongest connections apart. And when something feels wrong, don't be afraid to speak up—because silence only makes the pain last longer.

Chapter 39

A Letter to Mother (Part Two)

Dear Mother,

The first and second years after your passing were extremely hard for me. You find out a lot of things about yourself during that time. You find out your inner child also dies. Grief doesn't get easier over time—you just get better at managing the pain of you physically not being here anymore.

Many years prior, I made the decision to spend one year with my own family during the holidays, and every other year, I spent it with you. Getting together with you during the holidays was always a great time. Now, those times are just great memories. Holidays just don't seem the same anymore.

I try to stay away from social media when it gets closer to Mother's Day. I feel so much pain on that day. At the same time, I truly understand the feelings of others who have lost their mothers.

When I finally realized that I was never going to see my dear mother again, the pain became enormous. I can't even tell you how many days in a row I shed tears—I still do today. Your loss will forever be a part of who I am.

Nothing lasts forever, but for some reason, I thought I would leave before you. I still carry you—the laughter, the love, and the things you've said to me over the years.

I ask myself: what is a feeling that I will never forget?

The feeling of angels slowly taking you away, and there's nothing —absolutely nothing—I could have done about it.

Long after everyone goes back to normal, long after everyone goes their separate ways, you're still in an altered state of mind, and for a while, you feel lost.

To others, you look normal, but in reality, you're in a deep depression, a mirage of sadness. At least, I was. There are so many things you don't say to a person grieving their mother:

- "Are you okay?" That's one thing I didn't want to hear. I was absolutely not okay.
- "She's in a better place." Now, that statement got under my skin. I felt the better place was still here with me, Ma.
- "If you need anything, let me know." Well, those people are never around. Besides, you're gone. You were my everything. My Super Shero. What could anyone possibly do for me that you hadn't already done?

Trying to cut my speech short at your funeral was another thing that pissed me off. I had so many good memories to share. Because of your children, all your funeral expenses were paid in full, and now the funeral home was ready to end the ceremony and go home.

Mom, I hope you understand—I couldn't let that happen.

While you were here, I enjoyed using sign language to communicate with you. I loved making you laugh and hearing you call me crazy. I cherished your first plane ride, comforting you and making sure you knew everything would be okay. I truly enjoyed us just sitting down and catching up.

I also want to apologize for all my mishaps. But I also want to thank you—for everything you've done for me. Thank you for your life lessons and your loving care throughout my life.

I hope I've done good by you. Because of you, I became a better man.

To My Mom in Heaven,

The pain of your absence still lingers, but so too does the love you showered upon me throughout your time on this earth. Your memory is a cherished treasure, and your presence, though physically gone, lives on in my heart and in the echoes of your laughter that linger in my mind.

241

You were more than a mother—you were a confidant, a guiding light, and a wellspring of unconditional love. Your wisdom and warmth shaped my world, and your strength remains an enduring source of inspiration.

While I can no longer hold your hand or communicate with you, I find solace in the countless memories we shared together. Your love and your spirit are eternal, and I carry them with me always.

Though you may have passed away, the love and bond between us will never fade.

You are forever in my heart.

I love you.
[Hearts]

1984 My very first apartment

An eleven story building built In **1902**. The Pasadena Apartments on East Jefferson Avenue and Dubois Street. Just seven blocks away from Downtown's Renaissance Center and two miles from Belle Isle Island.

Oh the time I had back in the early to mid 80's. Life was so good. But boy! Did I had to grow up quick.

Grown up responsibilities kicked in high gear.

Chapter 40

1984 Moving Forward, Remembering Marvin

After a few years living with this woman and helping care for her children, I finally reached the breaking point. The chaos in that house—the constant arguments, the emotional manipulation, and the overwhelming responsibility—had drained me. I knew I had to find a way out, to regain some sense of control over my life.

By **1984**, I had saved up just enough money to make my escape. It wasn't easy, but I finally moved into my own place—a modest apartment downtown. The feeling of walking into that apartment for the first time, knowing it was all mine, was indescribable. For the first time in years, I felt a sense of freedom.

I can still vividly remember that April week in **1984**. It was a milestone, a turning point. On the morning of April 1st, I had just finished moving the last of my things into the apartment. I handed over the keys to the woman's house for the final time. As I stood in the doorway, ready to leave that chapter of my life behind, a news bulletin caught my attention. The television was on in the living room, and I heard the words, "Entertainer shot to death."

Curiosity froze me in place. I stood there, listening intently, and when the name was announced, my heart sank.

Marvin Gaye.

It felt as though someone had punched me in the stomach. I was devastated.

Transition to Personal Reflection (1984 Timeline)

What should have been one of the most exciting mornings of my life—a day of new beginnings—had suddenly turned into one of sorrow.

Marvin Gaye's music had been a constant presence in my life.

My brother and I spent countless hours at my aunt's house in the early '70s, with his voice filling the air as her record player spun his albums. Those moments with my aunt were some of the happiest of my childhood, and Marvin's music became a soundtrack for that joy.

As I stood there in shock, the memories came flooding back. Marvin wasn't just a singer to me—he was part of my upbringing. His songs were like a time capsule, reminding me of those innocent, carefree days. His music carried lessons, emotions, and truths that resonated with my soul.

For years, I had told myself that I needed to see him live in concert while he was still in his prime. But every time he performed in Detroit, something would come up, and I'd miss my chance. Now, that chance was gone forever. It was my greatest regret of **1984**— never getting to witness his magic on stage.

Marvin's death at just 44 years old was a tragic loss for the world, but for me, it was deeply personal. He would never grow old in our eyes, never create another album, never grace a stage again. To this day, his album *Here, My Dear* remains one of my all-time favorites. From it, I learned that honesty can create greatness.

Closing Reflection

As I moved forward in **1984**, I carried both joy and sorrow. The joy of finally reclaiming my independence and the sorrow of losing an icon who had shaped so much of my life. That year marked the end of one chapter and the beginning of another. It taught me that life is full of contradictions—freedom and loss, hope and regret.

But most importantly, it reminded me to cherish the moments and the people who matter because you never know when they'll be gone.

To this day, one of my favorite albums is *Here, My Dear*. It's more than just music—it's a testament to raw emotion, vulnerability, and the power of truth. Marvin poured his heart into every track, and through his honesty, he created a masterpiece that continues to resonate with me even decades later.

From this album, I've learned that honesty, even in its most painful form, can lead to greatness. It taught me that expressing one's truth, no matter how complicated or challenging, can leave a legacy that touches lives and inspires others to reflect on their own experiences.

Marvin's ability to channel his struggles into art has always stayed with me. It reminds me that even in our toughest moments, we have the power to create something meaningful and beautiful.

Chapter 41

The Most Beautiful Hazel Eyes I've Ever Seen

It's the dance club era, and I'm all in. At one time, Detroit was known for its dance clubs in the late '70s and early to mid-'80s, especially around the downtown area. Sure, there were awesome clubs all over Detroit—The City Club, Chuck's Millionaire Club, The 20 Grand, Babes, and The Diamond Shaft, just to name a few. We even had our own Cotton Club on Livernois near Ewald Circle back in the early '90s.

But in my opinion, these danceries had nothing on the clubs around the downtown area. Once again, it was all about the music, and I lived in the middle of all the hype. Back in the day, we even had our own Studio 54, which was located in the basement of the old Leland Hotel on Detroit's Cass and Bagley Street near downtown.

Let's see if I can jog some more Detroit memories. If you're around my age and clubbed as much as I did, you might remember the old River Rock Bar. You could go in, socialize, buy a few drinks, or dance in a man-made boxing ring.

Or how about the Underground after-hours bar on Van Dyke and Jefferson Avenue? You'd drive up into a building until you got to the top floor, park your car, and then enter the bar to dance on a colored lit floor—just like the one in the movie *Saturday Night Fever*.

The Warehouse was famous for its extensive house music. Even The Fox Theater was once a dance club before its renovation and rebuild. I remember dancing on the stage with several televisions behind me playing the latest videos. Saint Andrews also brought me some incredible nights.

My favorite lounge was a place called The Climax 2, which later became The Dancery on Mount Elliot and Lafayette.

I was once tagged with the nickname Eddie Murphy because I had a high-top fade, a neatly cut mustache, and always wore leather.

This spot became my go-to hangout three nights a week—it was within walking distance from my building. Whenever I threw parties in my apartment, my friends and I would include a visit to The Climax 2 to finish the nightlife.

Other legendary clubs that deserve a mention:

- The dance parties on the Boblo boat
- Legends on Congress Street
- The Leland City Club
- The Key Club
- Club U.B.Q.
- The Industry
- Monroe's inside Greektown's Trappers Alley
- The Roostertail on Marquette Drive
- And, of course, the legendary Club Taboo

A Night at Club Taboo

I'll tell you a story that happened at Club Taboo.

One summer night, I decided to walk home from work. Instead of taking Jefferson Avenue, I took the back way down Woodbridge Street. For several blocks, I could see a small crowd forming and a long line of cars slowly trailing each other.

As I got closer, I saw the commotion growing—cars being valet parked in a lot near some old train tracks and people rushing to get in line to pay their entrance fee. Excitement was definitely in the air.

As I approached my apartment building, I discovered that Club Taboo was right behind it. I was surprised to learn that this place was so close by.

Curiosity got the better of me, and I wanted to see what this club was like on the inside.

The following Saturday, I rushed home from work, cleaned myself up, and made my way to this exclusive club. I joined the line with everyone else, and when it was finally my turn, I paid the forty- dollar entrance fee. I was told the fee was usually twenty dollars, but because of a guest performance that night, it was slightly higher.

This would be my third downtown club experience in my young life. The first was Studio 54, and the second was The Underground.

As soon as I entered Club Taboo, I posted myself at the bar. The structure inside this place was stunning. That night, it was packed, and I couldn't help but become a people watcher.

I was new to the area, didn't know anyone yet, and had to keep things in chill mode.

I didn't want to get myself into any unfamiliar situations, so I kept to myself.

I also couldn't help but watch this beautiful woman on stage performing some of her biggest hits. This woman was amazing, with a voice only sent from the heavens. Although the mixed crowd was enjoying her masterful songs, I was a bit surprised that she was performing at such a small venue.

In the middle of her show, she informed the crowd she would be taking a short break but promised to return to sing more songs.

"Will that be okay with you?" she asked.

The crowd erupted with loud cheers and claps. "Yes! We'll be right here waiting!"

She and her bandmates left the stage and walked toward the bar. That's when it happened—she was standing right next to me.

I can't remember if she ordered a tall glass of ice water or a cocktail. All I know is that this attractive woman was shoulder to shoulder with me.

I began to sweat profusely through my new outfit and prayed she wouldn't notice how much I was shaking.

"Hi, are you enjoying the show?" she asked with a pleasant smile.

I stuttered a bit.

"Yes, yes, I am."

Her amazing eyes captivated me. Brown with a little bit of gold and a splash of green—the most beautiful hazel eyes I had ever seen. I remember being completely fixated on them. Those eyes seemed to look right through me, almost as if they were in control.

"I wish my aunt was here to share this moment with me," I said, almost to myself.

"Excuse me?"

The crowd was so loud she couldn't hear me the first time.

"I said, I wish my aunt was here to share this moment with me. She would have loved seeing you in person."

"You think so? Well, you tell your aunt I said hello. What's your name?"

"My name is Eric."

"Nice to meet you, Eric. I gotta get back on stage. Enjoy the rest of the show."

I couldn't believe it.

I got this close to a beautiful, living legend and even had a small conversation with her. I was able to look deeply into those amazing, piercing hazel eyes, and I'll never forget them.

When I was about five or six years old, my dad and I met the legendary wrestler Bobo Brazil, and I couldn't believe how big his hands were compared to mine. This moment felt similar—except this time, I got to meet an attractive woman face-to-face, and I was completely star-struck.

As she stepped back onto the stage, the band was re-tuning their instruments. We all sat patiently for her to begin. She led an almost silent countdown for the band to start playing.

"One, two, three."

The band began a familiar song, and the crowd went wild.

"This will be an everlasting love."

Man, what a moment in time for me. I had no idea being on my own would start off like this. This one highlight in my life has become one of my greatest memories over the years.

Looking back, I kind of understood why she chose Club Taboo as one of her venues. It was a very nice club, and she was likely making a comeback, deciding to sing in smaller, more intimate venues.

Today, Club Taboo no longer exists. There isn't even a sign to show it ever stood at 1940 Woodbridge near the train tracks. Instead, there's an old warehouse where the club once stood.

Also, back in the early '80s, pictures or videos from these clubs were rare. The first camera phones weren't even out yet. Don't believe me? Go online and try to find any videos or pictures of your favorite hangout spots from the early to mid-'80s. You might find two or three, but that's it—unless they're connected to a known Detroit DJ. Then, you might discover a little about the club that particular DJ played in.

It seems like some of the greatest times of the '80s in Detroit are kept hidden. The only thing you can rely on is your experiences and memories.

This legend is no longer with us. She passed in 2015, and she deserved all her flowers. She will forever be embedded in my memory.

Continue to rest in peace, Hazel Eyes.

You and your dad's songs will live on forever.

Man, was she gorgeous.

Today, Club Taboo on Woodbridge Street no longer exists. The vibrant club that was once filled with music, laughter, and memories has been replaced by an old warehouse. There are no signs, no plaques, or anything to suggest that the legendary club ever stood at 1940 Woodbridge near the train tracks.

It's almost as if the history of the place was erased, leaving nothing but the faint echoes of what it once was. For those of us who lived it, though, Club Taboo was more than just a venue—it was an experience. It was a place where the energy of the crowd, the pulse of the music, and the magic of the performances came together to create unforgettable nights.

To walk past the warehouse today is a bittersweet reminder of how time moves on. If you didn't know any better, you'd never guess that one of Detroit's legendary nightclubs used to stand there, hosting some of the greatest artists and creating memories for so many people.

This absence speaks to a larger truth about the '80s in Detroit: much of the city's vibrant nightlife, its culture, and its history are tucked away in the hearts and minds of those who were there. Without pictures, videos, or signs to document those moments, all we have left are our memories—and those memories are treasures that no time or change can erase.

Chapter 42

The Housewarming Party That Almost Ruined Me (1986)

Two years after I moved into my apartment, I was finally comfortable enough to have people over besides my close friends. So, I decided to throw a housewarming party—a decision I would later regret.

I was overly excited about my accomplishment of having my first apartment. So, I decided to invite friends and co-workers to celebrate with me. Keep in mind, not only was I one of the young managers at our restaurant, but I was also what employees called "the cool manager." Hell, I was friends with everybody. Everyone thought I was really dope at the time.

Not long after I moved into my place, I created fliers for my housewarming party and secretly invited almost everyone at work. Whoever I gave an invitation to, I had them promise not to tell any of the higher-ups, and I surely didn't want the corporate office to find out about this particular get-together.

The following Saturday, I prepared some food items for my guests to enjoy: stuffed baked salmon, shrimp salad, and a garden salad. A few appetizers like potato skins, cheeseburger sliders, and pizza bites were also on the menu. I even baked a chocolate cake the night before.

I filled my bathtub with cold water and four to five tall bags of ice to chill cans of beer and soda before my guests arrived. By around 6 pm the celebration was set, and friends and co-workers began to pile into my tiny apartment. People brought their own bottles and cans of liquid poison, adding them to what was already in my icy tub. My final estimated count of guests was around 13, with not enough seating to spare.

"Hey! Do you have any playing cards?" one of my cooks asked.

I found a pack of standard playing cards, and we took turns playing Rise and Fly or three-hand Spades. It was great to finally have the chance to really get to know each other outside of work.

All of the food was eventually gone, but the entertainment didn't stop. There was a lot of dancing to some good music, cracking jokes on each other, and, of course, a lot of drinking. Boy, oh boy —did we drink.

"Hey! You all ever heard of a club called The Climax 2 Lounge? It's just down the street and around the corner," someone suggested. "We should all leave here and continue our fun there," they added.

It was well after 10 pm. by that time, and everyone was already half-wasted. I wanted everyone to leave, and this was the best way to finally get everyone out of my apartment.

"That's a good idea, but before we go, let me ask a question. How many of you have to work tomorrow?"

Some had a shift to work in the morning, and a few had the evening shift. I also had to be at work by 8 am. to open the restaurant.

I came up with a serious suggestion. "Okay, I'm sure this club closes at 2 am. Let's all agree to leave by 12 so we can all make it to work."

Everyone agreed, and we all gathered our belongings and headed straight to the lounge.

My plan was to just stay a half hour with everyone and then come back home to get a few hours of sleep before opening the restaurant.

The Climax 2 was packed with people inside. It was nicely structured with a lot of room to dance.

The place had two dance floors—one in the front and one in the back. The back dance floor seemed to be the most popular, considering you could see yourself dancing in the tall mirrors.

In between the dance floors was a long bar.

While Freddie Jackson's hit song *"Have You Ever Loved Somebody"* played through the speakers, my housewarming guests continued their drinking at the bar.

"I gotta go, guys. I have to get up in the morning—and so do you. Promise me you all will make it back home safe and get to work on time," I said.

I gave my last soulful handshakes to the fellas, soft hugs to the girls, and made my way back home to get some much-needed sleep.

The next morning, the assistant manager and I were the first to arrive at work. An hour later, no one else had shown up yet.
Another hour passed, and it was still just the two of us in the restaurant.

The assistant grabbed the employee phone book and started calling people, but there were no answers. By 10 am with only two hours until opening, we were panicking. Not a single employee had called off or come in late.

At this point, I was getting very nervous. Guilt was eating away at me as I started to blame myself for having the party. Should I tell the assistant manager what happened the night before? I wrestled with the decision until I couldn't hold it in any longer.

"Listen," I began, "I have to tell you something about last night." The assistant manager looked up at me with concern.
"I had a housewarming party, and most of the employees attended," I confessed.

"Why didn't you tell me this hours ago?" she asked, visibly frustrated.

"To be honest, I was afraid to," I admitted. "It was a housewarming party, and there was a lot of drinking."

"This doesn't look good. You could get into serious trouble for this," she warned.

"I know, and I feel so bad," I replied. "But there's something else I need to tell you."

"What's that?" she asked, now bracing herself.

"After the gathering, we all decided to continue the fun at a lounge down the street from my apartment. I didn't stay long, but before leaving, I made everyone promise to get home safely and be on time for work," I explained.

"You've got to be kidding me," she said, shaking her head. "Let me share something with you. You're a good kitchen supervisor, but you're not here to make friends. You have to learn how to separate business from pleasure. You're not just a regular employee—you're part of the management team here."

She paused for a moment before delivering the kicker.

"Now I have no choice but to call the corporate office and tell them why we can't open and why we don't have any employees here," she said, turning and walking back into her office.

As the door closed behind her, I stood there alone in the kitchen, feeling a wave of shame wash over me. Everything she said was true. I should have been more responsible.

I began to mentally beat myself up.

"I should've stopped the gathering by 9 pm. I never should've allowed so much drinking in my home. Now I might lose my job, my apartment, and I'll have to start all over again," I thought.

Just as I was spiraling, the office door reopened. The assistant manager walked out with a blank expression on her face.

"Okay," she said.

"Do you want to hear the good news or the bad news first?" "The bad news," I replied, bracing myself.

"Well, the bad news is you'll have to stay and fully prep the kitchen for the afternoon shift. Corporate wants us to open at exactly 3 pm," she said.

"And the good news?" I asked, my heart pounding.

"The good news is, I told corporate that most of the staff got together for dinner somewhere, and they all got food poisoning at the same time. That's why no one could come in for work," she said, managing a faint smile.

"They suggested that we reopen this afternoon," she continued. "I want you to know something. I would never put my own neck on the line and lie for someone else to keep their job. But I believe in you. I believe you will do well and go pretty far in this company. Yes! I could've told corporate that the party was at your place and everyone got shit faced there, but I didn't. You owe me, and I hope you've learned your lesson. Now let's just hope that most of the afternoon employees show up for their 3 o'clock shift. Remember, you are not here to make friends. You're here to manage your kitchen staff and put out awesome food."

I couldn't believe what I was hearing. This lady took the risk and told a complete lie for me, and she didn't have to do that. If the truth didn't get back to corporate some type of way, this could be my second chance, and I was so grateful for it.

This woman believed in me, and from here on out, I would never let her down. Yes, I absolutely learned my lesson, and at that moment, I matured a little bit more.

I went back into the kitchen, put on my apron, and quickly got my preparations ready for the afternoon shift. 3 o'clock finally came around as the evening crew slowly arrived.

Three of the employees that came to my gathering entered the restaurant but couldn't look me in the face. I guess they got word that no one from the morning crew showed up for their shift.

"Looking back on that time, I realize how much I had yet to learn —not just about leadership but about life itself. Each misstep, like the housewarming party that nearly cost me everything, shaped the person I was becoming.

It taught me that being responsible wasn't just about the tasks at hand—it was about owning the choices I made and their impact on others.

Moments like these reminded me that personal growth often comes from the most unexpected situations, and the people who believe in us, even at our lowest, leave lasting impressions. That housewarming party may have been a near disaster, but it became a pivotal chapter in my journey, one that set the tone for how I'd approach challenges moving forward."

Moral of the Story: Mistakes are inevitable, but what defines us is how we learn and grow from them. Trust is fragile and must be earned, especially in leadership. The most valuable lessons often come from moments of failure, and second chances are gifts we should never take for granted. It's not about avoiding missteps entirely—it's about owning them, making amends, and becoming better because of them.

Chapter 43

A Kentucky Short Story

Let me tell you a story that happened to me and my family. I want to share this story because it serves as a reminder that events like this still happen today. I included this story in my book to show how cruel people can still be in this present day and age.

It has been said that together, we will all reach the mountaintop one day. People say that things are a lot better today than they were yesterday, but I say we still have a long way to go. They say that love overcomes all hatred, but in my opinion, I've lost all hope. We will never reach that mountaintop together. The world will end as it is now—consumed by money, greed, war, power, and, of course, racism.

There are even attempts to whitewash history from our books. I've always believed that to move forward, we must confront the past, search for solutions, and find ways to live together in peace. But in some cases, it seems like some people would be much happier if we reverted to the early 1960s. Let's face it—racism will never end. And in my experience, the worst kind of racism a person of color will ever encounter is what I call "silent racism."

What is silent racism, you ask? Well, it's everything I've experienced when it comes to hatred. It's generational. Here's my own definition of silent racism: It's when a person does or says something to you that is completely racist, but it's so subtle and transparent that no one else sees what you see or feels what you feel. No one else witnesses the racism because it happens in a normalized setting. It's camouflaged. But your gut, heart, body, mind, and soul can easily detect it when it happens.

Silent racism is not meant for everyone to see when the evil shows its face. It's direct and specific. It angers you but makes others wonder why you're so upset.

To others, it's never a big deal.

You're often considered to be at fault, labeled as someone who took it the wrong way. Maybe you're even told you have anger issues or that you're bipolar. What's done or said is rarely thought out, and the apologies—if they come at all—are usually false.

The eyes, though—they tell you everything you need to know about a person. Jealousy, sabotage, gaslighting, and privilege all play a role. And that's my definition of silent racism.

A Word About Self-Hatred

While I'm at it, let me address something else: self-hatred among our people.

I want to say this to my brothers and sisters—we as a people have been brainwashed for centuries to hate each other. The bad energy we direct toward one another is ignorant and self-destructive. Poverty, the lack of education, and the absence of job opportunities are all designed to create chaos between us.

People no longer need a reason to be angry with someone else. Being hateful has become a bad habit. Instead of coming together to create greatness for one another, we find reasons to tear each other down. We've become selfish. A smile held too long at someone can spark hostility. Accidentally bumping into someone or stepping on their shoe might lead to an argument or even a fight. Saying "hi" can sometimes result in silent rejection or an unwarranted glare of anger.

Today, correcting a child's wrongdoing could cost you your life. They might take it the wrong way, and you could end up on the wrong side of a bullet. There's so much hate among us.

But I wasn't brought up that way.

I was raised in a housing project on the northwest side of Detroit, where we turned hopelessness into excellence. We did everything together.

We looked out for one another, we loved each other, and we had mentors to guide us. In return, we mentored the children who came after us. We cared for one another like family.

But times have changed since my childhood.

People have become sinister toward one another. Most times, we can't even hug each other, lean on each other's shoulders, or even say, "I love you, brother." If there's anything I despise the most, it's the fact that we can't seem to unite like other groups of people do. Not all of us, but many of us step in our own way.

If my statements in this chapter upset you or ruffled some feathers, it only means that we need to change these narratives and do better. Be a part of the change. Let's face facts: we're the most athletic, the most creative, the most loving, and the most copied. Yet, we can't unite and love each other. We don't understand that unity is power. Some of us fail to comprehend that we come from descendants of kings and queens. In other words, we come from royalty but refuse to act like it.

Instead, some of us choose to look ridiculous—stepping out of our homes with sagging pants, underwear showing, and no belt in sight. Others come out in public wearing hair bonnets, pajama pants, and house shoes. What has happened to us? Dignity and respect are rarely taught these days. These two virtues are such a pet peeve of mine.

Our own colorism continues to separate us. It's been a color barrier and a serious emotional and psychological battle within our community. It can even be a form of racism between one another. This, too, is generational. Colorism began with the slave masters, who harshly mistreated their darker-skinned slaves. The darker the skin, the more intense the abuse.

Over centuries, this cycle of abuse continued. We adopted this learned behavior and started to mistreat one another simply because our skin is darker or lighter.

Fair-skinned people are often treated better than darker-skinned people, and this plays out in countless ways—even while being stopped by the police. Our skin color can still become a factor.

The most closely watched and hated group of the 1960s was the Black Panther Party. Yet, they protected their communities, fed children, and provided for their people. They believed in unity. Why can't we break this curse today? Why can't we find that same strength within our communities now?

I don't know about other parts of the world, but in Western society, I don't see us getting any better. The real question is: will we ever wake up? I guess we'll never know. There aren't enough good people—Black or white—to make this change. Just imagine if we all worked together for a common, human goal. Life would be amazing for everyone.

So, I guess I've just described three types of hate: racial hatred, hatred of your own people, and self-hate. These observations come from my experiences as a Black man on this earth. They're my opinions, shaped by years of personal encounters and reflections.

I'm sure your reality may be a little different from mine. I didn't write this to stir anger within you but to open up a broader perspective that we can all learn from. If we could just understand each other, this world would be a much better place for all of us. But first, we must be honest with ourselves. Otherwise, we'll never be able to fix these social problems.

And even though I've given up hope for humanity, I can still be proven wrong one day. But I guarantee it won't happen in my lifetime. Sure, it's better than past decades, but we still have such a long way to go.

— **Eric Wright**

A Kentucky Short Story

We had planned a road trip for my mother to visit two of her children who had moved to Atlanta, Georgia. I'm not sure if she ever traveled outside of Michigan when she was younger, but this was the first time the rest of us, as a family, traveled with her outside of the state. I was proud to share this moment with her.

The long, 12-hour scenic drive was beautiful, but we hit a couple of unexpected bumps along the way—bumps we surely weren't prepared for.

As we made our way through Kentucky, someone suggested stopping for gas before continuing the journey. We veered off the highway and pulled into a roadside gas station. While filling up both cars, some of us decided to head inside to buy chips, candy, and pop.

"I noticed your license plates say Michigan. Are you all from there?" the male cashier asked, his tone tinged with something I couldn't quite place.

We wondered why he was asking. "Be careful driving through Kentucky," he added. "Police don't take to your people too kindly out here."

I asked, "What do you mean by that?"

"Well, what I mean is that the authorities tend to watch outsiders who don't live in this great state of Kentucky more closely. Just thought I'd give you a heads-up," he said, his words laced with thinly veiled malice.

I immediately told everyone to pay for their items and get back to the cars. There was no doubt in my mind that this cashier was the type to call the police and give them our license plate numbers and car descriptions, tipping them off to trail us as we traveled through the state.

We drove for another two to three hours before deciding to stop for a meal. An Elias Brothers restaurant seemed like a good choice. As soon as we entered, a waitress greeted us, led us to a table, and handed us menus.

We were having a great time—making my mother laugh, cracking jokes, and doing what fun families do. But after about 40 minutes, my sister began to notice something odd. Other patrons, who had arrived well after us, had already gotten their food and left, while no one had come back to take our orders.

Almost an hour had passed, and our waitress still hadn't returned to our table. Frustrated, I asked for a manager. The manager came over, apologized for the "mishap," and finally took our orders herself. But even after that, there was no sign of our food. No one came back to check on us.

At this point, I was beyond upset. Something wasn't right. I decided to walk over to the kitchen window to see what was going on with our food. What I saw shocked me.

Our meals had been prepared, but the plates were stacked haphazardly on top of each other like garbage. The food was a mess, and the kitchen staff was laughing hysterically. It was clear that no one had any intention of serving us.

I glanced around the restaurant and noticed we were the only Black family there. The stares from other diners confirmed my suspicions. I couldn't believe we were being treated this way. I was devastated—not just because we hadn't been served, but because I never wanted my mother to experience something like this again.

She had already been through enough in her life. Born in the early 1940s, my mother had likely witnessed and endured more racism and discrimination than I could ever imagine, especially as a young Black woman with a physical disability.

At this stage in her life, she deserved to be treated with dignity and respect—not to see bigotry rear its ugly head in such a blatant way.

Returning to the table, I told my sisters what had happened to our food. We quietly gathered our belongings, and I quickly escorted my mother out of that toxic environment.

As we walked back to the cars, we noticed a Wendy's across the parking lot and decided to eat there instead. As we sat down to eat, my mother finally asked me, "What happened at the other restaurant? Why did we leave?"

I didn't really go into detail because I didn't want to upset her while we were on this trip. In the back of my mind, I was still furious, and my blood was boiling. The only regret I had about that day was that I never called their corporate office to explain what had happened to us. I shouldn't have let them violate our rights like that or allowed that restaurant to get away with their blatant racism.

Anyway, we finally arrived in the beautiful city of Atlanta and had a great week with my mother and family. We got to witness the laser show at Stone Mountain Park and visit "The City Beneath the Streets," Atlanta's underground shops and entertainment district.

I would like the reader to please forgive me if it seems like I've lost all hope for humanity. But I've witnessed, experienced, and read so much during my childhood and as an adult that life has steered me far from optimism. Decades of ugliness seem to never end—and they continue to this very day.

I also want the reader to guess what year this terrible event happened to me and my family. If you knew, some of you would be shocked, and others wouldn't be surprised at all.

My Final Thoughts

This chapter is a reflection of where we are as a society, and unfortunately, it shows how far we still have to go. Moments like these are painful reminders that even though some things have improved, the shadows of hatred and discrimination remain.

It's heartbreaking to think that my mother, after everything she endured in her lifetime, had to witness such blatant racism in what should have been her golden years.

She deserved better. We all do. Experiences like these make it hard to hold on to hope, but perhaps by sharing stories like mine, we can inspire others to think differently and act with kindness.

If anything, I hope this chapter reminds readers of the importance of standing up for what's right—not just for ourselves but for the generations that follow. We can't change the past, but we can strive to create a future where these kinds of stories no longer exist.

Chapter 44

The Foster Child Next Door
(Part One: A Situationship)

When I was a kid, I had the privilege of always being by my mother's side during visits to my grandparents. I say it was a privilege because I was always chosen to keep her company on those long road trips from the northwest side of Detroit to the industrial southwest side of the city. Maybe it was because I was the oldest child in my family.

If memory serves me correctly, we took the Fenkell Avenue bus, transferred to the Livernois Avenue bus, and then transferred again to the Fort Street bus just to get to their house. Once we arrived, I would search for my cousins, friends, or kids I knew on my grandparents' block to play with. If no one was around, I would wait for the foster kids next door to come outside.

These kids could never go beyond the front yard, and that's where we used to play until they were called back in for dinner. Once they went inside, they never came back out until the next day.
They had a yard curfew that kicked in well before the streetlights came on. At the time, I thought it was strict, but looking back, it was a good way to keep them out of trouble.

Another way we communicated was through the backyard fence. My grandparents and the foster mother next door had beautiful backyards—grass always neatly cut, with plants and flowers everywhere. We never crossed into each other's yards, but we had plenty of playful conversations through the fence. We played children's games together, each staying on our respective sides.

On one visit to my grandparents' house, I noticed one of the little girls next door was gone. She had moved away, and I never knew what happened to her. Maybe she was sent to another foster home or reunited with her biological family. I remember we were about the same age, and we had so much fun together.

Fast forward to many years later.

At the restaurant, I had the back of the house fine-tuned. Everyone knew exactly what to do to ensure a successful shift. The front of the house, however, was a different story. With no guidance, it was a mess every day.

We desperately needed someone mature enough to replace the lead waitress who had been transferred to Eastland Mall. None of the waitstaff on our team seemed like a good fit, so we decided to look elsewhere for an experienced leader. For two weeks, we collected applications but found no great potentials or suitable candidates to fix our failing system. The waitstaff was simply terrible.

Then, on the third Monday, management came across an application that stood out. The person had significant leadership experience, so we scheduled an interview.

A couple of days later, she walked in—this beautiful, fair-skinned, Afro-style-wearing, hip-switching, 6'2" bombshell.

"Excuse me. I'm here for my interview," she said.

My voice started to shake nervously. "Oh! Let me get the restaurant manager for you," I stammered.

Sometimes you get clumsy at the worst moments, and I embarrassed myself by walking into a wall on my way to the office.

"Follow me to the back of the restaurant, and I'll show you the table where your interview will take place," I said. "Would you like a Coke or something else to drink?"

"No, thank you," she replied as I walked away.

It was love at first sight for me, but I felt like I was way out of her league. Besides, I thought, I'd be too short for her—we wouldn't look right together.

About half an hour later, I saw her gathering her things to leave.

"Did you get the job?" I asked.

"Yes, I did," she replied, "and I start next Monday."

I took that moment to introduce myself. "I'm Eric, and I'm the lead cook around here."

She shook my hand and introduced herself.

Boy, was her hand soft. I didn't want to let go, but I didn't want to seem weird.

"I'm looking forward to working with you. I heard a lot of nice things about you during my interview, Eric. Well, I have somewhere else I need to be. Take care of yourself, and I'll see you next week," she said.

As she walked out of the restaurant, something clicked in my head —I'd seen this young woman somewhere before. My next thought was, *Man, oh man! Does she have a hip switch out of this world. The way she walked was amazing, and I was all in.* (laughing)

A few weeks went by as she worked tirelessly, day after day, hour after hour, getting the front-of-house waitstaff to work together as a team. It was amazing working with her, and together, we had the restaurant running like a finely tuned machine.

One evening, I suggested we go downstairs to one of the bars to celebrate her accomplishment. She thought it was a wonderful idea.

After we sat down, I ordered my usual— a toasted almond with a splash of rum. Back in those days, I loved my liquor-laced ice cream drinks. She ordered white Chardonnay.

The more I looked across the table at her, the more familiar she began to seem.

The more we drank, the deeper our conversation became, covering topics like our backgrounds.

She told me, "When I was a child, I went through foster care."
"Where did you live as a child?" I asked.

"Well, I lived in many places, but one of them was in Southwest Detroit with some other kids."

"Oh yeah? When I was a kid, I used to play with some foster kids right next door to my grandparents," I replied.

She asked, "What street did the kids live on?"

When I told her, curiosity overtook her, and she asked even more questions.

"Wait a minute. What were your grandparents' names?" When I told her, she froze in shock.

"What's wrong?" I asked.

"You're not going to believe this, but I lived right next door to your grandparents."

Her words hit me like a ton of bricks. Suddenly, I knew why she had seemed so familiar—she was the little girl I used to play with.

I almost shed a tear as I took in the realization. I quickly got up from the table to hug her.

When I sat back down, she began to open up. She shared that her childhood wasn't a happy one, as she moved from home to home.

Finally, when she came of age, she reunited with her biological family, but even then, things didn't turn out well for her.

"Sometimes life is still tough, but I'm managing," she said.

After we talked about our lives growing up and shared many drinks, I asked, "How are you getting home?"

"I walk across the street and catch the city bus," she replied. I offered to take her home, and she accepted.

When we pulled up in front of her building, which was actually an apartment complex and women's shelter, she gave me a friendly kiss on the cheek and thanked me for the drinks and the ride.

She then handed me her apartment number. "You can come visit anytime you like—just check in at the desk first. They'll call up for me, and I'll meet you in the guest room."

I thought it was a little strange but agreed to do just that.

For the next few weeks, I visited her regularly to check in and see how she was doing. Strangely, no men were allowed in the apartments. I thought it was sad for an establishment to control women this way, but I never pried into why she lived there. It was none of my business.

Over the next several months, I continued visiting my new friend. Each time, I signed my name on the visitor's list, waited for her call, and met her in the guest room.

On one visit, I surprised her with two tickets to see Prince and The Revolution at the old Masonic Temple. I remember this concert being my very first one. We even bought matching outfits, attended the concert, and had an incredible time.

Even then, I felt like I was out of her league.

I never had a crush on her when we were kids, but now she had my full attention. I pictured her dating someone taller, more sophisticated, and much better off.

After the concert, we had dinner downtown before I took her home. When we arrived in front of her building, I did something I thought I'd never be brave enough to do.

I thought she would laugh at me and politely say, "No, thank you." I thought she'd tell me I was too short for her.

But I gathered my courage and asked her to be my girl. She looked at me, surprised. "Are you serious?" she asked.

"I am," I replied.

She turned to look out the passenger side window for a few moments, and when she turned back to me, she said, "Yes."

I was stunned but thrilled. I didn't stop there, though. I was about to move into a new apartment on Jefferson and Marquette, nearly a mile past Belle Isle and just down the street from the well-known Roostertail Event Venue. I asked if she would like to move in with me.

To my utter surprise, she said yes to that, too.

We finally moved into our new apartment together, and for the next few months, life was a blast. I was madly in love with this woman. She had been my playmate as a child, became my best friend, and now she was my girlfriend. I even began to imagine her as my young bride in the near future. For a while, life was good between us.

But in hindsight, I should have stayed in my previous apartment building and dealt with the slowly rising rent. The new building always seemed to have something strange going on.

The elevator was frequently out of order, fights and arguments echoed through the hallways, and domestic violence incidents were a weekly occurrence. We lived on the sixth floor, and one evening, as we sat at home watching television, something horrifying happened. Suddenly, we saw a man's naked body fall past our window to his death.

We rushed to look out the window, and there he was, lying lifeless in the back parking lot. Rumors swirled about what had happened.

Allegedly, the man had been visiting a woman in the apartment directly above ours. It was said that he waited until her husband left for work before being let into the apartment. The two allegedly began having sexual intercourse.

Unbeknownst to them, the husband had been told he didn't need to work that night and he decided to return home.

Allegedly, while the husband was opening his apartment door, the guy inside quickly climbed out the seventh floor window and held himself on the window ledge for dear life.

This part of the story quickly reminded me about the time I had to hide in a closet and wait for a male individual to fall asleep before I could make my escape as a young teen back in the day.

Allegedly, the husband took a quick shower and afterwards had gone to bed.

The guy outside the window couldn't hold on any longer and fell to his death.

As we looked out our window, we were both in complete shock to see a motionless body lying on a hard cement pavement.

This was the type of craziness that was going on inside this old building.

Soon we would have our own personal craziness to deal with.

Part Two: You Never Know a Person Until You Live With Them

There's always two sides to a story. This is mine. After about five months of a wonderful and loving relationship, I started to see signs of depression and psychotic behavior. Working at the restaurant together became unbearable.

The arguments at home grew toxic, but I tried to show her in every way possible that she was loved. She couldn't stand another female being close to me at work. She always felt that I gave them a reason to be near me.

Her trust issues were extreme, and they caused problems between us. I was constantly accused of secretly talking to other women. This wasn't the case at all. I loved her, and I didn't want these misunderstandings to destroy us. Unfortunately, these issues even began to affect my ability to do my job. It got so bad that other female employees started to notice how she was acting and began playing mind games with her just to get a kick out of the situation.

Arguments would often erupt in the restaurant, and there were times when I had to physically restrain her from getting into a fight with another woman.

"I don't want your man," I'd often hear the other woman say. I was so embarrassed. I tried so hard to show her that she was everything to me.

I used to always say that I would never have kids and I would never marry, but she was the person I wanted to do all of that with. Yes, she had trust issues, and I believe that her experiences of going from foster home to foster home as a child were coming back to haunt her in some ways.

But I just couldn't wrap my mind around it. She was a beautiful person—smart, tall, attractive, curvaceous, funny, and very talented.

It should've been the other way around. Other women should have been jealous of her.

One Saturday morning, she decided she wanted to give up on me. She went into the kitchen drawer, grabbed a knife, and locked herself in the bathroom.

"What are you doing in there?" I asked. "Unlock this door before I break it down."

"Get away before I slice both wrists," she screamed.

"Baby, why do you want to do this to yourself? No one loves me. You don't even love me. You pretend to love me, but you really don't."

I tried to respond in a softer tone. "Baby, you know that's not true. You know you mean the world to me. Please, just put the knife down and open the door. Open the door and let me give you a hug. Baby, if you do this, I'll never be the same."

At this point, I was saying everything I could to stop her from committing serious bodily harm to herself—worst-case, suicide. She insisted that I didn't care about her anymore.

"Honey, you know I care about you. Just put down the knife and open the door. Let's talk this out in the open. Taking your own life is definitely not the answer.

Just tell me what you want from me. What do you want me to change?"

I was willing to do anything she asked me to do, whether it made sense or not. Suddenly, I heard the knife drop to the floor, and the door unlocked. She was sitting on the toilet, crying.

I rushed in and gave her the biggest hug I could. For a moment, we cried together and discussed what I could do better as her man. I couldn't fully understand why she felt this way, but I agreed to work on it.

I helped her out of the bathroom, got rid of the knife, and called off work.

We had a long, extensive talk that day. Afterwards, I took her to dinner. All I kept thinking was how close that call had been between life and death. It was a very scary moment for me. I realized that she was very possessive about me, and I had to be cautious and careful. Because of her past, I always felt like I was walking on shaky ground. But I refused to give up on her.

I wanted to be the one to give her a better life. Having a family and marriage was just around the corner for the second time in my young life.

Part Three: A Near-Death Experience

Within a few months, she had another episode. This one happened when she saw me taking part in interviewing a candidate for the night shift floor manager position. I guess she didn't like the laughter and smiles exchanged during the interview.

Let me be clear—I didn't want to do this interview in the first place. I was asked to step in because the restaurant manager was busy on a corporate call in his office. I knew that speaking with this woman alone at a table in the back of the room would cause a problem. The person I was interviewing was also tall, very attractive, and Caucasian. The fact that she was white only added to my girlfriend's extreme possessiveness and anger.

When we returned home from work, I got the silent treatment. She wouldn't say a word to me. At this point, I was tired of the constant arguments and mistreatment for no reason. I had done everything I could to make the relationship work.

I tried to show her that she was the only person I loved and cared for. But she had a mental problem, and I wasn't a psychiatrist.

I could no longer help her with our relationship. I was finally tired of it all. After a speechless night, we both turned in for bed.

Well, we didn't exactly have a bed. We were sleeping on the carpeted floor, waiting for a new bed to be delivered. She was tired too, but this time, she turned her agony and defeat onto me.

It was 3 or 4 a.m.—hell, I don't remember exactly what time it was. All I know is that it was really early, the apartment was quiet, and everything was dark. I was in a deep sleep, dreaming about the funk rock band Morris Day and The Time.

Something told me to wake up, and when I looked up, I couldn't believe my eyes. My own girlfriend had picked up the television over her head and was about to let it go—committing murder over some frivolous bullshit. I quickly rolled over as the television violently crashed to the floor near me.

She immediately ran out the door. I scrambled to put on some clothes and chased after her. Once again, the elevator wasn't working, so I had to run down the many flights of stairs to catch her.

As I got outside the building, I saw her running toward a waiting city bus across the street. I tried to catch up, but the bus quickly pulled away, leaving me breathless and defeated. My guess is that she told the driver a strange man was chasing her.

She never returned to work, and I never saw her again. I later learned that she had family nearby that I didn't know about. The girl broke my heart so badly—and she also tried to kill me.

276

Years later, I reflected on the situation and realized she could have benefited from psychiatric help.

But back in those days, people in my community didn't seek mental health treatment like we do now. It was largely unheard of, and mental health wasn't a topic we openly discussed or understood.

Well, that's my side of the story. On a positive note, I was so depressed the following night that I decided to stop at a liquor store and play a three-digit lottery number. I flipped through a *Three Wise Men* lottery book and found a number associated with shoes. It reminded me of my dream about Morris Day's Stacey Adams wing-tip shoes. To my surprise, it was the very first time I hit a three-digit lottery number. (laughing)

Looking back, the experience taught me lessons I didn't realize I needed to learn.

Relationships can be a reflection of our own vulnerabilities, and hers brought to light the importance of recognizing when someone's pain runs deeper than love alone can heal. It showed me that no matter how much you want to save someone, they must first be willing to save themselves.

That chapter of my life, as painful and chaotic as it was, became a turning point.

It forced me to confront not only my own choices but also the cultural silence around mental health that often leaves people in our communities without the help they so desperately need. The heartbreak was immense, and the trauma of nearly losing my life left an imprint I carried for years. But it also gave me a clearer perspective on the importance of boundaries, self-preservation, and knowing when it's time to let go for the sake of your own well- being.

Though her departure was abrupt and left me with unanswered questions, it prepared me for the next stages of growth and healing. I realized that love isn't just about holding on but also about knowing when to release someone with the hope they find their own peace.

And for myself, it became a moment to recalibrate, refocus, and start charting a path forward—one that valued not only my happiness but also my safety.

Chapter 45

A Letter to My Daughter
(An Unforgivable Sin)

I had a daughter who was born in **1987**, and it makes me sick to my stomach that I don't have a relationship with her. I can't blame anyone but myself. I destroyed that relationship, and I don't think I can ever repair it. It's the one single sin that I may have to pay my debt for—other than not being able to see her again.

Years ago, I tried to reach out on Facebook, but it was years too late. I finally faced those hurtful words: "Don't ever try to contact me ever again." Those words from her were very painful to see, but I understood that I deserved them. I was once a proud father who would have given her the world.

I remember being in the room when she was born at Riverview Hospital in Detroit. The doctor had to take me out of the room because the flow of blood from her mother made me pass out. The very last thing I heard was, "Get him out of here; I can't take care of two people at the same time." I had to lie on a couch outside her hospital room.

Boy, oh boy, did she cry a lot. At home, I would wrap her in a blanket, take her outside, and walk her up and down the driveway. The late-night summer air coming off the Detroit riverfront would calm her down and make her fall back asleep.

As she got a little older, she became my hanging buddy, my backseat rider. I took her everywhere with me. If I went to the store, she was with me. If I hung out with my buddies, she was with me. If I went to visit family, she got to see her grandparents. If I just wanted to cruise the city, she was in the backseat riding with me. I can remember one time when I wasn't paying close attention and accidentally closed the car door on her tiny finger.

I'm so sorry—I didn't mean to do it.

She yelled so loud and cried so hard. I felt terrible, and her mother cursed me out so badly after I got her home and explained what happened.

I think that's when the distrust began.

But sometimes you make mistakes. Again, I didn't mean to hurt her or cause her so much pain. Her mom was right—I should've paid closer attention. I also understand that you make innocent mistakes with your first child. From that point on, I was extremely cautious with her.

But something changed. Each time I came to visit, I wasn't allowed to take her anywhere. I wasn't even allowed to take her off the porch and walk her to the store anymore, even though I was still taking good care of her. I was her father, but I couldn't do the normal fatherly things with her. That really upset me.

I tried to file for child support on my own, but I went about it the wrong way. I tried to file in the city I lived in instead of the city where she and her mother lived. I didn't know this at the time. Child support was finally filed by her mother, and the courts set visitation. I could have her at her grandmother's house two days a week, and her mother would bring her to my mother's house on Fridays and Saturdays.

It was really an inconvenience for both of us—me traveling from Pontiac to the east side of Detroit and her mother traveling from the east side of Detroit to my parent's house on the northwest side. It was so much of an inconvenience that her mother took me back to court to see if I could pay for her travel expenses back and forth every weekend.

The judge denied her case, considering I was the one with the farthest travel to be with her. This angered me as well.

I can remember having a birthday party for her at my parent's home, and what a fun evening that was.

My mother bought her birthday cake, and my whole family was there to enjoy it with her.

It was such a sight to see her and my other daughter playing together on her special day.

When I finally gave you your gifts, the smile on your tiny face was priceless. A few two-piece outfits and some new tennis shoes that you couldn't wait to put on. "Daddy, can you put these shoes on for me?" you asked with excitement. I sat you on my lap and placed the new shoes on for you. Once I set you back on the floor, you ran back and forth in the living room, convinced you were running faster than before. That was so funny to me.

When your mother came to pick you up, you gave me a kiss on the cheek and the biggest hug before leaving out the door to go home.

The next morning, while sitting in my office, I received a phone call from your mother. She proceeded to tell me that she didn't appreciate what I had bought you for your birthday. "She needs dresses and dress shoes, not two-piece outfits and tennis shoes," she told me. I was so irritated—nothing I did was ever good enough.

Another time, I received a letter from the Friend of the Court stating that I had fallen behind on my child support payments. I appeared in court, only for them to raise my payments so I could catch up. The following week, I received another letter to appear in court. There must've been a mistake, I thought, because I had just been in front of a judge the week before. Assuming it was an error, I didn't go that time, but the court raised my payments again.

When I called to clarify the situation, the woman on the phone told me that nothing could be done about it and that the judge's final order couldn't be changed. This time, the payments started coming directly out of my paycheck. Yeah, the Friend of the Court wasn't so friendly.

By this point, I was furious.

While I was trying to catch up on my payments, I was called to court again because someone had decided they needed a raise in support.

I don't know who she was, but the woman I sat across from looked me over from head to toe, as if trying to find jewelry she could take from me. She even asked how I had gotten to court and whether I had driven my own car. She was going to attempt to take that too.

One year, I claimed you on my taxes. I thought that since I was paying child support, I could claim you at the end of the year. I didn't know that wasn't allowed. I didn't know that you had to live with me and go to school in the same city for me to claim you. I ended up having to pay all that money back to the federal government, the city, and the state.

Trying to love you got me deeper and deeper into trouble. Again, no matter what I did, it was never good enough. You were my first child, and I was doing my best to take good care of you without the courts.

I finally caught up on my payments and continued to pay, but by this time, I was so fed up. This was when I made the biggest mistake of my life. I became uninvolved in your life, and that was the dumbest thing I could have done.

No matter what, I should've been man enough to stick it out. I should've fought harder for you. I should've been the father figure you needed. Instead, I became the coward you know today.

I deserve your hatred of me, and I can only blame myself for the bad decisions I made. I cheated my family out of a relationship with you, and I'm so, so sorry.

You were my parents' first granddaughter. I think about you every day, and it makes me feel so sick to my stomach.

This continues to be very painful for me, and sometimes I privately cry. This is my punishment.

We all miss you, my riding buddy. I love you so much, and I'm truly sorry for not repairing us.

This terrible mistake may stop me from entering the pearly gates.

No matter what, I shouldn't have given up on us. I'm so sorry, and I don't blame you for hating me. I was careless and selfish.

I personally think this is the greatest sin a man can commit.

My Final Thoughts

To my beautiful daughter,

If you ever come across this book one day, I want you to know something that words can never fully express. Despite the time and distance that have separated us, my love for you has never wavered. You are always in my thoughts, and there isn't a single day that goes by where I don't wonder how you are, what you're doing, and who you've become.

I know I failed you. I know I made choices that hurt you and that created a distance I cannot bridge. For that, I am truly sorry. I would give anything to go back and do things differently—to be the father you deserved, to fight harder for us, and to never let my frustration, pride, and mistakes get in the way of loving you the way you needed me to.

You are and always have been a part of my heart. I remember the way your tiny hand felt in mine, the sound of your laughter, and the light in your eyes. Those memories are etched into my soul, and they remain some of the happiest moments of my life. You were my world, my little sidekick, my riding buddy. I was so proud to be your father.

I never stopped loving you, even when I let my own shortcomings overshadow my responsibility to you.

I wish I could explain how deeply I regret the choices I made.

I let my frustration with life and my struggles with circumstances get the better of me. I allowed myself to retreat when I should have fought harder, stood taller, and been more present for you.

I was young and flawed, and in my immaturity, I didn't realize how precious my time with you truly was until it was too late.

You are loved. You have always been loved. You were my first child, and the bond we shared, though short-lived, has remained with me every day since. I wish I had the chance to tell you in person how much you mean to me and how much I miss you. My life has not been the same without you in it, and it's a void that I carry in my heart.

If there ever comes a day when you feel ready to talk, I will be here—always. My door is open, and my arms are ready to embrace you. I know that I can't undo the pain I've caused, but I hope that maybe, just maybe, we can create something new—a chance to reconnect, to heal, and to make up for lost time.

Wherever you are, I hope your life has been filled with love, joy, and everything good that the world has to offer. You deserve nothing less. You are an incredible person, and I have no doubt that you have grown into someone extraordinary.

Please know that you are forever in my heart. You are my daughter, my blood, and my love for you will never fade.

With all the love and hope I have,

I also want you to know that my mother adored her first grand daughter. [Hearts]

Your father,
Eric Wright

[Hearts]

Chapter 46

Three Superstars

So anyways, it was now time for our restaurant to move into a much bigger space, which meant that the capacity to hold guests would be larger, more people would be employed, and we needed to do another grand opening to let folks know about our new relocation. Three of us were up for promotions and transfers to other restaurants in the company. But first, we assistant managers and supervisors had to train almost an entirely new kitchen and wait staff, learn how to make the new menu items, and get acquainted with our new digital registers. The company gave us three weeks to accomplish this, and whoever we had for staffing, we were stuck with by the end of training. So, they had to be good at what their position required.

Me and an assistant manager were in charge of training the kitchen staff. We had to train at least 100 potential candidates just to get 10 outstanding individuals. The third person, who was also an assistant manager, was in charge of training the new waitstaff. Chosen managers from other restaurants took notes every day just to see if we were cut out to be the next three superstars of the company.

Training these potential cooks was extremely hard and time-consuming. There were a lot of mistakes being made in the beginning of preparations. For example, I was teaching a guy the proper way of using a knife to slice meat. For whatever reason, he wanted to show off in front of the rest of the group, but instead, he slightly sliced part of his wrist. Luckily, he didn't cut any major tendons, but we still had to immediately send him to a nearby hospital. Another time, a young lady filled a basket of fries to go into the fryer. Not paying close attention to what she was doing, instead of carefully placing the basket into the grease, she dropped the basket, and the hot grease splashed up her arm, giving her second-degree burns.

After several mishaps, we finally picked the best cooks, waitstaff, dishwashers, bus persons, and cashiers. We were prepared for our big grand opening, and the three of us passed for our promotions. One of my buddies went to a mall on the east side of Detroit, the other went to a mall in Southfield, and I ended up at a mall in Troy. The three of us would become the best in the company, and we took pride in being just that.

The grand opening was a huge success. The company gave us a budget, and some of the food was free or either half-priced. It was a pretty fun weekend. I was so proud to see all three of us accomplishing our goals. We were anxiously waiting to move on to the next phase in our lives. I worked very hard. I went from several days of washing dishes, to a line cook, to lead cook, to kitchen supervisor, to being promoted as an assistant manager, all within eight years. I was made for this. Yes! I finally found my own lane and was proud of my achievements.

On the last closing day of the grand opening, the staff received their new uniforms and helped the remaining managers clean up the whole place before leaving for the day. I stayed and chopped it up with one of my manager buddies. We sat in the office laughing at the mistakes that were made throughout the week in the kitchen. We talked about how cute the two newly hired hostesses were. We even shared discussions about how the company was expanding, the new menu items, and how much we would miss working together.

"Hey man! We can still call each other and get together every once in a while. We can call each other's restaurants and see how each of us are doing," I told him.

"So, it's not a goodbye, my brother. It's an I'll see you later," he replied. It was good working with him those past few years, and it was bittersweet knowing we'd all be parting ways to lead different teams in new locations.

As I was walking out of the restaurant, I gave my buddy a soulful handshake and a brotherly hug.

"Do you have your keys to lock the front gate?" I asked. He assured me that he did, so I headed out, taking the long walk toward the parking lot.

Once I reached my car, I realized I had forgotten my briefcase. Sighing, I turned back and took the same long walk to the restaurant to retrieve it. When I left earlier, I had pulled the gate halfway down, and some of the dining room lights were still on. Now, the gate was pulled all the way down and locked, and all the lights were shut off. "Hmm," I thought, "he must've left right after I did."

I unlocked the gate, pulled it halfway up, and walked toward the dark hallway that led to the office. Sliding the key into the office door, I opened it and flicked on the light—only to freeze in complete shock.

There on the hard office floor were my buddy and one of the company executive's wife, both completely naked. They had clearly just finished having sex. She frantically scrambled to her feet, but I was frozen in disbelief. I couldn't take my eyes off her as she hurried to gather her clothes, with evidence of what just happened running down her leg.

I grabbed my briefcase as quickly as I could, avoiding their frantic explanations. Without a word, I bolted out from under the gate and ran straight to my car. My heart pounded in my chest, and my mind raced with disbelief over what I had just witnessed. For years afterward, I wished I had never gone back for that briefcase.

It was embarrassing for all of us.

Looking back, I was stunned that this married woman would risk her career, her marriage, and her family like that—and with one of us, no less. But I have to admit, as a young man, she looked damn good for her age. (Laughing.) What did she see in him that made her risk it all? And him—he should've been ashamed of himself. Or should he?

After all, she was a stunning woman with a beautiful, tanned body, clearly determined to get her groove back. (Laughing.)

The next day, he called me. "Hey man, I'm sorry you had to see that. Did you tell anyone?"

I assured him, "First off, it's none of my business. Second, I'm not a snitch—I keep secrets well. But let me ask you something: How many times were you intimate with her?"

He admitted it had happened at least twice before. I made it clear that I would keep his secret, but I strongly advised him to stop immediately. "You've got to cut this off before someone gets hurt —or worse, killed."

I think he took my advice, because I never heard anything else about them after that.

I remember telling my mom about my promotion and where I was working. The first thing she did was hold out her hand for some money. I was able to give her some, and we both laughed about it.

There was one individual at the restaurant who quickly took to me —a very attractive young woman who always seemed to be around to help me accomplish my goals at just the right times. She was kind, sincere, and mild-mannered. She became the sweetheart of the restaurant, adored by everyone, including the customers. Some customers would even request to have her wait on them. Her kindness and generosity earned her great tips every week.

What stood out most was her concern for me.

She was always willing to go the extra mile to ensure the dining room was spotless, the trash was taken out, and any other task I needed done was taken care of—every single night she worked. The strange thing was, she wasn't even the lead waitress. She did all of this because she had a thing for me, and, to be honest, I started to let her creep into my head.

I could tell she was aiming for my heart.

One day, I decided to sit her down in my office to ask her why she was doing all of this for me. Why was she going out of her way to take such extra effort? Her answer surprised me.

"Well, to be honest, I didn't like the way you were being treated when you first got here. I didn't think it was fair, so I made a vow to myself to always be there to help you whenever I could," she said.

"That's very sweet of you," I replied. "But I think everyone has gotten used to me by now, so I should be fine. You don't need to do all that work. That's why we have a full staff. Besides, it's not a good look. People might start to think we're involved in some way, and I could get into serious trouble if some silly rumor got back to the main office."

"I understand," she said. "But can you do me a favor and take me home? I don't have a ride today."

I hesitated. "Sure, but this has to be the only time I take you home."

I locked up the restaurant, and we got into my car to head to her place in Sterling Heights. As we approached her neighborhood, she asked me to drive one block over from her house.

"I can walk the rest of the way from here," she said.

Before getting out of the car, she leaned over, grabbed my face, and kissed me on the cheek.

"You have a good night, and thanks for the ride," she said.

The kiss caught me off guard, and it didn't feel right. I thought maybe she was visiting a friend before heading home. As I drove from Sterling Heights back to Detroit, I couldn't stop thinking about that kiss. I realized I had to figure out a way to stop whatever was starting to happen between me and this waitress.

I had once been in a relationship with a lead waitress when I was a kitchen supervisor, but this situation was different. I was now an assistant manager, and any involvement with a waitress could put my salary-paying job at risk. I couldn't afford to let that happen.

And how would I even explain it to my mom? Worse yet, how could I bring this up to my dad? I could already hear him saying, *"All these pretty Black girls out here, and you choose a white girl? BUUULL SHITTT!" (laughing)*

Despite my initial attempts to maintain professionalism, the bond between me and the waitress grew stronger over time. Eventually, we crossed the line and became involved with one another. What started as a simple connection quickly turned into something far more complicated. While our relationship blossomed in private, it faced immense challenges, especially when it came to her parents. Their views, rooted in deep-seated racism, cast a shadow over what could have been a beautiful story. What unfolded next was a harsh reminder of the realities we still face, even in moments of personal triumph.

Chapter 47

Once Upon A Time In Sterling Heights

Sometimes life hurts & you gotta go through some shit before you're able to flush the toilet.

— Patricia "Ms. Pat" Williams

It was now the early part of winter, November 1989. The restaurant had completely turned around and had become one of the top restaurants in its district. The place was clean, very organized, and running like a fine-tuned machine. At this point, I was in love and infatuated with this young woman. She had won me over, and we were now secretly dating.

She once had a curiosity about what urban nightlife was like in downtown Detroit, so I took her to a couple of dance clubs. Before I knew it, she was having the time of her life. I was glad I could provide her with fun and the opportunity to dance and enjoy music as I did. Even though she was white, she never felt out of place in any majority-black nightclub.

Besides, she was with me, and she loved just being herself. Sure, I got some weird looks from the black women, but I never let anyone disrespect her. She loved that. She loved the protection I gave her. We continued visiting social spots downtown, and soon everyone got used to seeing me with this young lady.

Afterwards, I would take the long drive back to Sterling Heights. She would fall fast asleep in the passenger seat until we made it to a block over from her parents' house. I never understood why I couldn't drop her off at her home. She told me she couldn't explain why but would tell me later. "Will I ever meet your parents?" I asked one night.
"When the time is right, I will introduce you to them," she said. "But right now isn't a good time."

I didn't press her on it, but I couldn't understand why she was so hush-hush about her parents, why I kept dropping her off a block away, or why we always ended up on a dead-end street for a passionate kiss.

Why did we always have to drive to Detroit to have fun instead of staying close to Sterling Heights?

Was she afraid her family and friends would find out she was dating and in love with a Black man? Would she be embarrassed?

I loved her, so I was patient. I stopped asking and decided to wait until the time felt right, like she asked.

Looking back, I was so naive. Love blinded me, and I didn't want to see the signs. One night after work, she finally decided the time had come to introduce me to her parents.

She had me drive to her parents' house and park in their driveway.

"When we go in the house, don't say a word," she said. "Let me do all the talking."

As we entered, her parents were sitting at the kitchen table. "Mom, Dad, this is my new boyfriend, Eric," she said.

Her mother responded, "Nice to meet you, Eric."

Her dad didn't say a single word. In fact, he didn't even acknowledge me.

To break the obvious tension in the house, my girlfriend suggested we go down four stairs into the living room to play some video games.

"Have you ever played *Tetris*?" she asked.

At the time, I wasn't really into video games, but I was so nervous that I sat on their couch and picked up a controller anyway.

As she showed me how to set up the game, I heard her dad's threatening voice behind me.

"Why is this boy in my fucking house?"

"Quick, fast, and in a hurry, I want this fucking nigger out of my damn house."

I couldn't believe what I just heard behind me. I remember sitting there on the couch, frozen in time.

It was such an embarrassing moment, not only for me but also for their daughter. She had to know her parents were racist.

I started to question my girlfriend. Why hadn't she ever mentioned her parents' prejudices before? Did she truly understand the weight of what had just happened? Why didn't she warn me or at least prepare me for the possibility of their reaction?

Suddenly, I began to wonder if I was more of an experiment than a partner. Was I someone she cared for deeply, or was she just curious about what it was like to be with someone so different from her? Did she love me for who I truly was, or was I merely a bold statement, a way to challenge her parents' views without fully understanding the consequences?

The questions raced through my mind, leaving me feeling hollow. The love I had for her began to feel tainted by the doubt planted by her parents' hateful reaction. It was hard not to feel used, even if her intentions had been genuine.

I was devastated and felt a little ill. I had never felt so out of place in someone else's home.

She should have at least shared this information with her parents beforehand to see how they would react.

"I'm so sorry, but my parents would like for you to leave," she said softly, looking down at the floor. I quickly put on my coat and followed her to the snow-covered porch.

"I'm so sorry," she repeated. "I never meant for this to happen. I'll see you at work tomorrow, and I promise to straighten out this misunderstanding. Please don't worry. I'll talk to my parents and explain that we're in love and are going to be together whether they like it or not."

She kissed me, hugged me tightly, and kept saying, "Everything will be okay."

I got into my cold car, deeply disappointed, and drove off.

On the long winter drive back to Detroit, my devastation slowly turned into anger and rage.

Why would her parents treat me like that? Granted, they had just met me for the first time, but they didn't even give themselves a chance to know me.

Why didn't my girlfriend tell me how her parents felt about Black people?

I had been so good to her—protective, caring, loving. Besides, they didn't know me from a city hood rat or a distinguished gentleman.

I thought to myself, *It's **1989**. Aren't we past racism?*

I had so many questions. I was also a little angry at myself for not detecting that this meeting with her parents could go so terribly wrong.

I should've known. This was why we kissed on dead-end streets.

This was why I always had to drop her off a block away from her house.

Once again, love blinded me. My strong sense of dealing with someone culturally different never kicked in.

I was so naive.

I didn't see this situation coming—maybe because I didn't want to. I refused to believe that the love we had between us wouldn't work, no matter what forces worked against us.

I refused to believe I was only restricted to my own kind. Love didn't work that way. God wouldn't want me to believe that. I had been inside her parents' house for no more than twenty minutes, and they hated the very sight of me.

1989 was definitely a tough year for me.

That Sunday morning, she was a no-call, no-show for her shift. The following week, I couldn't contact her to save my life, and she never showed up for any of those shifts either. I started to worry that something had happened to her.

Finally, I received a letter from her at the restaurant, basically telling me how much I meant to her and how much she loved me. The letter went on to say that her parents had bought a one-way plane ticket to her grandparents' home in San Francisco. It ended with:

"I won't be able to see you for a while, but I'm determined to be with you again when I come back next summer. I love you, Eric. Take care of yourself, and I will see you again sometime in June or July."

P.S. Please wait for my return. I'll understand if you find yourself in another relationship, but when I get back, get rid of her, 'cause I'm still your girl.

I was heartbroken, and my world was crushed. I never saw or heard from her again after that.

She was abruptly taken away from me. Yes, that's what hatred did. It took someone I truly loved and cared about. [Hearts] Her beliefs weren't her parents' beliefs, but that didn't matter. No one at the restaurant knew we were a couple.

We did a fantastic job of keeping our business and relationship on the low. But I was never the same after that devastating experience. I continued working in the city of Troy until my next destination.

I heard through the company grapevine that there was an opening for an assistant manager position in another part of Oakland County. I desperately needed a new challenge and new people. I needed my mental stability back.

So, I took my briefcase and headed for the city of Pontiac.

Racism is a taught behavior or an ideology. No one on this planet is ever born a racist. When you're an infant, you have no idea what racism is. Children grow up to become what they see and hear.

Someone has to teach you that you're inherently superior or inferior to other ethnicities or races of people. You're taught to look down on others. You're taught that it's okay to hate people who don't look like you.

You're taught that slavery was once okay. You consciously wish that you could go back to those times. You're taught as a child that it was okay to own other people.

You're taught to discriminate and antagonize individuals who don't look like you.

Racism can grow and develop into many forms of hatred. You're taught that equality is a no-no.

It's a complex social issue that affects societies worldwide.

Racism can be intentional or unintentional and is often rooted in stereotypes. It can be physically, socially, and mentally harmful.

As a child, you're taught to be prejudiced toward others.

It either puts fear in you or makes you feel disdain. Racism has been around for centuries and many generations.

Racism is not limited to overt actions or attitudes. It can also be subtle and systemic.

Personally, it can be very tiring to see people continually act like this for no true reason other than to use racism as a tool to hurt.

It serves no purpose but to hold every one of us back.

Over the many years on this earth, I loved who I loved, no matter what color or nationality a person was.

We have achieved many advancements in life, but it's that one thing that holds us all back—hatred, discrimination, and racism.

Life has a way of presenting unexpected challenges, and sometimes, those challenges force you to confront uncomfortable truths. Just when I thought I had found my rhythm—both in my career and in my personal life—fate threw me a curve ball that I never saw coming.

What started as an exciting new chapter filled with love and possibilities quickly turned into a harsh reminder of the barriers that still exist between us as people.

This is a story about love, resilience, and the painful reality of what happens when the world refuses to change.

Personal Timeline 1989

- The Berlin Wall came crashing down, marking the end of the Cold War.
- Ted Bundy, one of America's most infamous serial killers, was executed.
- The handheld Game Boy was released, revolutionizing portable gaming.
- The Central Park 5 were wrongfully convicted of crimes they didn't commit, spotlighting racial injustice.
- Madonna's *Like a Prayer* album sparked global controversy.
- Spike Lee's *Do the Right Thing* hit theaters, challenging viewers to confront racial tensions in America.
- The devastating Exxon Valdez oil spill released 10.8 million gallons of crude oil into Alaska's Prince William Sound, causing widespread environmental damage.
- The San Francisco earthquake, also known as the Loma Prieta earthquake, struck during the World Series, leaving a lasting impact on the Bay Area.

Personal Reflections:
1989 was a year of immense change for me. Professionally, I witnessed success and growth as the restaurant thrived. On a personal level, I experienced the highs of love and the lows of heartbreak, with a relationship that faced challenges I never anticipated. This year tested my resilience, shaped my perspective, and reminded me of the progress still needed in both personal relationships and society at large.

Chapter 48

The Rise And Fall Of Three Men

*"Some people will never like you
because your spirit irritates their demons."*

— **Denzel Washington**

Downfall Number One

So here I am, in my 4th restaurant, thirty miles from Detroit. The manager I'm working with was really an awesome guy. He was one of the guys who helped train me before the grand opening downtown, so I had worked with him before. He was mild-mannered, always calm, and extremely nice to others. He was known for his measured responses to crises. His store was always busy, which also made him very tired and stressed out. He hadn't had an assistant manager in his store for several weeks until I got there.

I quickly noticed that being too nice to his dysfunctional staff was his biggest downfall. They would often take advantage of his kindness—taking breaks on the clock whenever they wanted to, and coming back to work hours later. Employees' closing duties were also a joke. Oftentimes, when the store closed, employees would half-clean their stations and run out the door. The manager would stay after and finish cleaning behind them before he got to go home. I thought that was crazy. He never fired anyone and never demanded anyone do their job. I never understood why he put up with so much riff-raff and the lack of respect from his employees.

But he loved his staff and didn't mind showing his misunderstood gratitude at the end of every summer. The restaurant was making so much money, and every month, the manager would somehow shave a little off the cash, falsely fix the paperwork, and turn in incorrect bank deposits and statements.

By the end of the summer, he would put together this huge picnic for his employees and their family members at a nearby park. The picnic was always held on a Sunday evening after the store closed. Unlimited amounts of food, pop, and chips were at these fun turnouts. Now, I must admit, I also had the time of my life at my first picnic.

Allegedly, the company caught wind of these picnics and wanted to investigate where the money was coming from to cover the high costs of these gatherings. Allegedly, the company's investigation concluded that the manager was using company money to pay for the picnics and immediately fired him. It was a very sad day to see this man pack up his personal belongings and walk out the door for the very last time. It was tough for some employees to hold back their emotions. Some even broke down and cried. This man was generally loved by so many throughout the company because of his generosity and kindness.

We ran without a store manager for a week before the open position was offered to me. I accepted my fourth promotion within eleven years of service, but I had to make drastic changes in the store after my takeover.

There would be no more going on break without permission, no more breaks for hours at a time, no more breaks on the clock, no more coming to work whenever you felt like it, no more giving free food to friends and family, and no more leaving the shift before your cleaning or closing duties were done. By now, I had a reputation for turning a terrible staff around. It was either my way of doing things or the doorway. I had no problem hiring new staff and getting rid of all the bad apples. In the beginning, the staff couldn't stand my guts, but their feelings about me would eventually change.

Downfall Number Two

I had begun retraining and testing my cashiers, cooks, and dishwashers. I had a group of pretty smart kids, and everyone passed their food exams with flying colors.

Slowly, I eased up a bit from being a strict drill sergeant. I felt I didn't need to be this way anymore with my staff. I regained control of the restaurant, and the staff began to think I was a pretty cool dude. They finally understood that I wasn't there to make their work environment unpleasant. I just wanted the place to run efficiently while having a pleasant work experience every day.

I used my old tactics and appointed a day and night-time lead cook and a day and night-time lead cashier. This place didn't use waitresses and had no need for them. Once again, this tactic worked out. It also lightened my load of work since my district manager hadn't assigned a permanent assistant manager for me just yet.

I had no one to permanently assist me for at least two and a half weeks. Different managers volunteered to drive out from other stores to help and relieve me on my off days. Even my old buddy from the grand opening came out a couple times. Finally, my district manager filled the position and gave me a permanent assistant. In this story, we will call him Dan. Dan was a pretty strange guy, and I would find out later how sneaky he could be. Dan had already known the rundown on me. He knew about my achievements and that I was beloved in the company.

Dan didn't like me from the start. Maybe because I was much younger than he was, and I was his boss. He would override some of my decisions with certain employees, and behind the scenes, we would get into heated arguments. Once, I said something he didn't like, and he took a swing at me.

I quickly moved out of the way, and he hit the ice machine, fracturing his arm.

I never told my district manager what really happened because I wasn't a snitch. Dan almost breaking his arm was enough satisfaction for me. Looking back, I should have said something. The company would have fired him or replaced him.

The store continued making money hand over fist. My store was running like a fine-tuned machine.

My boss decided to give me a raise, but jealous Dan didn't receive one. He privately told one of my staff members that he would make sure I didn't receive another pay raise again. As I said earlier, this guy was very sneaky. He went behind my back and told my boss that I was coming in late every day, even though I had moved to Waterford, just three miles away. I was on salary, but suddenly had to punch in on a clock to prove what time I came in for work. He even went behind my back and told our boss that I wasn't training any of the new employees. I soon discovered that Dan was ratting me out and spreading false lies just to get me fired. He hated me that much.

I arrived for work one day, and my boss met me at the door. "Let's sit out here and have a talk," he said.

First off, I would like for you to hand over your store keys. You two just can't get along, and it's not a good look for your employees. So I'm afraid I'm going to have to demote you and transfer you to another store. He handed me my last check and told me to report to my new place that Saturday morning. I was devastated. How could you get a substantial raise, along with praise, and get demoted and transferred in the same month?
Twelve years and four promotions, I devoted my life to this company—only for it all to come crashing down.

Saturday morning, I decided not to go to the other place. Just like that, I was done with the company.

I left management behind and went on to learn how to cook different types of cuisines. Yes! Jealousy and hatred made me lose the job I loved for so long. My ex-boss promoted Dan, and he was now the new manager.

What a sneaky dude. But karma would come back around and have its day with Dan.

Downfall Number Three

The following story is based on what I was told by one of my former employees, who later became one of my closest friends.

After I left, Dan, the new manager, started becoming unusually friendly and a bit too familiar with some of the younger employees. One young woman in particular, a cashier, had a difficult home life and often ran away from home. One day, after she had run away again and refused to return, she found herself with nowhere else to go. After work, Dan offered her a place to stay at his home, where he and his wife lived.

Later, Dan's wife went upstairs to bed, leaving them in the living room. Allegedly, when she came back down to check on them, she found them in a compromising situation on the couch. This caused a massive argument between the couple. During the confrontation, Dan had a health scare and was taken to the hospital. Allegedly, the young woman's parents found out about the situation and filed a lawsuit against the company. Dan was let go immediately, though he didn't face legal consequences. Allegedly, his wife also filed for divorce.

Again, I wasn't there to personally witness everything, so this part of the story is based on what I was told.

The last time I saw Dan, he was working as a manager at a pizzeria. I couldn't help but wonder if the same behavior was happening again.

My thoughts on the situation? Now I realize the real reason Dan wanted me out of the way. My district manager let me down by promoting Dan instead of addressing the issues.

How could he praise my work and loyalty to the company, only to demote and transfer me in the same month? I also began to question whether race played a part in it.

Looking back, I regret not addressing my issues with Dan sooner. I had a strong relationship with the vice president of the company, and I should have reported the problems I was having. Instead, I let the situation fester, and my store was given to Dan.

I worked hard for the company, turning around struggling locations, improving food quality, and training the best kitchen and front-of-house staff. After twelve years of dedication, this was the way things ended.

So, my thoughts now? I believe both the company and Dan got what they deserved. At the time, I didn't know this was the push I needed, but I eventually moved on to better things. Though I no longer worked for the company, I continued to hire some of my old staff over the years.

And after all that happened, I was also preparing to marry my new bride. [Hearts]

The events that transpired during that time were a mixture of heartache and hope, leaving me in a place of reflection. Losing my job, something I had dedicated twelve years of my life to, was an incredibly difficult experience. The feelings of betrayal, frustration, and confusion weighed heavily on me.

I had poured my heart into the company, turning stores around and building relationships that I thought would last. To have all that stripped away in a single moment left me questioning everything.

But, as time passed, I began to see things differently.

Although I was devastated by the loss, I was also filled with a sense of relief, like a heavy burden had been lifted.

I could no longer ignore the internal struggles and the toxicity that had been building within the company. And while I was let down by my district manager and the company's handling of the situation, I couldn't ignore the silver lining that had started to emerge. In the midst of all the uncertainty and pain, I found a new chapter waiting to unfold.

That's when I realized that sometimes, what feels like the end of one path can be the beginning of another. While I may have lost my job, I gained something much more precious — my best friend. Marrying my wife was a pivotal moment that forever changed my life. It was exciting, it was new, and it was everything I had been waiting for. Amid the turbulence, I found peace, love, and a partnership that gave me strength. The journey to this point had been challenging, but in her, I found someone who truly understood me, someone who had my back no matter what.

Our marriage brought a sense of joy and fulfillment that was far beyond anything I had ever experienced. As much as I mourned the loss of my job and the years I had invested, I quickly realized that the real reward was in the love I had found. My wife became my rock, my constant, and my best friend. The excitement of beginning a new chapter with her by my side far outweighed the loss I had felt earlier.

It was a bittersweet time — part of me was still grieving the career I had built and lost, but another part of me was embracing the future. For the first time in a long while, I felt like I had a true sense of direction, and it was one I was walking with someone who would be there for me every step of the way.

Looking back, I see that those difficult moments, as painful as they were, were necessary for me to truly understand what was important.

Losing my job was not the end, but a catalyst for change.

It forced me to reevaluate my life and the relationships that mattered most. And in the end, the greatest gift I received wasn't a promotion or a paycheck — it was a love that would last a lifetime.

1992 was a challenging time, but it was also an exciting one. Seeing the expression on my mother's face as she watched me get married was one of the most unforgettable moments of my life. It was a mixture of pride, love, and joy that I will always cherish.

New Beginnings and Enduring Lessons

Chapters 33–48 encapsulate the culmination of struggles and successes, where every challenge paves the way for transformation. These stories delve deeper into the complexities of identity, love, and resilience, reflecting on the courage to let go, the value of hard-earned wisdom, and the power of starting anew. This section serves as a reminder that every ending brings the possibility of a brighter tomorrow and that, through it all, growth remains at the heart of the journey.

- **Chapter 33: King of Detroit**

  A tribute to Detroit's first Black mayor, whose summer jobs program changed lives, including the author's.
  Through hard work and resilience, young Detroiters found purpose and independence under his leadership.

- **Chapter 34: An Old Man's Story**

  A chance encounter with a former firefighter reveals a shocking confession of racial hatred and neglect during emergencies in the 1930s and '40s. This encounter shatters the author's view of heroism and underscores the deep scars of systemic racism, leaving a lasting lesson on the importance of breaking cycles of hate.

- **Chapter 35: A Different Kind of Lesson**

  A falling out with the author's mother led to staying with a woman from your past as a live-in babysitter.
  This chapter reflects on navigating trust, boundaries, and the lessons learned from complex relationships.

- **Chapter 36: Finally Finding My Own Lane**

  The author transitions from dishwasher to lead cook at the Renaissance Center, embracing hard work and new responsibilities. Despite witnessing workplace struggles, tragedies, and dangers, he finds his footing in the restaurant industry, learning resilience and leadership. This chapter underscores personal growth and the value of lifting others up when opportunity arises.

- **Chapter 37: Mama's Salmon Burgers and Croquettes**

This chapter honors the author's mother, who turned humble ingredients into comforting meals for her family. Her Saturday salmon dishes—especially her salmon croquettes—left a lasting impression.

Inspired by her creativity, the author introduced her salmon burger recipe at work, which became a customer favorite for over 25 years. This chapter celebrates family, resilience, and the legacy of making something extraordinary out of simplicity.

- **Chapter 38: An Urban Ninth Grade Love Story**

The author recounts his first high school romance with Lynne, a sweet and shy classmate. Despite their connection, jealousy and miscommunication caused their relationship to end painfully, teaching him the importance of honesty, trust, and speaking up in relationships.

- **Chapter 39: A Letter to Mother (Part Two)**

A heartfelt tribute to the author's late mother, reflecting on grief, cherished memories, and the lasting impact of her love and guidance. Through pain and gratitude, he honors her legacy and the lessons that shaped his life.

- **Chapter 40: 1984 Moving Forward, Remembering Marvin**

In 1984, the author gained independence, moving into his first apartment. On the same day, Marvin Gaye's tragic death shook him deeply. Marvin's music, a constant through his childhood, taught lessons of joy and truth.

Here, My Dear remains a powerful reminder of the beauty in vulnerability and the importance of cherishing moments before they're gone.

- **Chapter 41: The Most Beautiful Hazel Eyes**

  At Club Taboo, the author met a legendary singer with stunning hazel eyes and a heavenly voice. That brief encounter became an unforgettable moment in Detroit's vibrant dance club era. Though the club is gone, the memory lives on as a cherished highlight of the city's nightlife history.

- **Chapter 42: The Housewarming Party That Almost Ruined Me (1986)**

  Hosting a housewarming party with coworkers led to chaos when no one showed up for work the next day. An assistant manager's lie saved the author's job, teaching him hard lessons about responsibility, leadership, and second chances.

- **Chapter 43: A Kentucky Short Story**

  A family road trip to Atlanta turned sour in Kentucky, where we faced silent racism at a gas station and blatant discrimination at a restaurant.

  Despite the hurt, we protected my mother from the pain of such cruelty. This experience reminds me how far society still has to go, urging us to strive for a future of respect and unity.

- **Chapter 44: The Foster Child Next Door**

  A childhood connection resurfaced when a former foster kid became my coworker and then my girlfriend.

  While love blossomed briefly, her unresolved trauma led to toxicity and a terrifying near-death experience. She left suddenly, ending our relationship.

  This chapter taught me the value of boundaries, self-preservation, and the importance of mental health awareness.

- ## Chapter 45: A Letter to My Daughter

  The author reflects on his relationship with his daughter, born in 1987, and the mistakes that led to their estrangement. He recalls cherished moments, his struggles with child support, and how frustration drove him away. Despite his regrets, he expresses unconditional love and hopes for reconciliation, acknowledging his failures as a father.

- ## Chapter 46: Three Superstars

  The Author and two colleagues successfully train staff and earn promotions during the restaurant's grand opening. A shocking discovery about a colleague's affair and an evolving bond with a kind waitress complicate his professional and personal life, highlighting challenges in career and relationships.

- ## Chapter 47: Once Upon A Time In Sterling Heights

  The author's love for a coworker ends painfully when her racist parents force her to leave. Despite her promise to return, he never sees her again. Heartbroken, Eric reflects on how deeply racism divides and hurts, seeking a fresh start in Pontiac.

- ## Chapter 48: The Rise and Fall of Three Men

  The author recalls managing a restaurant where a kind but lenient manager was fired for misusing funds. The author replaced him but faced sabotage from an assistant manager, Dan, who ultimately caused his demotion. The author left the company after 12 years.

  Dan later lost his job and marriage due to inappropriate behavior.

  Despite the setbacks, Author found peace and joy by marrying his best friend, turning his challenges into a fresh start filled with love and hope.

A Message for the Reader

This journey has been one of reflection, growth, and revelation—not just for me, but hopefully for you as well. These stories, though rooted in my personal experiences, speak to universal truths about resilience, love, and the strength found in overcoming life's challenges.

As we approach the final chapters, I encourage you to take with you the lessons woven into these pages. Let them remind you of the importance of perseverance, the value of connection, and the hope that exists even in life's darkest moments.

Thank you for walking this path with me.

Let's see how these final stories unfold as we move forward together.

Chapter 49

There's A Stalker in the Mall

Before all the drama with me and my so-called assistant, I kept getting these strange phone calls at the restaurant. The calls came sometimes two or three hours apart—all day, every day. This went on for at least three weeks. Every time I got on the phone, whoever was on the other end would hang up. It was very annoying.

The caller always asked for the manager, so I had to answer every call. It could've been a new carryout order, a customer complaint, the main office, or my district manager checking in.

"Hey, you have a phone call," my lead cashier told me again. This time, the person whispered, **"I'm watching you."**
Click.

Two hours later, the person called right back and whispered, **"I'm sitting in the food court, and I'm watching you. I can tell you everything you're doing."**
Click.

The caller hung up again. This time, I could tell it was a female voice. Now I was starting to get nervous.

I had been promoted just two years prior, lived in Detroit, worked in Troy, but had transferred to a store in Pontiac. My boss had been fired, so now I had to step up and take over the daily operations of the restaurant. I didn't know too many people here.

I had a little baby mama drama in my life, but she wouldn't play on the phone like this. I hadn't mistreated any woman I had dated in the past. So, who could this be?

I looked out into the food court, trying to guess and spot who this person might be, but there were so many people walking around that it was impossible to figure out who my stalker was.

The Mystery Deepens

One early morning, I answered the phone in my office.

"Is this the manager?"

"Yes, it is. May I help you?"

The woman finally revealed who she was.

"I'm the person that's been playing on your phone, and I'm so sorry. You see, I have a crush on you. My name is Samantha, and I work at the bank where you make your deposits. Today, when you make your money drop, ask for me. I'm one of the bank tellers.

And please forgive me for being so rude and hanging up on you every day. You see, every time you get on the phone, I freeze and don't know what to say. So I hang up."

I accepted her apology and told the strange woman I was flattered. I also told her I would ask for her when I went to the bank. That evening, I finally got the chance to make the restaurant's money deposit and physically see who this woman was.

When it was my turn to walk up to the next available window, I asked, *"How are you today? Excuse me, but do you have a bank teller by the name of Samantha that works here?"*

"Who?" "Samantha."

"No, sir. I'm afraid we don't."

I was puzzled and pissed off at the same time. I thought this woman had lied to me.

The Chase Continues

She called back the very next day. The woman proceeded to tell me that she was very shy and that's why she had lied about working at the bank.

"I wasn't quite ready to meet you yet, but I'm for real this time. I really work at a clothing store in the mall. The next time you go on your break, come to Winkleman's Department Store and ask for me there."

Still curious, I set out to track down this mysterious woman.

On my lunch break, I walked to the other side of the mall and into the clothing store. A salesperson approached me.

"Can I help you?"

"Are you Samantha?" I politely asked.

"No, sir, I'm not."

"Do you have a person by that name who works here?"

"No, sir, we don't. But I can help you look for something if you'd like."

At this point, I was very disappointed that this unknown person had lied to me for a second time. I really didn't have the time for these childish games, and the next time she called, I planned to have a few choice words ready for her. I thanked the salesperson and stormed out of the clothing store. A week went by, and all the strange phone calls stopped. I was no longer chasing this elusive mall stalker.

One day, I had a JCPenney payment due, and since I could pay it right around the corner in the mall, I decided to stop by. Up the escalator I went. I noticed a few nice men's sweaters before reaching customer service when, all of a sudden, I heard a lot of giggling.

Two young ladies were looking at me and laughing hysterically. "May I ask, what's so funny?"
"Oh, nothing. This girl right here just told me a funny joke."

I paid my bill and made my way back toward the escalator. Right before stepping on, I quickly turned around to see what the two ladies were doing. They were laughing even harder.

They must know something I don't, I thought. *Or one of them is the actual stalker.*

The next afternoon, I was sitting in my office when my cashier stepped in to tell me that someone up front wanted to talk to me.

"Hi, may I help you?" I asked the young girl. "My sister would like to meet you."

"Where is she?"

The young girl explained that her sister was very shy and that she had to go get her. Ten minutes later, the two came back.

"Here she is!" the young girl yelled.

It was one of the women who had been laughing at me when I paid my bill. A 4-foot-11 cutie pie. Suddenly, I felt pretty excited, and we finally got the chance to talk a bit.

"So, what's your name?"

She laughed and told me her real name this time.

"I'm Eric, but away from work, everyone calls me Ezee."

"Oh, you're easy with the ladies, huh?"

"No! It's just my nickname. I adopted it back in high school."

As we talked, I couldn't believe how attractive this woman was. I wanted to find out immediately if she was a good kisser.

One kiss could tell me a lot about her.

She asked, "Do you live in Pontiac?" "No, I'm in Detroit."

"Maybe one day soon, you could come home with me," I said.

"I'll have to get to know you first. Plus, you'll have to meet my dad."

I told her I understood. I wanted to kiss this woman really, really bad, so I came up with a game of my own. Let's see how shy she really is. My carryout line was getting pretty busy.

"You can sit in my office if you like while I help my staff get these orders out," I said. She agreed. I invited her into a back corridor that led to all the restaurants and retail stores.

Right before we got to my door, I gently turned her toward me, closed my eyes, and stuck my whole tongue in her mouth.
In complete shock, she ran like a bat out of hell.
I thought I'd never see her again, but she came back an hour later.

And that, my friends, is how I met my wife. *[Hearts]*

What began as a series of strange phone calls and a whirlwind of playful curiosity ended up changing my life forever. That bold moment in the corridor—a mix of impulsiveness, humor, and raw attraction—sparked something neither of us could have anticipated. At the time, I couldn't have imagined that the shy yet captivating woman standing before me would one day become my rock, my best friend, and the love of my life. But as fate would have it, that daring kiss and her unexpected return marked the start of a love story I'll treasure forever. The journey to get to this point wasn't always straightforward, but sometimes, the best things in life are the ones that come when you least expect them.

1992

Chapter 50

Cancer

From personal experience, cancer is such a strange and cruel disease. It doesn't just attack your physical body—it also works against your mind and spirit. I now know what people go through when they've been diagnosed with this disease. The sleepless nights, the relentless worry, and the haunting words "what if" that echo endlessly in your mind.

What if cancer takes me out—will my family be okay?
What if the operation or radiation doesn't work—how much time do I have left?
What if I had prayed more, eaten healthier, or exercised regularly —would I be in this position?

These thoughts are like shadows that never leave your side. You find yourself reflecting on family and friends who left this life too soon, entertainers and public figures who succumbed to the disease, and the staggering reality of how long this battle against cancer has been fought—with no definitive cure in sight.

You think about everything you'd leave behind: family, friends, milestones yet to come, and your legacy. The thought of losing all of it weighs on you heavily. You try to put on a brave face around others, but in private, the sadness often consumes you. You cry more than you ever thought you could, and you pray harder than you ever have before. The emotional toll is relentless, and the fear of the unknown keeps you up at night.

In the days leading up to my surgery, I felt a desperate need to finish things—projects around the house, chores that couldn't wait, and lingering tasks I wanted to cross off my list. I worked tirelessly to make sure everything was in order.
I even had to clean up after a broken underground pipe that flooded half of my basement, destroying everything in its path.

With the help of my amazing neighbor, I cleaned, rebuilt, painted, and replaced everything. I gave myself a three-week deadline, and with God's grace and support from those around me, I got it done.

But no matter how much I accomplished, the worry never left me. It loomed in the back of my mind, robbing me of sleep and peace. Cancer doesn't just challenge you physically—it challenges your will to keep going. It isolates you, leaving you feeling alone in a battle you never asked to fight. At times, I felt like I needed a psychiatrist just to cope with the mental strain.

My diagnosis was prostate cancer, and I had three options to remove it: freeze the cancer cells, undergo radiation, or have it surgically removed. I chose surgery. They removed my entire prostate, and the experience was more painful than I could have imagined. Six incisions across my abdomen, a Foley catheter to carry, and sleepless nights lying on my back were just the start. The pain and discomfort were unrelenting, and many nights, I sat in the dark and cried, wondering, *Why me?*

One particularly difficult night, I found myself thinking about my mother and her battle with cancer. As a child, I had watched her go through unbearable pain and depression. Surgeries in the 1970s were nothing like they are today, and I could see how much she suffered. She would slowly walk around in her housecoat, barely speaking to anyone. I knew she felt alone, and it broke my heart.

But one day, she made a decision. She refused to let the disease define her. She chose to fight back. She chose strength and endurance. She chose to hold on to life for her children. With God's helping hand, she beat cancer—and it never came back.

That memory gave me strength. I stopped crying, sat up in my chair, and thought, *If my mother could battle and overcome cancer, then so can I.*

Though she's been gone for years, I still rely on her spiritually.

Her courage, charisma, and unwavering strength continue to inspire me.

I now understand the physical and emotional toll that cancer takes on a person. The pain, the endless doctor's visits, the surgeries, and the recovery process—it's all-consuming. Wearing adult diapers and dealing with skin rashes, struggling to stand in the shower, and needing constant assistance—it humbles you in ways you can't imagine.

But cancer also changes you. It forces you to reevaluate your priorities and your perspective on life. It teaches you to let go of grudges, to forgive, and to cherish the moments you have. It reminds you of the importance of love, kindness, and being present for those who matter most.

My mother exemplified all of these lessons. She became a beacon of hope and love in our community, cherished by everyone who knew her. She fought back and won, choosing to live and be there for her children. She was my Super Shero—the strongest woman I've ever known.

Even now, I draw on her strength and courage to face my own challenges. I remind myself that if she could overcome the odds, so can I. I strive to be an example for others, to lead with resilience and hope, and to be someone else's Super Hero in their time of need.

What I've learned through this journey is that we are only given one life, and it's up to us to make the most of it. Don't take it for granted. Live fully, love deeply, and create memories that will outlive you. My mother understood that—and now, so do I. Life is precious, and every moment is a gift. Choose to live it today.

As I slowly began to recover, regaining my physical strength and emotional balance, I couldn't help but view life through a new lens. Facing cancer had not only tested my resolve but also forced me to redefine what truly mattered—family, love, resilience, and the memories we create. The pain I endured became a teacher, reminding me that every moment is a gift, and every challenge is an opportunity to rise stronger.

Though my scars—both physical and emotional—remain, they now serve as a testament to my fight and my faith. They remind me of my mother's strength and the courage it took for her to choose life. Her example fueled my determination to be a beacon of hope for others, just as she had been for me.

But as I stepped back into the rhythm of daily life, I realized that the battles we face don't always come with warning signs. Some challenges appear suddenly, testing our strength in unexpected ways. Little did I know, the lessons cancer taught me would soon prepare me for the twists and turns still waiting ahead.

Chapter 51

The Difference Between Then and Now

Unstructured Outdoor Play:
Man! Through all the struggles and hard times, I still had an awesome childhood, and I wouldn't trade it for the world. My past has made me who I am today, and I have never forgotten where I came from. But I think it's sad how drastically times have changed. I also understand that nothing can ever stay the same.

I truly believe that technology and greed have cheated our children out of creativity and imagination by constantly bombarding them with instant gratification rather than encouraging them to explore the vast depths of their own minds. The answers to life's challenges have become too easy.

As a child, we didn't have all the things available today, but we figured out how to have fun and enjoy each other's company. Back then, kids spent hours outside playing games like hopscotch, center tag, or flag football. Streets and parks were alive with activity, and there was a sense of freedom to explore without constant adult supervision.

We played childhood games that had been passed down for generations. Let me ask you something—when was the last time you saw children playing with jacks, four square, or hide and seek? Instead, you see kids glued to their cell phones, sitting on the couch all day playing computer games or spending hours online playing Fortnite.

Imagination and Simplicity:

With fewer toys and no electronic distractions, imagination played a big role in our childhoods. A simple cardboard box could become a fort, a spaceship, or anything our minds could create. Homemade activities were the norm. Now, ask a kid today to build something out of a box and watch their reaction.

Community Connections:

Neighborhoods used to be tight-knit. Parents knew each other, and it wasn't unusual for all the kids on the block to gather and play. The sense of communal support and safety has diminished over the years.

The phrase, "It takes a village," protected children and kept us all out of trouble back in the day. Besides your own mother, you had other mothers in the community looking out for your well-being.

Family Time:

Mealtime was often a family event, free of distractions. Conversations at the dinner table were a time to bond and share. Today, many kids don't have the time—or interest—to sit at a dinner table and talk about their day.

Hard Work:

So much has changed. When we were kids, we didn't receive allowances, but we couldn't wait to go out and make our own money by running errands, cutting grass, raking leaves, or shoveling snow from sidewalks and driveways. That was our thing to do every year.

Nowadays, it's rare to see kids going door to door, asking if anyone needs their yard cleaned. Then again, these are dangerous times. You don't see children doing that anymore because parents fear for their safety. When we were kids, we didn't have to worry about someone snatching us up because we were smart enough to hang in groups.

A Safer Time:

Speaking of dangerous times, I remember how, in the summer, my dad used to open all the windows and doors to let in the cool night breeze. We never had to worry about someone breaking into our home while we were asleep.

If you live in an urban community today, you wouldn't dare trust doing that.

Halloween:

Halloween is so different for children now. Most kids group together in cars to go house to house, collecting as much candy as they can in a two-hour span—or they don't go trick-or-treating at all. Some kids attend Halloween parties or visit stores just to get their candy.

When I was a kid, we used to head out at 8 p.m. with a pillowcase, fill it to the brim with candy, come home to empty our bags, and then go out again until midnight. It was such a thrill!
Unfortunately, it's way too dangerous for kids to do that now. Times have changed so much. I just wish today's kids could experience the fun and freedom we had back in the day.

What Kids Watch:

Television today is a far cry from what we grew up with. Kids can now see sexual acts on almost every channel, and the cursing in cartoons is just ridiculous. Kids don't even have to talk to their parents about the birds and the bees anymore—they can just watch a TV show. When I was a kid, television and radio were restricted from that kind of content. There were limits to what you could hear or see— unless you were me. (laughing)

What Kids Listen To:

Music has changed drastically, too. When I was growing up, songs were about togetherness, companionship, makeups and breakups, and the art of making love. Songs celebrated the beauty of a woman and how to love and respect her. Today, the music is full of disrespect and vulgar language.

Rap lyrics are saturated with words like "bitch" and "whore," and the "N-word" is thrown around so loosely. Back in the day, we didn't hear that in music. Our songs had fun beats, awesome lyrics, and meaningful slow jams. Back then, the fellas were nervous to ask a girl to dance. If she said yes, it was a win, and you'd feel brave enough to ask her again. But if she said no, it was embarrassing, and your friends would laugh at you.

Today, some guys lean on walls while girls dance alone or with each other.

In our day, we danced with purpose, often mimicking strippers or male dancers to entice the ladies sensually and sexually. Girls would take these opportunities to ask you for another dance, and if you were lucky, you could exchange phone numbers by the end of the night.

Today, the dance phenomenon is twerking, where young women use their bodies to entice men. Thanks to social media, this dance has become popular for all the wrong reasons. As a longtime people-watcher, it's amusing to see different generations dancing in the same space. The older crowd still loves to slow dance, while the younger generation often stays "too cool," holding up walls. It's funny watching young ladies dancing alone or with each other —it just doesn't look the same.

Patience and Problem-Solving:

When we were kids, we learned patience through delayed gratification, whether it was waiting for Saturday morning cartoons or figuring out how to fix a broken toy.

Hands-On Activities:

We learned practical skills by helping our parents or grandparents with cooking, gardening, or repairing things around the house. In my family's case, it was helping my grandmother attend to her farm. These activities built resourcefulness and a sense of accomplishment.

Physical Activity:

Without video games or endless TV, we were more physically active by default. Walking to school, riding our bikes everywhere, and playing sports were part of our daily lives.

Discipline in the '60s, '70s, and '80s

The Infamous Butt Whippings

Physical punishment was widely accepted and considered an effective way to enforce discipline. Belts, switches, and extension cords were commonly used, especially in communities where parents believed in the saying, *"Spare the rod, spoil the child."*

Discipline back then was immediate and directly tied to the perceived wrongdoing. And it wasn't just your parents who could whip you—other adults who knew your parents, as well as teachers, had full authority to discipline you if you stepped out of line.

Today, physical punishment is seen as harmful by many psychologists, and laws prohibit this form of discipline outright. Discipline has shifted toward non-physical methods like time-outs, loss of privileges, and positive reinforcement. The emphasis now is on understanding and fostering open communication.

But looking back, I have to admit—my dad used to whip my ass. (laughing) My dad was physically fit and very strong. He would hold us in the air by one leg and beat the breaks off of us! And look at me now—I didn't turn out so bad.

Those butt-whipping experiences shaped me in a positive way. Crime was lower back then, and children had more respect for authority. Look at the crime rate now. Some argue that the absence of corporal punishment has led to increased defiance among today's youth. Others counter that non-violent discipline creates emotionally healthier and more empathetic adults. Either way, times have certainly changed.

The Changes Over the Years

Young teens today are missing out on so much fun. We went beyond sleepovers and pajama parties—house parties, yard parties, and basement parties were the real thing back in the day!

Word would spread that someone was having a party on their block, and you and your friends would show up—even if you didn't know the homeowners. The more people that showed up, the more exciting the party became. We didn't have social media back then, so we walked from the projects into urban neighborhoods in search of yard parties.

We partied until midnight—that's when most gatherings would end. But today, you can't just walk into a party uninvited. Two things might happen: either you'd get jumped by a bunch of hoodlums, or someone might take a few shots at you. The distrust and uncertainty among people today is understandable, but it's also sad.

These fun times are far behind us. If memory serves me right, the era of basement parties started dying out in the early '90s. It just became too dangerous to invite strangers into your home. Even block parties have become risky—something always seems to go wrong.

Not in a million years did I think I would see so many schools boarded up or demolished. My preschool, **Little Angell**, no longer exists. An empty lot stands where my elementary school, **Big Angell**, used to be. My middle school, **Warren G. Harding**, is gone. And my high school, **Redford High**, has been replaced by a Meijer superstore. It's heartbreaking to know that all I have left are the memories of these schools that played such a big part in my life.

The Price of Everything & The Cost of Greed

Greed has taken over, and the price of everything has skyrocketed. Kids today missed out on the simple joys of affordable treats— 15- cent Faygo pops, 25-cent bags of chips, and candy bars for as little as 10 to 25 cents.

I remember my favorite thing to eat was **Banquet pot pies and white rice**. In 1974, you could buy **five** pot pies for a dollar.

Today, that same dollar will only get you **one** pot pie, and you'll need some change on top of that. In 1984, I got my first car, and gas was around **$1.25 per gallon**. My friends and I could ride around all day without worrying about fuel costs. My mother could go to the grocery store and bring home **five bags of food for $50**. Today, those same **five bags would cost close to $200**.

Yes, greed has taken over. And you know what they say— *"Money is the root of all evil."*

This is what kids are left with today—the lack of creative things to do and the high cost of everything. The world has changed in ways we never could have imagined, and I can't help but wonder if we've lost more than we've gained.

The Lost Treasures of Detroit's Past

And are there any dollar movie theaters around anymore?
Ah! Detroit's Norwest and the Mercury Theater—so many great memories in these two theaters. Back then, you could catch a movie for a dollar, enjoy some snacks, and still have money left in your pocket. Today, the theaters we have are built in malls, and it costs **$20** just to see a movie flick.

At one time, Detroit had its own **23-acre amusement park, Edgewater Park**, located on Seven Mile and Berg Road near Grand River Avenue. That park was a haven for kids, filled with thrilling rides, games, and unforgettable summers.

There was also the **indoor amusement park at the old Cobo Hall** downtown—another exciting spot that brought joy to so many children. And let's not forget the iconic **boat rides to Bob-lo Island**, a historic amusement park that was a dream destination for Detroit families.

Kids today will never experience these incredible places. They've missed out on a lot of the fun and magic that made childhood so special back then.

It's too bad and oh so sad.

Transition: A Childhood Filled with Joy

Looking back, I realize just how amazing my childhood truly was. I was blessed to have a family that made sure I experienced every ounce of fun life had to offer. My aunts—on both sides of the family—played a huge role in that. They made sure I had every opportunity to enjoy myself, explore new things, and take part in experiences that would later become some of my most cherished memories.

Whether it was a trip to an amusement park, a day at the movies, or a simple adventure around the neighborhood, they made sure that I never missed out on anything that had to do with fun. Their love and dedication gave me a childhood filled with excitement, laughter, and unforgettable moments—memories that I still hold dear to this day.

I truly understand that every generation had its own time for fun, and each era brought something special to those who lived through it. But I can confidently say that growing up in the '80s was something truly amazing. The experiences, the freedom, and the sense of togetherness we had during that time were unmatched. It was a generation built on creativity, adventure, and pure enjoyment of life—before technology and modern conveniences began to change the way kids experience fun.

I can't help but feel for the kids today, who may never know the kind of childhood I was lucky enough to have. They'll never know the thrill of running wild in a neighborhood where everyone knew each other, where summer nights were spent playing tag under the streetlights, and where weekends were filled with simple joys— climbing trees, racing bikes, or just gathering with friends for a game of *Go/Stop or Center Tag.*

So many of the experiences that shaped my childhood are disappearing. The family outings to dollar movie theaters, the excitement of amusement parks like Edgewater and Bob-Lo Island, and even the fun of something as simple as drinking a 15-cent Faygo and grabbing a bag of 25-cent chips on the way to the playground—all of it is gone or drastically changed.

I think about how my aunts went out of their way to ensure I had the best childhood possible, filling my world with joy, discovery, and adventure. I only wish today's children had those same opportunities—to be carefree, to explore without fear, and to experience the world the way we once did. But sadly, times have changed, and the childhood I knew is now just a memory of a different era.

I truly thank the ones who were deeply involved in my life.

Chapter 52

An Extraordinary Woman / My Mother

My mother was an extraordinary woman. She lived her whole life deaf and mute, facing challenges that would have seemed insurmountable to many, but she never let her disabilities define her. Despite our family being very poor, she made sure that we never went without the essentials. Each morning, no matter how tight things were, we were fed and dressed for school, ready to face the world because of her tireless efforts.

She was a pillar of love and kindness in our community, never making enemies and earning the admiration of everyone who knew her. Her warm smile and generous heart left a lasting impression on all who crossed her path. The holidays were especially meaningful to her. She cherished those moments when the whole family came together, laughing, sharing stories, and filling the house with love. She also loved being updated on what was going on in everyone else's life during our holiday times together. Those memories are treasures I hold dear.

In her later years, Mother was finally able to break free from taking care of all of us and just enjoy a calm and peaceful life. She was able to travel with my brother and sisters, a dream she never imagined would be possible. I still remember our first plane ride together. She was so scared, gripping my hand tightly for the entire three-hour journey to Atlanta. I didn't let go, knowing how much courage it took for her to step into the unknown. That moment was just one example of her incredible strength and resilience.

Raising five children, she did the best she could with what little she had. Her love, determination, and sacrifices built a foundation for us that continues to support us today. My mother's life is a testament to the power of perseverance and unconditional love.

I love and miss her dearly.

Her legacy lives on in every lesson she taught her kids and in the hearts of everyone who was fortunate enough to know her.

Eleven years ago, my mother received her wings and left this world, but her presence has never truly left me. Before she departed, she instilled a part of herself in each of her children, like pieces of a puzzle that fit her enduring legacy. She didn't just raise us; she shaped us, each in her own way, with lessons that were as practical as they were profound.

One of the greatest lessons she taught me was to mind my own business and stay in my own lane. Watching her react to certain people seemed so simple, but as I've grown older, I've realized just how much sense it made. Life is full of distractions, gossip, and unnecessary drama, and if you let yourself get caught up in things that don't concern you, you lose focus on what really matters. The memory of her actions has guided me through countless situations, reminding me to keep my priorities straight and my energy directed toward my own goals and responsibilities.

It wasn't just her reactions toward others that taught us.

My mother led by example, navigating her hard life with quiet dignity despite the challenges she faced as a deaf-mute woman. She didn't let negativity derail her. Instead, she focused on her well-being and family, living her truth without apology or complaint.

I can clearly see her lessons reflected in my siblings as well. Each of us carries a part of her spirit. Whether it's the kindness she showed to others, her ability to stretch a little into a lot, or her unwavering love for family, her values live on in all of us.

I'll give you an example.

Last year, a pipe broke under my house, flooding my entire basement. My brother didn't hesitate to help. He gave me the money and showed me exactly what to do to get my floor redone. He did it purely out of the kindness of his heart.

He didn't have to do it, but that was the love and spirit of our mother in him.

She privately and secretly did so much for people—acts of kindness even my siblings never knew about. I'm still at a loss for words, but I'm so grateful my brother did that for me.

Even though my mother is no longer physically here, I still feel her guidance every day. When I face challenges or difficult decisions, I often ask myself, **"What would my mother do?"** In those moments, I see her in my mind, communicating through sign language, telling me to stay focused, to rise above, and to always do my best.

Losing her was one of the hardest moments of my life, but I take great comfort in knowing that she left us with everything we need to carry forward her legacy.

I am also deeply grateful to God for my sister, who stayed behind with our mom and ensured that her later years were peaceful and full of love. My sister's devotion and care gave our mother the comfort and dignity she deserved after a life of sacrifice and hardship. Knowing that our mother was surrounded by such love in her final years brings me immense peace.

My mother was such a wonderful person, and both her family and in-laws truly showed her so much love. She was cherished not just by her children but by everyone who had the privilege of knowing her. That love was a testament to the kind of person she was— humble, generous, and full of grace.

She created a home that radiated warmth, and her presence brought people together in a way that made everyone feel welcome and valued.

I wrote this chapter to show who my mother really was—a woman of quiet strength, boundless love, and unwavering dedication to her family. She may not have been able to hear or speak, but her actions and her heart spoke louder than words ever could.

She was a light in the lives of everyone who knew her, a source of wisdom and comfort, and a living example of what it means to love unconditionally. My mother was more than just extraordinary—she was our foundation, our teacher, and our greatest blessing.

This chapter is my way of honoring her life, capturing the essence of who she was, and sharing her story with the world. Her love continues to guide me, and I hope her story inspires others to see the **beauty in kindness, the strength in sacrifice, and the power of a mother's love. [Hearts]**

I truly miss you, Ma.

Throughout my life, I have been blessed to cross paths with many incredible people—mentors, friends, and loved ones who have shaped me into the person I am today. But no one, not a single soul, has had a greater impact on my life than my mother.

She was more than just a parent—she was the heart of our family, a wellspring of unconditional love and wisdom.

Her presence, though soft-spoken, commanded deep respect and admiration, not just from us but from everyone who had the privilege of knowing her.

The lessons she instilled in me are etched deeply in my soul. They were taught not through words but through the quiet power of her actions—her strength in the face of adversity, her kindness even when times were tough, and her unwavering devotion to her children. These lessons are my guiding light, shaping how I face challenges and how I approach life's uncertainties.

Now, as I reflect on her remarkable journey, I want to take a moment to honor the woman who gave me life, who sacrificed so much without hesitation, and whose strength continues to inspire me to this day. Her story is not just mine to tell—it's a story of love, resilience, and the boundless power of a mother's legacy.

Chapter 53

Inspirations and Thank You Page

I was born and raised in what I personally like to call the great middle era—beginning with the hatred of the 1960s, transitioning into the feeling-out period of the 1970s, and culminating in the best of times in the 1980s.

I would like to thank the individuals, groups, places, events, treasures, and memories that inspired me as a child in some way, shape, or form. Some of these names will forever remind me of my childhood. Others have served as powerful reminders to do better, become a better person, and contribute positively to this Earth.

There are so many things and people in my life I need to be grateful for. I thank you all for being a part of my childhood, teen years, and young adult journey.

First and foremost, I would like to thank the God within me, my mom and dad, my brother and sisters, my grandparents, my uncles and aunts, my amazing cousins, my Smith Homes Projects family, my best friends and brothers, and my project mothers and mentors.

I would also like to express my gratitude to my preschool and elementary schools, Little Angell and Big Angell, as well as my middle and high schools, Warren G. Harding and Redford High (Go Huskies!). Special thanks go to the Brightmoor Community Center, Crowell Recreation Center and boxing team, and the communities of The Jefferies, Brewsters, and the Herman Gardens Projects.

To my best friend and brother on Dumbarton Street, and to The House of Prayers, I am forever grateful. I also extend my appreciation to all my art instructors, music teachers, and the real history teachers who didn't shy away from teaching the truth.

As strange as it may sound, I want to thank the racists for showing me what racism looks like and teaching me how to detect and confront it. To my haters—thank you as well.

I will never change who I am, no matter how much the world tries to dictate otherwise. I am a modern day king with great gifts and personal royalties. I am a special human being. So deal with it.

I also want to acknowledge Dr. Martin Luther and Coretta Scott King, Malcolm X and Betty Shabazz, Elijah Muhammad, Muhammad Ali, Medgar Evers, Huey P. Newton, Angela Davis, Rosa Parks, Maya Angelou, John Lewis, Jesse Owens, Fannie Lou Hamer, Alex Haley, Nelson Mandela, Mahatma Gandhi, Andrew Young, James Baldwin, Stokely Carmichael, John F. Kennedy, Robert F. Kennedy, Thurgood Marshall, Ruby Bridges, Julian Bond, and Billie Holiday (Strange Fruit).

Thank you for your contributions, Harry T. Moore and his wife Harriette Moore, the first civil rights activists to be assassinated. Thanks for the fight in social justice. I also want to recognize James Weldon Johnson, who wrote our Black national anthem, and the great Black author Toni Morrison. Most of all, I thank myself for celebrating Black Excellence every day, not just during the shortest month of the year.

The brain is a tremendous gift. A song, a phrase, a television scene —anything can trigger memories and transport you back in time, whether to a moment of regret or to a cherished experience.

I can still remember my dad getting frustrated with me when I struggled to tie my shoes as a little boy. I recall my parents sitting me down on newspapers so I could learn how to eat on my own.

I can even remember the mood in our home when Dr. King was assassinated. My parents were shocked and devastated—it was probably the first time I ever saw my mother cry. My father had to explain to her what had just happened.

My uncle was also with us that night. I still remember his complete silence as the news bulletin interrupted our program on our black- and-white television, sitting on a four-wheel cart.

I am a firm believer that memory is a powerful gift, and I thank God for blessing me with it.

As a kid, I also used to think that Coretta Scott King was the most beautiful woman in the world. She moved on this earth with grace, compassion, and strength. To me, she embodied royalty. Watching her on television was mesmerizing. Thank you for your contributions to the fight. You are never forgotten.

I would like to thank Princess Diana. You were an incredible human being. The world needed someone like you.

Detroit's Guardian Angel

During my lifetime, I have read many books and watched many documentaries on the most influential women of the 19th, 20th, and 21st centuries. Women like Coretta Scott King, Mary McLeod Bethune, Josephine Baker, Maya Angelou, Ida B. Wells, Mother Teresa, Shirley Chisholm, Ruth Bader Ginsburg, Sojourner Truth, Diahann Carroll, Hattie McDaniel, Harriet Tubman, Jacqueline Kennedy Onassis, Angela Davis, Rosa Parks, Fannie Lou Hamer, Toni Morrison, Wilma Rudolph, Susan Rice, Phillis Wheatley, Michelle Obama, Princess Diana, and my favorite woman right now, Senator *Alexandria Ocasio-Cortez* and so many others.

But I would like to personally thank a person who had a direct connection to me and my family's life. *Mother Waddles* was the most influential person I ever met during my childhood years on Dumbarton Street. She was once called the **Guardian Angel of the Ghetto**, a divine Detroit legend. This woman was absolutely extraordinary with a heart of gold. Whether my family remembers or not, we were linked to this amazing woman's helping hand.

She is the main reason why I am so giving and caring toward people who are less fortunate—because I remember when **we** were the less fortunate and what that felt like. I remember all too well when my own family relied on the help of this great woman.

Twice a week, we would walk up Dumbarton Street to her food

bank on Grand River Avenue and receive bread, cakes, pies, cookies, canned goods, frozen meats, and even clothes.

She also provided hot meals for forty cents, and if we didn't have the change, she would let us eat for free because she never wanted us kids to go back home hungry.

These memories have kept me humble throughout my life.

I would like to thank The Scene Dance Show, Soul Train, James Brown, The Jackson 5, the group Switch, Depeche Mode, Kraftwerk, Cybotron, DeBarge, Evelyn "Champagne" King, The mighty, mighty O'Jays, The Ohio Players, Parliament-Funkadelic, Hall & Oates, The Gap Band, the beautiful Stevie Nicks and Fleetwood Mac, and Detroit's own Dramatics and The Bee Gees.

I would also like to thank Joe, The Mighty Clouds of Joy, Mahalia Jackson, Joe Tex, The Staple Singers, the iconic Barry White, Isaac Hayes, Martha "Jean" The Queen, Prince and The Revolution, Earth, Wind & Fire, Freddie Jackson, Joe Simon, Lou Rawls, and Lenny Williams. Special thanks to radio stations W.C.H.B, W.D.R.Q, and W.J.Z.Z., as well as Detroit's first Black- owned radio station, W.G.P.R. Thanks for the memories.

I once had this strange crush on Stevie Nicks of the group Fleetwood Mac. I even gave her a personal nickname: The Beautiful Witch. Her voice and the lyrics of her songs were so mesmerizing. Watching her performances on television made me pay close attention to the words of her music. Other Black students in high school thought I was weird for singing her songs out loud, but I didn't care.

I thought I was in love with this mysterious, musical artist. My peers thought I was crazy, but they never understood how extremely talented and amazing she was. Thanks for the memories, Stevie.

I thank my wife, my ex-wife, and my kids, my high school sweetheart, and the foster children next door to my grandmother.

I want to thank all the people who were very close to me but are no longer here. Rest in peace. Thanks to all my old coworkers and friends from the past.

I would also like to thank the old Hudson building downtown, Sibley's Shoe Store, Cunningham Drug Store, S.S. Kresge, Grandland Shopping Center, Sonny's Restaurant, Northland Shopping Mall, Fairlane Shopping Mall, Dave's Store, D&C Supermarket, Michael and Richards Liquor Store, The Side Store, The Norwest Theater, The Mercury Theater, The Palms Theater, The Bel-Air and The Ford-Wyoming Drive-In, The Fox Theater, The Broadway Lounge, The Diamond Lounge, The Diamond Shaft, Babe's After Hours Club, The Underground, The Broadway Lounge, The Climax 2 and later The Dancery, the short-lived Cotton Club, U.B.Q., The River Rock, The City Club, Club Taboo, Studio 54, The Brass Key Lounge, The Roostertail, Sinbad's Restaurant, Belle Isle Island, Boblo Island, McShane Park, Chene Park, Stopel Park, The Eastern Market, and River Rouge Park.

Thanks for the memories.

Detroit's Broadway Lounge on Schaefer Road—this was the pickup spot back in the day. Go in, have a few drinks, dance, pick up one-night stands, or turn girls you just met into girlfriends. This place was highly talked about in my first book. I would like to thank this place for the fun memories. Man! Was I ghetto fabulous back in the day.

I would like to thank these individuals from my memories: Author Donald Goines, Bruce Lee, Dr. J, Reggie Lewis, Darryl Dawkins, Spud Webb, Dominique Wilkins, Muggsy Bogues, Ralph Sampson, Hakeem Olajuwon, Penny Hardaway, Mr. Basketball from Southwestern High and Michigan University sensation Antoine Joubert, and Larry Johnson "Grandmama."

Special thanks to Mayor Coleman A. Young. Southwest Detroit,

Whittaker, Michigan, Ypsilanti, Willow Run, Belleville, Michigan, Olympia Stadium—a special thanks to food stamps. Thanks for government cheese, government peanut butter,

The Salvation Army, The Goodwill, Detroit summer jobs, The Detroit Art Institute.

Special thanks to film star Jane Kennedy, Thelma from Good Times, The Wild, Wild West, Lost In Space, Star Trek, Perry Mason (My Dad's favorite TV show), Laugh-In, The Sonny and Cher Show, the TV show Kung Fu, The Flip Wilson Show, The Benny Hill Show, The Carol Burnett Show, Sanford and Son, the first Black female television show, Julia. The American Bandstand, Smothers Brothers, The Richard Pryor show, Jackie "Moms" Mabley, Billy Dee Williams, Soupy Sales, The Jeffersons, The Tom Jones Show, The Wild, Wild West, Fat Albert, Kimba the White Lion, Mighty Mouse, Speed Racer, and the show Fame. The Little Rascals, Sir Graves Ghastly, Bill Kennedy at the Movies, New York Undercover, The Three Stooges (all six of them), and Roller Derby (The Detroit Thunderbirds). The Ed Sullivan Show, The Pearl Bailey Show, and The Beverly Hillbillies. Thanks for the memories.

A funny childhood story just occurred to me. One summer afternoon, my friends and I rode our bikes to the McDonald's next to Grandland Shopping Center on Grand River. We went inside, placed our orders, and then decided to eat outside next to our parked bikes.

One of my friends, the only one who ordered fries, was happily munching away when he noticed a few birds circling nearby. At first, he ignored them, but soon they became bolder, swooping in closer with every bite he took.

In an effort to protect his fries, he started waving his hands, shooing them away. The birds weren't having it.

One particularly bold bird must have taken offense because, out of nowhere, it dropped a perfectly aimed surprise right into his bag of hot fries. The look on his face was priceless—disgusted, frustrated, and defeated all at once.

We all burst out laughing while he stood there, staring at his ruined fries. If there was ever a lesson to be learned, it was this: Sometimes, it's better to just share your McDonald's fries before nature takes matters into its own hands! (laughing)

Thank you Phyllis Hyman, Phoebe Snow, Brenda Russell, Roberta Flack, Bobby "Blue" Bland, Nick Ashford and Valerie Simpson, Patti Austin, Angela Bofill, Dionne Warwick, Otis Redding, Al Wilson, Lenny Williams, Oran "Juice" Jones, Natalie Cole (Hazel Eyes), Deniece Williams, Nancy Wilson, the incredible David Ruffin, Was (Not Was), Minnie Riperton, Bob Marley, Roger Troutman and Zapp.

Thank you Stoepel Park, Herman Gardens Projects, The Jefferies Projects. Thank you Southwest Detroit, Northwest Detroit, and East Detroit. I would like to thank my favorite deejays: Steve "Silk" Hurley, Deejay Jeff Mills, and Frankie Knuckles. WJZZ's Rosetta Hines, Deejay Assault, Deejay of The Climax 2 Donafay Collins, and Kid Capri. Thanks to Mason for continuously telling us musical stories of the past. Thanks to Electrifying Mojo and the Midnight Funk Association, the making of cassette tapes, Smith Homes Center lunches, chopper bikes, boom boxes, Walkmans, jingle boots, and Sibley's Shoes.

I would like to thank my dad for his old station wagon with the side wood panels. I would like to thank all my mother's best friends, my dad's best friend with the 1967 candy apple red convertible Ford Galaxy 500. Man, I always wanted one of those. Redford High's school bus tickets, Redford school dances, Harding's talent shows, Mr. London & Mrs. Archie—these teachers inspired me to be healthy and athletic.

Thank you, Mrs. Seltzer, my art teacher. Love you forever. I also miss the talks we used to have. I hope California was good to you.

That Blue Goose paddle with the holes in the middle of it, the haunted houses in the country—the city haunted houses don't have anything on these. At least, they didn't when I was a kid. I would like to thank my puppies Chico and Rico.

My rabbit, which my aunt gave me. She also gave us a parakeet, but I don't think my siblings remember that (laughing). I thank the willow trees on my grandmother's farm. I thank my other grandmother for making her world-famous strawberry cakes and peach cobblers. The motorcycle rides with my auntie. I thank my other aunt for her music collection. I thank the baseball games on my grandmother's farm.

I would like to thank the family that lived directly across the street from us. We had so many things in common. I absolutely loved your mom. I would like to thank my next-door neighbors on Crescent Drive. You were the best neighbors anyone could have. Your families are always in my memories.

Thank you, Ernie Barnes, for your brilliant paintings and contributions to the world of art. (The Sugar Shack Painting). Thanks, Hitman Thomas Hearns. You made us Detroiters very proud. Thanks to whoever invented these old candies: Now and Later candy, Boston Baked Beans, Mary Janes & Squirrels. I thank God I had a chance to see 10-cent bags of chips and 25-cent Faygo pops. Thanks for the Towne Club pops, Auntie. (I was like 8 years old.) When gas was only 87 cents a gallon.

(Men weren't as greedy on this planet just yet.)

I thank God I was here to witness the snowstorm of 1973. Snow was up to my hips, and we had so much fun. And guess what? We still had to go to school, somehow, some way. Thanks to Sal's Fruit and Vegetable truck—me and my brother's first under-the-table job in the projects. Thanks for the memories.

Thanks for desegregated school busing.
It forced us to get along. (Some of us anyway).

A memory just landed inside my head. My dad once had a station wagon with wood panel siding. We were coming home from a late visit with my grandmother in Whittaker, Michigan. I remember it was snowing heavily that night.

As my dad was driving, we hit a patch of black ice, and the car spun violently in the middle of the freeway. We ended up on the side of a hill, upside down.

I thank God there weren't too many other cars traveling behind us at that time of night. I also thank God no one was seriously injured. What a vivid memory. I don't know if any of my siblings remember this, but yes, it did happen.

I want to thank the Pasadena Apartments on East Jefferson and Dubois, my apartment on East Jefferson and Vandyke, and my apartment on East Jefferson and Marquette, which once stood down the street from the historic Roostertail Event Venue. At that time, the cost of living was inexpensive, and I was having way too much fun. (I couldn't stay away from Detroit's downtown.)

At the very beginning of this book, I talked about being a very sick child. I would envision three beautiful angels floating across my bed. The third angel would suddenly stop, look at me with evil intentions, and rush toward me. I would be so terrified, lying in my bed, hiding under my covers.

I want to thank the person who told me what those visions meant.

I would like to thank these other musical artists: Slave, Aretha Franklin, The Spinners, Peabo Bryson, Special Delivery, The Persuaders, Mass Production, The Average White Band, The Commodores, George Michael, Tom Browne, Bohannon, The Intruders, Anita Ward, Anita Baker, The Floaters, The Enchantments, The Isley Brothers, Bootsy Collins, Al Green, The Temptations, Ray Goodman and Brown, David Bowie, The Stylistics, The Chi-Lites, Gladys Knight and The Pips, Curtis Mayfield, Harold Melvin and The Blue Notes Featuring Teddy Pendergrass, Blue Magic, The Five Stairsteps,

The Main Ingredient, the amazing Stevie Wonder, Elton John, Freddie Mercury and Queen, The Delfonics, Young & Company, D Train, Invisible Man's Band, Kano, Michael Henderson, The Jonzun Crew, Cameo, Rick James, Teena Marie, Twilight 22,

Johnny Kemp, Bloodstone, Newcleus, Tracie Spencer, Patrice Rushen, GQ, New Birth (my wife's favorite old group), Foxy, Rufus with Chaka Khan, Joe Sample, Kool and The Gang, Lenny Williams, Cheryl Lynn, The Intruders, DeBarge, Heatwave, Midnight Star, Cherrelle & Alexander O'Neal, Mary Mary, The Police, Sly & The Family Stone, Curtis Mayfield, Midnight Star, Rockie Robbins, The S.O.S. Band, The Gap Band, The Manhattans, Boosie Collins, The Brothers Johnson, Michael Franks, Michael McDonald, Glenn Jones, Bobby Caldwell, The Originals, Janet Jackson, Simply Red, Bobby Brown, Ready For The World, Colonel Abrams, Donna Summer, Rose Royce, The Moments, The Undisputed Truth, Stanley Clarke, Tears For Fears, George Duke, Lisa Stansfield, Terence Trent D'Arby, The Clark Sisters, Sade, Lisa Lisa & Cult Jam, Sybil, The Mighty Clouds of Joy, Genesis, The B-52's, Christopher Cross, Jean Carne, One Way, and Culture Club. Thanks for the musical memories.

Now, for some reason, I remember being stuck on the pop group Culture Club. Probably because of Boy George's vocals and the deep meaning of those wonderful songs. Clearly, I wasn't fond of the way Boy George wore his clothes, hair, and makeup, but his group from London had me way out there. Culture Club's Greatest Hits is still one of my favorites. ("Time Won't Give Me Time.") Thanks, Boy George.

Thank you, Tammi Terrell and Florence Ballard (the original lead singer). You were such a beautiful woman.

I continue to write Tyler Perry to do a movie about your life. Thanks to Johnnie Taylor and L.T.D.

Sarah Vaughn, B.B. King, Donny Hathaway, and Roberta Flack. Thanks to Little Milton, Charlie Pride and Jerry Butler.

Thank you, Toto ("Georgy Porgy" 1978). I would like to thank these genres: Disco, Soul, R&B, House Music, Techno, Funk, Jazz, Blues, hearing my uncle's Country Music, New Jack Swing, Pop, and Gospel. Thanks to the Motown Sound.

Thanks to my grandmother who introduced me to the music of James Cleveland. Hearing gospel on top of her refrigerator came in handy in life.

I would like to thank whoever created these dances: Detroit's own Schoolcraft, The Cabbage Patch, The Smurf, The Wop, The Reebok, The Prep, The Running Man, The Roger Rabbit, The Kid 'N' Play, The Robo Cop, The Biz Markie, The Tom and Jerry, The Fly Girl, The Bart Simpson, The Jit, The Robot, and The Errol Flynn. Boy! My childhood was fun. I remember doing all these dances. Thanks for the memories.

I want to say thanks to these Hip Hop legends and groups from back in the day: The Fat Boys, The Beastie Boys, MC Lyte, House of Pain, Monie Love, Digital Underground, The 2 Live Crew, J.J. Fad, Tag Team, Run D.M.C., Whodini, Heather B, Slick Rick, MC Hammer, Big Daddy Kane, Kool Moe Dee, L.L. Cool J, Tone Loc, Young MC, EPMD, 3rd Bass, Eric B. & Rakim, Roxanne Shante, The Real Roxanne, The Sugarhill Gang, N.W.A., Public Enemy, Afrika Bambaataa & The Soul Sonic Force, Dana Dane, Heavy D, Ice Cube ("Goddamn I'm Glad Y'all Set It Off"), Kurtis Blow,
A Tribe Called Quest, KRS-One, Grandmaster Flash and The Furious Five, De La Soul, Kid 'N Play, Rob Base and
DJ E-Z Rock, Arrested Development, Sir Mix-a-Lot, Geto Boys, Biz Markie, Special K, Queen Latifah, Newcleus, Doug E. Fresh and The Get Fresh Crew, The D.O.C., UTFO and De La Soul.

I would like to thank whoever invented these childhood games I used to play as a child. Some of these games had been around before I was even born: Go-Stop, Hide and Go Get It, Center Tag, Four Squares, Red Light, Green Light, Flag Football, Dodge Ball, and many more.

The entire Smith Homes Projects was a huge playground.

I thank my co-worker from back in the day who taught me how to dress to impress. Continue to rest in peace.

Thanks to the Detroit gangsters and pimps of the '70s and '80s—those suits were the bomb. My dad set an example back in the late '60s. My mom looked good as well. Most of all, I want to thank myself for creating my own classic style. Thanks to the old G-Men clothing store in Summit Place Mall, Louis The Hatter, Sibley's Shoes, the old clothing store in Northland Mall, Max Green's Men's Wear, Donna Sacs, Men's Warehouse, The Broadway, Suit Depot, Via Roma Fashions, Gator City, City Hatter, BHOGALLI Leather, Van Dykes, and Merry-Go-Round. Oh! I can't forget my high school days of shopping inside the Salvation Army for those old man suits back in the mid-'70s and early '80s.

Champions of the Detroit Pistons, Detroit Red Wings, and the Detroit Tigers—thanks for the memories and the good times. Your championships made us all proud. Thanks, Barry Sanders—you were amazing.

Here's another funny memory that just came to mind. Many moons ago, I was invited to this young lady's apartment for a couple of drinks and to keep her company. Anyways, the night had gotten really late, and instead of letting me out of her place, she took my hand and led me to her bedroom. She lit candles while the legendary gospel singer Mahalia Jackson was playing in the background. I started to take my clothes off, but I just couldn't get past the sound of the gospel singer. It reminded me of my grandmother's old radio on top of her refrigerator.

I asked the young lady if she could turn her cassette player off, and she refused. "I always play gospel music throughout my place every night."Tonight won't be any different, she said. I tried to ignore the music, but Mahalia kept shouting through those speakers so loud that she became a major distraction. It didn't make any sense to me.

We'd been doing the devil's work all night, and now this woman decides to play gospel music before engaging in a sexual rendezvous? I suddenly started to feel a major disapproval come over me.

Her spirit was trying to tell me not to do it. I was so spooked.

"I'm sorry, but I can't do this," I told the young woman. Hearing the voice of Mahalia Jackson terrified me, and I knew I was doing something wrong.

I put my clothes back on and ran out of the young lady's apartment, never to revisit ever again. (laughing) Mrs. Mahalia Jackson, I just want to thank you from stopping me from continuing doing the devil's work that night (laughing).

All music artists that were mentioned, thanks for your contributions to the world of music and life itself. Thanks for taking me back down memory lane while I was writing this book.

I thank all the people who have opened doors and stood for what's right. To the first Black woman to win an Oscar, Hattie McDaniel —thank you for not giving up. To my grandparents, thanks for the memories and the love you gave us all. I truly miss you. To all my cousins, things may be different now, but boy did we have a blast when we were kids. To The Smith Home Projects family—thanks for the memories. Whether it was good or bad, we had so much fun together.

To the city of Detroit and the city of Pontiac—thanks for the memories and opportunities.

Before I leave this earth, if I could just have one more Smith Home Projects reunion, I'll be in charge of the music. And besides, I would absolutely love to see everyone I used to play and go to school with as a child once again.

A very special thanks to the ones that are no longer with us. You are embedded in my heart and in my memories. I think about you quite often, and you have made my childhood a great one.

The names on my Smith Homes family list are so long, and I'm so grateful that I met you, prayed with you, played with you, went to school with you, did mischievous things with you, cried with you, and had so much fun with you.

To The Smith Home Projects—if I had to relive my childhood on Evergreen and Lyndon, I wouldn't change a damn thing.

You made me who I am today, you made me a decent man, you made me humble, and you made me a caring, giving, and wise man. I never forgot my beginnings and where I came from.

I know things aren't meant to stay the same, and those wonderful years will never return. Every once in a while, I pay a visit to the old neighborhood. I don't see kids playing the same games we used to play anymore. The neighborhood surrounding the projects used to look vibrant. Now, it's a bunch of empty lots where beautiful homes used to stand.

My middle school and high school no longer exist.

The Side Store, Michael's and Richard's liquor store, Dave's Store, and D&C Supermarket no longer exist. Northland Shopping Mall, Norwest, and The Mercury Theater no longer exist. The Cotton Club that stood on Livernois is now a junkyard. The Climax 2 that stood on Mount Elliott is now an empty lot. Boblo Island and Edgewater Park are long gone. Jack in The Box restaurant on Plymouth Road, A&W restaurant on Schoolcraft Road, 1940 Chop House,

The 20 Grand Lounge—where I saw Detroit's own Dramatics for the very first time on Mother's Day—no longer exist.

A lot of things I enjoyed as a small kid and as a young teen are no longer around, but my memories of these places are still intact.

Crescent Drive, I will always love you.

And to our favorite line some of us kids used to say in the

projects: "With a billy stick, I don't play that shit." (laughing)

Oh, and before I forget, Teddy Pendergrass was a bad dude, and in my opinion, Aretha Franklin was the greatest songstress that ever lived. Ron Banks and The Dramatics were absolutely amazing to watch when I was a kid.

And I don't care what anyone says, David Ruffin was the baddest Temptation. Before the madness, James Brown was once the baddest man on the planet. You will always be Soul Brother #1.

Amy Winehouse was such an amazing young talent. Bobby Caldwell, with all that soul, you made us all think you were Black. Queen, you lived throughout my childhood, and we truly were champions. Adele, I really enjoyed watching you connect with your fans—you're amazing. Celine Dion has one of the greatest voices of our time.

Whitney Elizabeth Houston had a voice that was sent by our ancestors. Marie Dionne Warwick was Mocha soul, Phyllis Linda Hyman was a sophisticated gem, and Donny Edward Hathaway was a musical genius.

In my book, there will never be a soulful and creative band like Earth, Wind & Fire. Teddy Pendergrass was magical on stage. There will never be another smooth Barry Eugene Carter (White). Chaka Khan, I absolutely love you. Heatwave, The Delfonics, The Dynamic Superiors, Special Delivery, Switch, and The Whispers—you all were the blueprint for us to try and follow.

'70s and '80's Soul music was such a special time.

Gerald Levert, talented but also funny. Teena Marie had a serious stage presence.

After your show at Detroit's Chene Park, I saw your limo coming towards me. I yelled your name, and you had your driver stop the car. You rolled down your window, and I was able to run up and shake your hand. What a moment. Continue to rest in paradise, Lady T.

Alanis Morrissette, why did you just disappear like that? A lot of us have missed your songwriting.

You were once my favorite breakout star.

And as far as I'm concerned, Sam Cooke wrote the greatest song ever recorded—"A Change is Gonna Come."

The song "I'll Always Love My Mama" by The Intruders is the best tribute to mothers ever.

"Dear Mama" by Tupac Shakur comes a distant second in my personal opinion.

"A Song for Mama" by Boyz II Men comes in third place.

Philip Bailey from Earth, Wind & Fire had one of the greatest falsetto voice ranges of our time.

I personally think Freddie Mercury from the group Queen had one of the best voices of our time.

Sade is one of the most beautiful songstresses in the entire world.

Little Richard, they tried to downplay and discredit your contributions to rock and roll music, but we all know the real deal. You were instrumental in this genre. Thank you.

Cameo and David Bowie, your music is also a part of my teenage years.

The song "Get Off" by Foxy was my Smith Homes Center party jam.

So was "One Nation Under a Groove" by Parliament-Funkadelic.

I was a dancing fool when I was just a young kid. (laughing)

My all-time favorite song by The Jackson Five: "I Wanna Be Where You Are."

I would like to thank Arthur "T-Boy" Ross and Leon Ware for writing these lyrics.

Prince, your first two albums were masterful.

True fact: One of your very first concerts was with the Rolling Stones.

People booed your performance at the Pontiac Silverdome. Thanks for not giving up, and thanks to Detroit's radio host, Electrifying Mojo, for introducing you to Detroit.

He also introduced us to Was Not Was, B52's, Cybotron, Kano, The Jonzun Crew, Kraftwerk, George Kranz ("Din Daa Daa"), and many more. And for that, I will always be a member of Detroit's Midnight Funk Association.

I remember events that happened in my life through music. Jerry Butler, Lou Rawls, Johnnie Taylor, The Isley Brothers, and

Frankie Beverly & Maze—your music flourished through my ears as a young teenager.

As far as the Hip Hop world, I really wished that rapper Nas and singer Kelis never divorced. They were my ultimate power couple.

I was at home watching HBO when they aired a documentary showing Lisa "Left Eye" Lopez's last travel to Honduras. At that time, I already knew how she was killed. What I didn't know was that this documentary would show the actual footage of what happened to Ms. Lopez. Watching this shocked me to the core for about three weeks. I'm still heartbroken about that devastating day. Gone way too soon. Continue to rest well, Lisa.

I could go on and on, but how much time do we all have?

Soul vocalist Betty Wright—was our family really related on my grandfather's side? Continue to rest in paradise.

Life has a rhythm, much like music. Each moment, each experience, every memory is tied to a sound, a voice, or a song that plays in the background of our minds. Music has been my constant companion, guiding me through the highs and lows, the triumphs and the heartbreaks. It has shaped my understanding of the world and allowed me to express emotions I couldn't always put into words.

From the soulful harmonies of Motown to the raw energy of hip-hop, each note and lyric tells a piece of my story, reflecting the depth of my experiences and the richness of my past.

As I look back on my life, I realize how much music has been a marker of time. The melodies of my childhood, the anthems of my teenage years, and the classics that still resonate with me today have each played a role in shaping who I am.

Certain songs take me right back to a moment—whether it was dancing in the living room as a child, hearing a song on the radio while riding through the city, or watching my favorite artists perform live. Each of these memories is a note in the grand symphony of my life.

But music is more than just sound. It is culture, history, and emotion intertwined. It connects us across generations and backgrounds, offering a sense of belonging in a world that often feels chaotic. The artists who poured their souls into their craft gave us more than just entertainment—they gave us wisdom, resilience, and truth. From the electrifying performances of James Brown to the poetic lyricism of Tupac Shakur, from the timeless ballads of Whitney Houston to the boundary-pushing creativity of Prince, these artists shaped not only the music industry but also the world around them.

In the same way, music has served as a reminder of where I come from. It echoes the voices of my family, my community, and the streets that raised me.

The sounds of gospel on my grandmother's radio, the rhythms of funk blasting from neighborhood parties, and the voices of legendary artists telling stories of struggle and success have all influenced my path. These sounds have been my refuge, my escape, and my motivation. Even as times change and the places of my youth disappear, the music remains, carrying the spirit of those moments forward.

As I continue to reflect on my journey, I recognize that my love for music is more than just appreciation—it is reverence. It is a celebration of the artists who dared to be different, who told our stories, and who gave us something to hold onto when words failed.

It is gratitude for the voices that comforted me, inspired me, and challenged me to see the world in new ways. It is a tribute to the memories that will never fade, no matter how much time passes.

Music is a time capsule, a bridge to the past, and a beacon for the future. It reminds us of who we were, who we are, and who we strive to be. And for that, I will always be grateful. The melodies may change, the artists may come and go, but the impact of their songs will live on forever. Just like the memories they bring back, music is eternal.

As I close this chapter, I find solace in knowing that no matter where life takes me, music will always be there to guide me back home. It has been my constant, my companion, and my reminder that every experience, good or bad, has a song to go along with it. And so, I continue to listen, to remember, and to cherish every note, for they are the soundtrack to my life.

Chapter 54

Musically Battle Tested
(Just Another Thank You Page)

Music in my life came full circle. By this point, I considered myself a connoisseur of the art of deejaying. Every night, I would ride past this bar, wishing I was the one rocking the house.

Because of a well-known radio station at the time, the parking lot and front door were always packed.

One day, I heard through the grapevine that the owner of the bar no longer needed the radio station's services. So they packed up and moved to a bar up in Flint, Michigan. It was a big mistake for the owner. Before long, the bar wasn't getting those crowds anymore, and he needed to come up with something quick. He decided to hold deejay tryouts every weekend.

I knew a waitress who worked at the bar, so I handed her a well-put-together deejay résumé. My résumé was pretty extensive. I had started in a few local bars around the downtown area and was the very first deejay to play at Detroit's Comerica Park when it opened. I even did parties for the Detroit Tigers and the Red Wings. Yes, I've touched the Stanley Cup a few times.

The following week, I got the phone call to sit down and meet with the bar owner.

"You are the very first person to give me a deejay résumé," he said. "I see you've rocked a few crowds in your life. Do you have your own equipment?"

I told him I had everything I needed, including lights to put up in the ceiling over his dance floor.

"I'll tell you what—I'm going to give you a shot. Come in next Saturday, play your set, and if everyone in my place likes you, the job is yours."

That next Saturday, I came in early, set up my equipment at the deejay booth, and installed my lighting in the ceiling.

I was so excited—but also nervous.

As the patrons began to come in, I started my set. After about two hours, I could hear some people in the bar begin to boo me. What I didn't know was that the original deejay, who had been playing there for years, was secretly going around the bar telling people that I was the one trying to take his job. That wasn't the case in my mind, but the misunderstanding upset a lot of people.

Now the boos were getting louder.

"Go back to where you came from!" I remembered a person saying.

Another person yelled, "Where did you get this deejay from?"

I was devastated. The original deejay even had some guys waiting to beat me up when the bar closed. I had to call for backup to protect me while I broke down my equipment at the end of the night.

Afterward, I sat down with the owner.

"Well, I think you had a rough night, and I've decided that I'm going to move on to the next candidate."

Those were some disappointing words to hear. But I didn't give up —I wanted this so bad. I just needed another crack at it.

"I'll tell you what," I said. "For the next two Saturdays, I'll play here for free. Just give me another chance."

The owner jumped on the idea of not having to pay a deejay for two weeks and agreed to give me the shot I needed.

At the time, I knew nothing about downloading music or creating my own CDs.

I was computer illiterate, but I also knew what songs were hot and would automatically make people get on that dance floor. I called my cousin and a co-worker to start making CDs for me.

I also needed to be different from everyone else—I needed a gimmick.

I used to be so shy to say anything on a microphone. I had a hype man, but he moved to Atlanta. This would be my very first time verbally getting people to dance.

If I wanted to be a premier deejay at this bar, I needed to become the loudest hype man ever. I needed to be known as that crazy deejay. I also needed to not give a damn about that other deejay's feelings and, once again, become the best at what I did.

I had no intentions of taking his job, but for what he did to me my first night, I had every intention of taking over the whole place and intentionally becoming the face of this bar.

I had two Saturdays to become the resident deejay.

My first free Saturday went well—no boos from the crowd, and I noticed more people entering the bar than before. So, I had that going for me.

On my second free Saturday, I was in **music battle mode**, and it was time to win some people over. Along with my vast collection of music, my first 20 CDs were made with some guaranteed bangers on them. My gimmick also had to work.

At the time, I was using a **Vestax CDX-12**, a two-CD cross mixer. I put in my first two CDs, and the dance floor finally began to fill up. At a distance, I could see the other deejay standing in a corner, hoping I would fail once again.

I decided to take my microphone, leave the deejay booth, and get in the middle of the crowd.

I pretended to have **dance floor interviews**: "Hey, what's your name?"
"Are you having a great time?"
"Does anyone have any song requests?"
Suddenly, I screamed at the top of my lungs,

"IS EVERYONE HAVING A GREAT TIME?"

The crowd went crazy and happily screamed back at me.

As I walked back to my deejay booth, I noticed a waitress waiting for me.

"Hey, this table would like to buy you a drink. What would you like?" she asked.

"A whiskey and coke, please."

I waved at the table and thanked them. As I continued playing my set, the **free drinks just kept coming.** The more I drank, the crazier I got.

I guess word had gotten to the streets that **this new crazy deejay was on overload.** People kept piling into the bar non-stop. It hadn't been this packed since the radio station had its parties there.

Before long, I was a little **buzzed from the whiskey and cokes**. I decided to **stand on top of the deejay booth** and take things to another level. I waved my white towel in the air, calling on the patrons sitting at the bar to join the dance floor.

To my surprise, **they did just that.**

After the night was over, the **security team** came up to shake my hand.

"Great job! Hope to see you here next weekend," one of them said.

I took my final CD case to the car before walking back in to talk to the owner.

"Great job, Deejay Ezee!" he said. "Well, the job is yours if you still want it. I'm willing to pay you **$200 every Saturday night** and give you **Ladies Night** on Thursdays. If you can get people in here on that night, I'll add an additional **$100** to your pay every week."

The following week, I used my **own money** to make posters and flyers, posting them all over the city in hopes that my **first Ladies Night** would be a success.

I also asked the owner if he could give out **tickets at the door** for every lady that came in that night.

The tickets would be used for **half off** on any first drink purchased. He agreed—**but only for the first night**.

"If I lose any sales, I won't do it again," he warned. I could tell he was a bit stingy, but at this point, he was willing to try anything to **save his business**.

My **posters and flyers actually worked**. A half-hour into my set, the **women started pouring in**.

"Good evening, ladies, my name is Deejay Ezee. Welcome to the all-new Ladies Night. Make sure you use your ticket for half off your first drink!"

I felt like I was influenced by the old deejay from **Detroit's Climax 2** a decade ago.

Two hours passed, and I **couldn't believe what I was seeing**—the bar was now **standing-room only**.

A couple of **Thursdays passed**, and the place **continued to be over capacity**. I received my **bonus** and was also **given Friday nights**.

The radio station crowds were back—but this time, it was me hyping the place up three nights a week.

I was the **Deejay** and the **Hype Man** all in one.

Since I was **packing the house consistently**, the owner gave me free rein to do **whatever I wanted on Friday nights**—as long as the place stayed packed.

So, I invented the **Friday Night Hot Body Contest**.

I created posters and flyers for this event as well.

This time, I asked the owner if we could have a **first and second place winner**:

- **First place** would win **$100**
- **Second place** would win a **bar drink of their choice**

The owner agreed to that, too.

At this point, **I was on a roll, and he knew it.**

If **Thursday's Ladies Night** drew the women, then **Friday's Hot Body Contest** would **surely bring out the fellas.**

And man, **did this night draw a crowd!**

Women would enter the bar wearing **trench coats with lingerie underneath** or **heels and a housecoat** with just a pair of **panties and a bra** underneath.

"If you're entering the Hot Body Contest, please sign up at the deejay booth!" I would announce.

The men in the bar had the job of picking the winner every week.

One time, my **sisters and their friend** came to see me at the bar.

I

convinced their friend to enter the contest by telling her,

"If you enter, I'll make sure you win the contest."

Now, she **wasn't wearing anything provocative**—just a **nice jean outfit** that night.

But she agreed to enter, and by the end of the contest, **I cheated and claimed her the winner.**

Boy, the fellas got really **angry at me**, but **I didn't care.** I had the

power to do whatever I wanted.

I was **the king of nighttime fun.**

I actually thought it was **hilarious** watching my **sisters and their friend leave the bar with the cash prize.** *(laughing)*

The Next Big Idea

Sometimes I would **get bored** and switch things up.
I turned the **Hot Body Contest** into a **Wet T-Shirt Contest**.

I had the privilege of **putting a tarp down on the dance floor** and
spraying the front of women's T-shirts with a water bottle. But

after a while, **I wanted something greater to promote.**

I no longer wanted to do a **Hot Body or Wet T-Shirt Contest** anymore.

I wanted to come up with something **new**. Something **big.**

Something **bold.**

And then, I came up with a **whole new contest**:

The Friday Night Freestyle Battles

Back in those days, **there was a lot of competitive talent in the city**, and I wanted to be **the one to showcase it.**

The **best in the city** would go after each other **every Friday night —both males and females.**

This contest was **extremely popular**.

At first, contestants only had **60 seconds** to rap. But I quickly realized that 60 seconds **was definitely not enough time to go hard in the paint**—if you know what I mean.

So, I changed it to a **full three minutes or less per person**. I set **very strict rules**:

- **Keep your raps clean.**
- **No using of the "N" word.**
- **No touching each other.**
- **No dropping my microphones.**

Breaking any of these rules would mean automatic disqualification.

The **last two participants** standing would **win a free bar drink**.

And if you lasted **five weeks in a row**, you would **win the cash prize of $300**.

The Rise in Popularity

Week after week, the **best rappers** battled it out.

This contest created **long lines down the side of the building**.

The **parking lot stayed full**.

The **money kept flowing**.

We had to **beef up security** and **hire even more bartenders and waitresses**.

My popularity kept growing, and I was starting to feel like a hometown celebrity.

The bigger the **weekend crowds**, the more **money all the employees got paid**.

But what I didn't realize was that the **bar owner's secret cocaine addiction was also growing.**

Total Takeover

I was given **another day to boost**. Now, I had:

- **Ladies Night on Thursdays**
- **Friday Night Freestyle Battles**
- **The Saturday Night Jams**
- **Old School Sundays**

Every night, I would get **8 to 12 whiskey and cokes** under my booth from patrons showing their appreciation.

I couldn't drink them all, so **I gave them away to my buddies**.

Meanwhile, the **other deejay**?

He was left with just **Monday, Tuesday, and Wednesday—the dead nights**. *(laughing)*

Nobody was coming out on **those** workdays.

The **crazy deejay had taken over the whole place**, to say the least. *(laughing)*

Security Hated Me—But Loved Me Too

The bar was **so packed** every weekend that **security would get pissed off at me** for playing certain songs.

These songs would **get everyone riled up**, making it **hard for security to control the crowd**. *(laughing)*

Yes, they would be so mad at me, but at the end of the night, every one of them would **shake my hand** and say,

"Ezee, you are amazing!"

Pajama Night—A Summer Sensation

Another **popular party** I used to promote in the summer was the infamous Pajama Night.

The Beginning of the End

The energy was electric. **Pajama Night** had become another wild success. People would **walk into the bar wearing pajamas and house shoes**, but once again, some women took it a step further—**wearing house coats with lace lingerie underneath**.

Man! There's just something about women wanting to wear lace outfits at a bar. That's so crazy to me.

One night, on my **birthday**, I decided to **take the party to the next level**.

I **rented a party bus** and invited **some of the bar's best patrons** to come party with me. We rode through **Downtown Royal Oak**, hitting a few bars before **bringing the celebration back to our home bar**.

That night was **unforgettable—pure fun**, just like the way it used to be.

But slowly, everything I had built in this bar began to fall apart.

- **No more crowds.**
- **No more party promotions.**
- **No more posters or flyers.**
- **No more contests.**

The **music that once kept the bar alive was fading into silence**.
It wasn't because the people stopped coming.
It wasn't because the bar lost its spark.

Cocaine.

Cocaine would **ruin the best local bar in the city.**
One night, the owner said he put the money bag in one of the ovens for a minute, and when he got back, the bag was gone. Not one employee got paid that night. I was so pissed.

It was one of my best nights.

I knew the real reason why that money bag disappeared.

Another time, the owner passed each employee their money at the end of the night in white envelopes. I didn't think anything of it, but when I got home and opened my envelope, I noticed I was short a hundred dollars. So, I called him.

There really wasn't any explanation.

All he said was that he shorted a hundred dollars from **everyone's** pay that night.

When I asked why, once again, he had **no explanation**.

I worked hard for my money, and I made him a lot of money as well. So, you know I was heated.

I was finally fed up and **threatened him**.

"I'll tell you what—if I don't have the rest of my money when I come back tonight, I'm going to **rip your whole bar apart**."

When I came back, he wasn't there, but a bartender handed me the rest of my money and also told me I was banned from ever stepping foot into the bar again.

I took down all my lighting, packed up the rest of my equipment, and **left**.

The Attempt to Bring Me Back

Two months later, the head of security called me and told me that the place **really needed me back**.

"Liquor sales are down, and people keep asking if you're playing. When we say no, they turn back to their cars and drive off. We really need you to come back, along with all your contest ideas."

I agreed to come in and talk about details for another **possible Pajama Party**, since my birthday was coming up again.

As I went over plans, the owner of the bar walked in. "What is **he** doing here?" he asked.
The head of security tried to explain that it would be a **great idea** to bring me back.

"No, no, no. He is banned from coming in here, and I **meant what I said**."

I was sure that I was going to make my big return, but it didn't work out.

The owner refused to admit that he made a **huge mistake**.
Two years later, he lost his place, and now the **bar no longer exists**.

Reflecting on My Time at the Bar

I'm **grateful** for the opportunity while it lasted.
I'm very **thankful** to the people who swelled my head up and made me feel like a **local celebrity**. *(Laughing)*

Every once in a while, someone will stop me and ask if I was that **crazy deejay** from back in the day. Every blue moon,

I would still hear a loud voice yell:

"We Want Ezee!"

Just like the lyric from the rap group **N.W.A.**

Thanks but no thanks.
Those days also got me in so much trouble with the **ladies** and caused a rupture in my **personal relationship**.

Today, I would **never** want to be another resident deejay at any club or bar.

Too many **temptations**, and **evil lurks in every corner**:

- **Outside shootings**
- **Sex & cheating**
- **Jealousy & bar fights**
- **Drugs & alcohol levels through the roof**
- **Women with bad intentions**

That bar had **it all**.

I was **musically battle-tested** and rocked the house **back in the day**.

I was once **the man walking these streets**.

I still **thank the owner** of that bar. I was able to **scratch this off my bucket list**.

The community continues to **keep the name Deejay EZee alive** and in their memories.

I often hear about my **heyday** at this once-popular entertainment spot.

At a gas station, grocery store—somewhere in public—I would sometimes hear:

"Hey, you look familiar. Aren't you that crazy deejay that used to play at that bar back in the day?"

"Man! I had so much fun when you were there."

"Deejay EZee is your name, right?"

The bar wasn't just a place to play music—it was a **stage for my creativity, my hustle, and my passion**. Every night I played, I wasn't just spinning records; I was **building an atmosphere**, creating an **energy** that made people want to stay, dance, and return week after week.

I saw it **all**—from the way music brought people together, to how fame could change a man, to how **temptations** lurked in every shadow.

I learned that **power in nightlife** doesn't come from the sound system or the size of the crowd—it comes from the **influence you hold** over people's emotions, movements, and memories. I had **built something special**, and for a moment, I was **unstoppable**.

But in this business, you're only as good as your **last great night**, and sometimes, no matter how much **hard work and dedication** you put in, things **fall apart**.

The **bar's downfall** wasn't because of the music or the energy we created—it was **greed, addiction, and mismanagement** that ultimately killed what we had built.

Moral of the Story: Success isn't just about talent—it's about trust, consistency, and smart business decisions.

No matter how much energy, love, and passion you pour into something, if the **foundation is weak**, everything will eventually **collapse**.

I had turned that bar into a **powerhouse**. People came from all over to experience the energy we created.

But in the end, **bad leadership and bad habits** will always ruin a good thing.

This experience taught me:

1. **Know your worth** – Never let anyone shortchange your value, no matter how much you love what you do.
2. **Not all money is good money** – If the environment is toxic, no amount of cash is worth losing yourself.
3. **Protect your legacy** – If you build something great, be smart about who you trust to run it with you.

Final Thoughts: Looking back, I can say that those days were some of the most **exciting and unpredictable** times of my life.

For a while, I was at the **top of my game**. I had the crowds, the attention, the respect—I had everything a deejay could ask for.

But I also saw **the dark side** of that world.

The **fast life**, the **temptations**, the **jealousy**, the **money games**— it all came crashing down, just like it always does when people get too greedy.

I'm grateful for the **memories, the experience, and the lessons**. I still love music, and I'll always have that **crazy deejay energy** inside me. But I've moved on to **bigger and better things**.

I no longer need the **crowds, the parties, or the flashing lights** to prove who I am.

I left my **mark** on that world, and my name still echoes in the memories of those who lived it with me.

This chapter is a testament to a **legendary time in my life**—a time when I **commanded** the nightlife and made an unforgettable impact on the scene.

Those nights, those crowds, those battles, those parties—they were all a part of something **bigger than me**.

I may not be on those turntables anymore, but the memories of **Deejay EZee** will always be a part of **nightlife history**. Life moves forward.

The deejay days were a **chapter**—an unforgettable one—but just one piece of my story.

As I stepped away from hyping crowds, I found myself stepping into **a new era**—one filled with **different challenges, greater responsibilities, and a deeper sense of purpose**.

The next phase of my journey would take me to **places I never expected**, teaching me even more about **life, love, and the things that truly matter**.

And that's where the story continues…

This is a Nursery Rhyme Productions

We Tried This With The Fellas. Now It's The Ladies Turn

BATTLE FRESTYLE FRIDAYS

With Your Host Deejay EZee

Ladies Here Are The Rules

1) The first four ladies that sign up at the Deejay booth will rap battle each other at 12 midnight.

2) Deejay EZee will pick the secret rap instrumental for that night.

3) Each lady will have 3 minutes to go head-to-head with each other lyrically

4) Keep it clean. No cursing or using the N-word, or you will be automatically disqualified. If you have real skills, you won't need to use that word.

5) Anything goes, but you cannot touch each other. Remember, this is just a battle. Nothing Personal.

6) Dropping the mic or screaming into the mic is an automatic disqualification.

7) The last two standing will rap battle for the drink of their choice at the bar. Win five weeks in a row and be named Champion with a $300 cash prize.

Bottled domestic beer: $2.00
Well drinks: $2.00
Special shots: $1.00

Look for Upcoming Events:
Denim Cognac Party
Pistons Jersey Party

Deejay EZee and Sheila's
Birthday Bash

Chapter 55

Today's Shenanigans

Trigger Warning: This chapter may make some readers feel a bit uncomfortable, Especially the ones that say their vote doesn't matter.

We live in a world that is far different from when we all were kids. Greed and racism have separated us today. Just like a bad case of asbestos growing inside the walls of our society, the toxicity spreads quietly, unnoticed, but always lingering, poisoning our relationships and communities until we find ourselves suffocating under the weight of hatred, division, and intolerance.

Although I've missed my mother dearly, I'm so glad she isn't here to witness how much the world has changed since she passed. Larger countries taking full advantage of trying to take over smaller countries, a felon is able to run for president, Medicare and Social Security being threatened for cuts, the widening gap between the rich and the poor, and the blatant disregard for the well-being of the most vulnerable among us. The love and unity she stood for seem so distant in a time when greed and division have taken the forefront, and it breaks my heart to think of how much she would have mourned these changes.

I'm glad she's not here to see more police killings of Black people on the rise, a tragic pattern that keeps repeating itself despite all the promises of change. The outrage that follows each incident seems to fade with time, only to be replaced by another story, another life lost. She lived through the struggles of racism in her time, but the magnitude of the violence and the systemic injustice we see today would have broken her heart all over again.

She would have been devastated by how little progress we've made in addressing the root causes of this violence and how some still refuse to acknowledge the humanity of people who look like me.

It's hard to watch, especially when I know how much she believed in the goodness of people and how she worked so hard to make sure her children could rise above all that.

I'm also sure my mother wanted to see all her grandchildren live in a much nicer world, one where they wouldn't have to face the same struggles she did—where their skin color wouldn't be a barrier to opportunities, where they could walk the streets without fear, and where their dreams wouldn't be limited by the harsh realities of prejudice. My mother worked tirelessly to provide for us, to create a better life than the one she had known. I know my mother wanted them to thrive, to be free from the chains of racism, poverty, and inequality. But I also know she would have wanted them to carry forward the lessons she taught us as kids.

We were just kids enjoying life, but we had no idea life would change so drastically. We never thought that we would have a president trying his best to destroy humanity. The games people play, the distractions, the manipulation—it's as if we've become numb to the reality of the consequences of our actions. People spew hate, the truth gets twisted, and we forget what it means to be kind, to be just, to look out for one another. We're so wrapped up in our own lives, in our own ambitions, that we've forgotten how to come together as a community, as people who care for one another.

But deep down, we all know better. We know the difference between right and wrong, between love and hate, between what should be and what is.

We've been taught these lessons—whether from our families, our communities, or from life itself. The problem is, we've gotten so used to the chaos that we've let it become normal. We've allowed ourselves to be desensitized to the pain and suffering around us.

And one of the greatest examples of this was the passing of

Supreme Court Justice Ruth Bader Ginsburg.

She was a titan of justice, a defender of the people, and a relentless advocate for equality. But after she left this world, the shenanigans that followed in the justice system were beyond comprehension. We saw the integrity of the Supreme Court come into question.

We found out that some justices weren't truly for the people, but for themselves. We found out that they could be bought—willing to make decisions that would drastically affect people's lives in exchange for money, lavish trips, and personal gain.

Justice Ginsburg stood for fairness, for justice, for progress. She spent her life breaking barriers, ensuring that women had rights, that equality wasn't just an idea but a reality. And yet, after she was gone, we witnessed corruption seeping into the very institution she fought to uphold. Some justices weren't continuing her fight for fairness and democracy. Instead, they catered to the highest bidder, making rulings that benefitted the powerful while crushing the vulnerable. It was a betrayal of everything she stood for, a revelation of how deep corruption runs in the highest court of the land.

The Democratic Party seems to not have a fight in them anymore, while the Republican Party has the every-man-for-himself attitude.

The majority of both parties are too old and very selfish, not wanting younger members to hold any high positions and not willing to listen to new ideas. The dysfunction in our government is more apparent than ever, and it has led us to the state we are in now—stagnant, divided, and losing credibility on the world stage.

We have a South African immigrant and an non elected official, dismantling our government and he has privileges to do so.

If my mother were here, she would shake her head at it all. She would see the deception, the greed, and the blatant disregard for morality.

And I know she would remind me, as she always did, that no matter how much darkness exists in the world, it's up to people like us to be the light. In my lifetime, I've seen it all on Television. From assassination attempts to actual assassinations to blatant buffoonery in the White House.

The injustices, the corruption, the loss of integrity—these are not just moments in history but lessons that should remind us all of what's at stake. It seems other countries are passing us by, and we are starting to become a third-world country.

But where do we go from here? How do we reclaim the unity we once had, the integrity that once defined our institutions, the love that once bonded us as a people? The answer is simple but not easy
—we must **acknowledge the brokenness before we can begin to fix it**. We can no longer afford to turn a blind eye, to pretend that things will get better on their own.

Our communities need us. Our children need us. They are growing up in a world where school shootings are at an all-time high, where children are being separated from their families due to deportation, where lunch programs that once ensured they had a meal are being taken away.

What did our children do to deserve this? The answer is nothing. They are the innocent victims of a system that prioritizes money and political gain over humanity.

The most heartbreaking reality is that no one seems to care about the child anymore. We live in a time where politicians are being secretly paid off to vote against the well-being of the people, where decisions that impact the most vulnerable are made in backroom deals fueled by greed. Where did we go wrong? How did we let the very foundation of our society crumble beneath us?

It's painful to think about, but even more painful to **accept it as normal**. And I refuse to.

I refuse to let the sacrifices of our ancestors, the blood, sweat, and tears of those who fought for our rights, be in vain. **We must wake up.**

The world I grew up in wasn't perfect, but it was a place where community mattered, where people looked out for each other, where children could be children without fear of mass shootings, political greed, and systemic injustice.

Now, it's up to us. Do we sit back and let the corruption, hate, and division consume us? Or do we rise up, take responsibility, and fight to leave behind a better world for the next generation?

It's time we all woke up and recognized the power we have to change things. To stop letting the shenanigans define us. To start acting with the empathy, love, and respect we know is right. It's time to take responsibility—not just for ourselves, but for the world we want to leave behind. Because at the end of the day, we all know better. We just need to start doing better.

In 2028, we have the greatest opportunity to at least bring back some type of normalcy. Vote and vote correctly. Consider your children's future.

And one more thing-this so-called, "ethnic cleansing" happening right before our eyes is beyond disturbing. It would be a damn shame if the United States played a role in forcibly removing 1.9 million Palestinians from the Gaza Strip, displacing families, erasing their history, and replacing their homeland with a luxury tourist destination. Does that sound familiar? It should. There's a long history of taking what doesn't belong to us. The same playbook has been used time and time again from stolen lands to broken treaties, from entire cultures being uprooted to histories being rewritten by the victors. And now, once again, the world watches as power and greed justify the removal of people from their homes, as if their existence is nothing more than an inconvenience to someone else ambition.

The parallels are impossible to ignore.

The displacement of Indigenous tribes from their ancestral lands in America, the forced removals that shaped history in Africa, the destruction of thriving Black communities in the name of progress in cities across the U.S. It's the same ruthless cycle, just wearing a different mask.

How many times will history repeat itself before we finally get it right? At what point do we stop allowing power-hungry leaders to redraw borders with blood and determining who gets to stay and who is pushed out? If this is the future of geopolitics, then humanity has learned nothing.

What's worse is that we keep pretending to be shocked by history repeating itself, as if we weren't warned, as if we didn't see the signs. The forced displacement of people, the rewriting of history to favor the powerful, the destruction of entire cultures in the name of so-called "progress"—these aren't new horrors. They are just the latest version of the same brutal cycle.

I've lived long enough to understand how this playbook works. First, demonize a group of people. Make them the enemy, strip them of their humanity, turn their mere existence into a threat. Then, erase their rights, their autonomy, their voices. Label them as invaders on their own land, as a burden, as an obstacle to whatever empire is trying to expand its reach. Finally, displace them, take what isn't yours, and act as if it was never theirs to begin with.

This is exactly what's happening to the Palestinians in Gaza. 1.9 million people being removed, their homes destroyed, their histories erased, their future stolen. And instead of stopping it, governments around the world are silently endorsing it—some out of fear, some out of greed, and some because they simply don't care.

But here's the part that infuriates me the most: how easily people accept it.

The same people who claim to love freedom, democracy, and justice turn a blind eye when those values are inconvenient. The same people who talk about never letting history repeat itself refuse to call this what it is.

And we know why.

Because acknowledging the truth would mean admitting their own complicity. It would mean admitting that the same hands funding these removals are the ones that fund our own broken systems. It would mean recognizing that the people we're told to trust, the leaders we're told to follow, are the ones signing off on human suffering.

But this isn't just about one conflict, one displacement, one injustice.

This is about a global pattern of destruction fueled by power and wealth.

This is about how corporations own governments, how billionaires decide the fates of entire populations, how war is manufactured and sold as if it were an industry like any other.

It's about the fact that we are watching people be stripped of their humanity in real time—and somehow, the world keeps spinning like nothing is happening.

And if we let it happen now, what's stopping it from happening again?

What's stopping another country from deciding an entire race, religion, or class of people are inconvenient and must be removed?

What's stopping another government from claiming that suffering is necessary for "progress"?

Because make no mistake—what is happening in Gaza is not an isolated event. It is a warning.

A warning that anyone can become expendable when those in power decide it to be so.

A warning that if you are not useful to the empire, you are disposable.

A warning that if this is the future of global leadership, then no one is truly safe.

So, where does that leave us? Do we keep watching, keep scrolling past headlines as if this is just another chapter in a book that's already been written? Do we shake our heads and say, "What a shame," while doing nothing to stop it?

Or do we finally wake up?

Do we finally accept that if we do nothing, we are just as guilty as the ones who pull the trigger?

Do we finally recognize that choosing to ignore injustice is the same as endorsing it?

Because if we allow this to happen—if we allow the forcible removal of millions to go unchecked—then what happens next? Who becomes the next target?

And when they come for us, who will be left to speak up?

—**Eric Wright**

Moral of the Story: The world is changing, but not always for the better. The values of unity, honesty, and justice that once guided us seem to be fading, replaced by greed, corruption, and division. The struggles of the past were not fought in vain, yet today, we see history repeating itself in ways that betray the sacrifices of those who came before us.

The lesson in all of this is clear—**we must not sit idly by and watch our world crumble.** We cannot allow ourselves to become desensitized to injustice or be fooled by the distractions that keep us divided. We must stay informed, hold those in power accountable, and continue the fight for fairness and integrity, just as those before us did.

At the end of the day, **we all know better, and we must do better.** It is our responsibility to push back against corruption, stand up for the vulnerable, and make sure that the future is brighter for the generations to come. **If we fail to fight for what is right, we are just as guilty as those who tear it down.**

Final Thoughts: The Cost of Reckless Choices

It shouldn't matter what color or gender a candidate is—what should matter is their **competence, integrity, and vision for the country.** Yet, in one of the most critical elections in history, the voters and the people in power knowingly and deliberately chose **the wrong person**—someone **unfit for the position, lacking the character, intelligence, and moral compass to lead.**

This wasn't a mistake made out of ignorance. **It was intentional.** A calculated decision, rooted in prejudice, greed, and a refusal to allow change to take place. **A woman of color was on the ballot —qualified, experienced, and ready to lead—but rather than embrace progress, you clung to the past.** You let fear dictate your choice, fear of what it would mean to have a leader who didn't look like the ones before.

And now, look at the mess we're in. **Look at the division, the chaos, the suffering that could have been avoided if only you had chosen wisely.** If only you had put the **country before your own biases,** before your refusal to accept that leadership can— and should—reflect the diversity of the people it serves.

Instead, you gave power to someone who had no business leading a nation. Someone whose **incompetence has damaged the very fabric of our democracy.** Someone whose **self-interest came before the people, whose corruption ran unchecked, whose recklessness put lives at risk.**

This is what happens when **you vote for the wrong reasons.** When you let **fear outweigh logic, when you choose to sabotage progress rather than embrace it. And now, we all have to suffer the consequences.**

Elections aren't just about party lines, personal feelings, or who "looks the part." They're about the future. And when you knowingly make the wrong choices, history will not be kind in its judgment.

1. Revelation 3:17 People Thinking They're Winning But They're Lost

"For you say, I am rich, I have prospered, and I need nothing, not realizing that you are wretched, pitiable, poor, blind, and naked."

Relevance:

This verse speaks to **self-deception and false confidence**—many people today believe they have everything they need because of wealth, success, or status, but spiritually and morally, they are **completely lost and blind to reality**.

2. Revelation 12:9 Mass Deception and Confusion

"And the great dragon was thrown down, that ancient serpent, who is called the devil and Satan, the deceiver of the whole world —he was thrown down to the earth, and his angels were thrown down with him."

Relevance:

This verse highlights **global deception**—the enemy's influence is everywhere, leading **entire nations, leaders, and cultures into confusion, division, and foolishness**. Lies are spread so easily today that many people **can't see the truth**.

3. Revelation 9:6 Chaos and Desperation

"And in those days people will seek death and will not find it. They will long to die, but death will flee from them."

Relevance:

This describes a time of **intense suffering, pain, and hopelessness**. With today's **mental health crises, violence, and moral decay**, many feel trapped in **desperation**, yet they refuse to seek true peace in God.

"The world I once knew as a child—a place of simplicity, joy, and boundless possibilities—has faded into something unrecognizable. What was once a society built on values, faith, and the promise of a better future now teeters on the edge of chaos. These three Bible verses are more than just ancient prophecy; they are a stark reflection of the times we are living in—the unraveling of democracy, the deception that blinds so many, and the growing darkness that signals the beginning of the end for mankind as we know it.

Though my heart aches for my mother every day, I find solace in knowing that she has been spared from the suffering that so many of us now endure. In an unselfish way, I am grateful that she is not here to witness the division, the greed, and the moral decay consuming the world. She left before the storm, and for that, I thank God."

Chapter 56

A Short Hospice Story

A mother is her son's first true love. A son, especially that first son, is a mother's last love.

Denzel Washington

"Mom, when I visit you tomorrow, what would you like for me to bring you to eat?" he asked, his voice filled with both love and quiet desperation.

His mother, frail but still holding on, thought for a moment before answering, "I have a taste for some Popeyes chicken."

"I'll tell you what," he said, trying to sound cheerful, "How about I bring you some chicken, mac and cheese, a biscuit, and a Coke?"

His mother smiled faintly, nodding. "That sounds good."

The next day, he arrived at the hospice center, balancing a bag of warm food and a cold soda in his hands. The scent of the crispy chicken filled the small room, but he noticed that, just like the last few times, she barely touched her food.

"Mom, I know it's been hard for you to eat," he said softly. "But let's try a little, okay? I'll help you."

She made a weak effort, taking small bites, sipping her Coke, but he could see the struggle. After a few minutes, he gently took the food and placed it back in the bag. "I'll leave it here. I'll tell the nurse to warm it up and feed you later."

Then, he sat beside her bed, holding her hand as they watched television. The air in the room felt still, yet heavy, as if time itself was slowing down to make space for something sacred.

About an hour later, as he absentmindedly flipped through the channels, he suddenly felt a soft squeeze on his hand.

He turned to look at her.

"What's wrong, Ma?" he asked, leaning in.

She didn't answer right away, but her eyes were fixed on the ceiling, her face illuminated by a quiet, almost childlike wonder.

"Ma?" he repeated. "What are you looking at?" A smile spread across her lips.

"Angels," she whispered.

His breath caught in his throat.

"Angels?" he echoed, his voice trembling. "Do you see anything else?"

Her eyes never wavered from whatever vision she was witnessing. "Just angels," she said softly, as if it were the most natural thing in the world.

His heart pounded as he gripped her hand a little tighter, his tears spilling onto the blanket draped over her frail body.

"Ma," he choked out, "Are you... are you trying to tell me that it's time to go?"

She didn't answer, but the look in her eyes—the peace, the acceptance—spoke louder than words ever could.

He bowed his head, tears streaming freely.

"Ma, if you want to leave, it's okay," he whispered through his sobs. "You've lived life to the fullest. And I know... I know there are people up there waiting for you. People you've missed for so long."

His voice broke.

"I know the pain is unbearable now. I can see it. And if you think it's time to let go... it's okay. We'll all understand. We'll miss you, but we'll understand."

For a moment, her smile remained, then slowly, it faded.

The warmth of her grip softened, her hand resting still in his.

Panic surged through him as he stood abruptly, his chair scraping against the tile floor.

"Ma?" he called, gently shaking her. No response.

His chest tightened as he rushed into the hallway, frantically searching for a nurse.

When he found one, she quickly followed him back into the room, checking his mother's vitals with practiced calm.

"She's just resting," the nurse assured him gently. "She's still here."

But he knew. He could feel it deep inside. He turned to the nurse, his voice hoarse.

"Can I talk to you?" he asked.

She nodded, stepping aside with him.

"I think my mother will be gone soon," he admitted, his words barely above a whisper. "She's comfortable with leaving. And I told her... I told her it's okay."

The nurse gave him a look of understanding, placing a hand on his shoulder. "We'll take great care of her," she promised.

That night, he went home, his heart weighed down by grief.

Throughout his life, this man had wrestled with faith. He had been unsure of what to believe—what was real and what wasn't.
Religion had always been a tangled web of contradictions, unanswered questions, and lingering doubts.

But in those last moments with his mother, something changed.

She had seen something.

Something beyond this world.

She wasn't afraid. She wasn't struggling. She had seen **them**—the angels.

And in that moment, it became real to him. The God he had questioned, the afterlife he had doubted—**it all had to be real.**

She wouldn't have smiled like that otherwise. She wouldn't have looked so **ready**.

And if there was one thing he knew for certain, it was this: He wanted to see her again.

To do that, he had to **do right by God**. He had to live with purpose, with faith, with love.

Two days later, his mother took her last breath. She had gone home.

— Eric Wright

Moral of the Story: Life has a way of teaching us the most profound lessons in the quietest moments—when words are few, but understanding is deep.

This man spent his life questioning, doubting, trying to make sense of a world that often seemed unfair and uncertain. He had witnessed struggle, loss, and hardship, and through it all, faith had been an elusive concept, something he could never quite grasp.

But in his mother's final moments, he found clarity in the one thing that needed no explanation—**her peace.**

She saw **something** beyond this life, something that made her smile, something that reassured her that she was not alone.

That moment wasn't just for her—it was for **him** too.

It was God's way of saying, **"I've been here all along."**

Sometimes, the proof we seek doesn't come in words, in books, or in closing arguments. It comes in **the undeniable presence of something greater than ourselves**—in the peace of a loved one's passing, in the way love transcends even death, and in the realization that there is more to this life than what we see.

Faith is not always built in churches or in sermons; sometimes, it's built in **care facilities or hospital rooms, holding the hand of someone you love, watching them leave this world with a smile.**

In the end, we are all searching for meaning, for purpose, for reassurance that this life is not all there is.

Chapter 57

My Final Chapter - My Legacy and My Mother

Life is a collection of stories, woven together by moments of triumph, struggle, and resilience. As I sit here reflecting on the journey that led me to this very moment, I am overwhelmed with gratitude. The road has been long, filled with twists, setbacks, and unexpected turns, but through it all, one truth has remained constant—I was always meant to tell this story. My story.

It began in the turbulent 1960s, during a time of racial unrest, political upheaval, and change. The streets of Detroit bore witness to a history that would define generations to come. The riots, the injustices, and the struggles were not just events that happened around me—they were experiences that shaped me. As a child, I was unaware of the magnitude of these events, but I felt their impact deeply. I grew up in a world where survival was an everyday battle, where love had to be stronger than hate, and where resilience was not an option but a necessity.

In this book, I have acknowledged the great individuals who worked, fought, and even sacrificed their lives under unimaginable circumstances to pave the way for a better future. Though they are no longer here, their bravery, resilience, and unwavering determination have left an everlasting impact on history. What they endured and accomplished was nothing short of extraordinary, and I carry their legacy with me every day.

Amidst the challenges, my childhood in the Smith Homes Projects was filled with memories that would define the person I became. but we made the most of what we had. We swam in the Swim Mobile, took long walks to Rouge Park, and played endless games in the project's big field. We rode all day on our chopper bicycles, turned on fire hydrants to cool off, and ran through the water with laughter echoing through the streets.

We walked to the train tracks to collect flares to carelessly play with, played center tag with our closest friends, and spent cold winters ice skating on a man-made rink. Our nights were filled with sleepovers in each other's homes, where bonds of brotherhood were forged. We may not have had much, but we had each other, and that was enough.

In the midst of chaos, there was my mother. A woman of extraordinary strength and grace, she carried the weight of our family on her shoulders without ever letting us feel the burden. She was deaf and mute, but her actions spoke louder than any words ever could. She was my protector, my provider, my unwavering source of love. Despite the poverty that surrounded us, she made sure we never felt deprived. The meals on our table, the clothes on our backs, the warmth in our hearts—it was all her doing. She had a way of making miracles out of nothing.

As a child, I watched her navigate a world that often refused to accommodate her. Yet, she never complained. Instead, she adapted, finding her own ways to communicate, to nurture, to ensure her children were given the best life she could offer. She taught me the most valuable lesson of all: perseverance. No matter what life threw at her, she found a way to push forward, and that resilience became embedded in me.

As I grew older, I began to find my own path. Music became my escape, my passion, my voice. From the streets of Detroit to being the very first DJ to play at Comerica Park, to the DJ booth of a packed club, I poured my soul into my craft. Every song played, every beat that made the crowd move, every contest I orchestrated —it was all part of a larger journey, a testament to my determination to carve out something meaningful in this world. But with that journey came challenges.

The betrayals, the setbacks, the moments where I questioned my worth—all of it tested me in ways I never imagined.

Still, through every success and failure, my mother's spirit remained with me.

Cancer came for me in a way I never expected. It was a fight unlike any I had ever faced before. The physical pain, the mental toll, the sleepless nights spent wondering if I would make it through—it was a battle that nearly broke me. But then, I thought of my mother. I thought of how she had fought her own battle, how she had endured hardships without ever giving in to despair. If she could fight, then so could I. And so, I did. With every painful step, every moment of doubt, I chose to keep moving forward. I chose to live.

Even in her final days, my mother continued to teach me lessons. Losing her was the hardest thing I have ever endured, but her legacy lives on—not just in me, but in every life she touched.

So here I am, at the end of this book, but not the end of my journey. I have shared my story, my struggles, my victories, and my pain, not just for myself, but for those who come after me. My legacy is not in the music I played, the clubs I rocked, or the battles I won—it is in the love I give, the lessons I pass on, and the impact I leave behind. My legacy is my mother's love, carried forward in everything I do.

To anyone reading this, know that life is a journey filled with ups and downs, with moments of joy and pain. But through it all, we must hold on to the lessons that shape us. We must remember where we came from, honor those who paved the way for us, and never stop fighting for the life we deserve.

My mother's story is my story. Her strength is my strength. Her love is my greatest inheritance. And as long as I live, her legacy will never fade.

Life is unpredictable. No matter how much we prepare, plan, or dream, it unfolds in its own way, pulling us in directions we never expected. If there's anything I've learned, it's that we are not defined by **what happens to us**, but by **how we respond** to it.

Looking back, I see a boy who grew up too fast, a young man searching for his place in the world, and a man who fought for everything he believed in. I see a journey filled with heartbreak and healing, loss and redemption, victories and lessons learned the hard way.

I think about all the people who crossed my path—some who walked with me, some who betrayed me, some who inspired me, and some who taught me lessons I never wanted to learn. Each of them played a role in shaping the man I became. Some taught me the power of loyalty, while others reminded me to never be too trusting. But through every encounter, one truth remained: **life goes on, and so must we.**

I think about the places I've been—the dark alleys and the bright stages, the quiet nights alone and the loud nights where the bass shook the room. I think about the times I stood in the spotlight and the times I stood in the shadows, doubting whether my story even mattered.

But it does.

It matters because every struggle, every challenge, every fight for survival led me here.

I sit here now, reflecting on all I've been through, and I realize that my journey is not just mine.

It belongs to the generations before me who fought battles I will never fully understand. **It belongs to the generations after me**, the ones who will read these words and see a reflection of their own struggles, their own hopes, their own resilience.

This book isn't just a story—it's a testament.
A testament to **hardship and perseverance**.
A testament to **love and loss**.
A testament to **the unbreakable spirit of those who refuse to be forgotten**.

One day, my name will be just another name in history.

But if this book—if my words, my experiences, my truth—can **inspire even one person to keep fighting, keep dreaming, keep moving forward**, then my story has done its job.

This is my final chapter, but my story will never truly end. This is my legacy—my journey, and the book I leave behind for my family to cherish and reflect on for generations to come.

Instagram: @author_eric_wright
Facebook: @Eric Wright (Author Eric Wright)
Tik Tok:@author_eric_wright

Continue resting in peace my brothers
K.O. L.K. and M.W.
And my sisters
L.O. Q.O. B.O. L.G. M.G. And K.G.
Rest in paradise

To my family members who have long passed away,
I love you and have truly missed your presence.

Visit my new website GhettoFabulousBooks.com

You can also purchase other merchandise on the site as well.

My books are also available on all book platforms including

Kindle.

I hope you enjoyed my short stories and I hope I didn't offend anyone in the process. After all, I'm just another writer.

This book was one of the most challenging projects I have ever taken on. This time around, I wanted to truly understand why editors and publishers charge so much for their work. So, I made a bold decision—I would do everything myself. From writing and formatting to ensuring proper grammar and structure, I took full control of the process, relying on A.I. as a tool to help refine my work. [This took a whole two years]

Looking back, I must admit, although my first book was an important accomplishment, it was also a personal disappointment —not because of the content, but because of the publishing experience itself. I invested hard-earned money, expecting professional guidance and support, but the reality fell far short of my expectations.

The editor I worked with was **difficult to communicate with**, often unavailable when I needed clarification or revisions. Instead of offering **detailed feedback**, she skimmed through my pages, **barely making corrections.** When I requested that she take another careful look at the manuscript, she became **frustrated** with me—**as if I was inconveniencing her for simply wanting my book to be the best it could be.**

She claimed to own her own **publishing company,** but in the end, it was clear—**she wasn't a real publisher.**

She didn't bring value to my work, nor did she treat it with the respect it deserved. That experience left me feeling cheated, but more than that, it fueled my determination to **never put my work in someone else's careless hands again.**

But through this journey, I have come to truly understand and appreciate just how tough and time-consuming this process can be. Writing a story—pouring your thoughts, memories, and emotions onto a blank page—is the easy part in comparison. The real challenge begins when it's time to bring that story to life in book form.

Formatting, structuring, and organizing an entire manuscript is an **entirely different beast.**

It's not just about making the words flow—**it's about making them fit within the technical confines of a book.** Margins, font choices, spacing, pagination, table of contents, image placement, and ensuring consistency across **hundreds of pages**—it all takes **precision, patience, and relentless attention to detail.**

There were moments when I wanted to **throw in the towel,** when it felt like no matter how much I fixed and formatted, **there was always another issue waiting to be resolved.** And unlike writing, where creativity flows freely, **formatting is a rigid, unforgiving process**—one mistake, one overlooked detail, and the entire layout can shift, throwing everything off balance.

I now have a **deep respect** for the professionals who do this for a living—not just because of the **skill involved,** but because of the **sheer amount of time, effort, and frustration** that goes into it. And while **I am proud** that I took on this challenge alone, I can say without hesitation that it has been one of the **most difficult tasks I have ever undertaken.**

I also had to come to terms with something important—A.I. is not a real person. It doesn't think, reason, or truly understand context the way a human does. While it has been an invaluable tool throughout this process, I quickly realized that it, too, makes mistakes.

There were times when **I trusted it to fix something**, only to later discover that it **introduced new errors** or misinterpreted what I was trying to say. It lacked the **intuition and human experience** that a skilled editor would have, and sometimes, it felt like I was constantly **revising and correcting the corrections.**

The frustration would build up. I'd spend **hours** trying to fix an issue, only to end up **right back where I started.** It became an exhausting cycle—one that led me to **quit several times**, convinced that I had wasted my time and money.

I even went as far as canceling my subscription and getting a refund, thinking I was done with it for good.

But each time, **I found myself needing it again.** Despite its flaws, **A.I. was still a useful tool**, and walking away from it meant making my job even harder. So, begrudgingly, I would resubscribe and try again, learning to work around its limitations and **use it as a guide rather than a crutch.**

This experience taught me that **technology—no matter how advanced—cannot replace human effort, patience, and creativity.** It can assist, but it cannot do the work **for** you. In the end, I had to rely on **my own determination** to get things done **the right way.**

That's an incredible sentiment—to want to help others get their own stories out into the world, despite the challenges you faced along the way.

But I had to recognize that this process wasn't easy for me, and I am not a professional editor, publisher, or English teacher.

Because of that, there were **many hurdles** I personally had to overcome, and each step of this journey tested my **patience, resilience, and determination.** Here's a breakdown of some of the biggest challenges I faced while putting this book together:

1. Formatting Nightmares

Writing the story was one thing—**turning it into an actual book was another.** I quickly realized that **proper book formatting is an art in itself.** From margins and page breaks to font consistency and paragraph alignment, **one wrong move could throw off the entire document.**

There were moments when I would fix one thing, only to **mess up something else in the process.**

Trying to get the layout just right felt like **an endless game of trial and error.** At times, I had to completely start over just to get everything lined up correctly.

2. The Never-Ending Page Count Adjustments

Every time I made a small edit—**adding or removing a single sentence**—it could **shift the entire layout, affecting the page count.** This meant I had to **constantly update the Table of Contents**, making sure all the page numbers were still correct.

It was exhausting, and I sometimes felt like I was **chasing my own mistakes, never truly catching up.** But in the end, I learned just how **precise** and **delicate** book formatting truly is.

3. The Struggle with Transparency & Printing Issues

Once I finally had the book formatted, **new problems emerged—** technical issues that I never even thought about. Lulu's system kept flagging **"transparency errors"**, and no matter how many times I tried fixing them, **the warnings wouldn't go away.**

I spent **hours troubleshooting transparency issues, flattening images, adjusting ink coverage, and making changes I didn't even fully understand.** At one point, I considered **removing all images from the book completely,** just to make things easier.

I was determined to **figure it out**, but this step alone tested my patience like nothing else.

4. The A.I. Struggle – A Double-Edged Sword

Using A.I. to assist with **grammar and structure** was a learning experience. **It helped a lot, but it wasn't perfect.**

There were times when it misinterpreted my words, reworded things incorrectly, or made changes that took away from my original message.

Instead of blindly trusting it, I had to **double-check everything—** which often meant doing **just as much work as before.** It was **a tool, not a solution**, and that's something I had to learn the hard way.

5. The Mental and Emotional Toll

Putting this book together wasn't just a **technical** challenge—it was an **emotional** one too. Writing about **personal experiences, struggles, and reflections** meant reliving some of the most **painful and defining** moments of my life.

There were days when I had to step away from the book completely, just to **clear my mind.** Other times, I felt **mentally drained** from spending hours fixing tiny details that no one else would even notice.

But through it all, **I refused to give up.** I had come too far to stop now.

Final Thoughts

This journey has **taught me more than I ever expected.** I now understand why **editors, publishers, and book designers** charge what they do—**because this process is no joke.** It takes **time, patience, and a deep commitment** to see it through to the end.

Despite all the obstacles, I know one thing for sure—I **believe in this book.** Every challenge I faced only made me more determined to **get it done, and to do it the right way.**

And now that I've **pushed through the struggle**, I hope that my journey can inspire others to do the same.

I would like to extend my heartfelt gratitude to my friends and followers on Facebook, who have been a constant source of encouragement and inspiration throughout this journey.

It was through their support, enthusiasm, and belief in my storytelling that I found the motivation to turn my urban short stories into a full-length book.

What started as **individual stories, shared piece by piece,** grew into something far greater—a complete body of work that captures **life, struggles, and resilience in a way I never imagined possible.** Every like, comment, and word of encouragement reminded me that **my stories mattered,** that they resonated with people beyond my own experiences.

Without that push from my **Facebook community**, this book might have remained just an idea, a collection of thoughts never fully realized. But their faith in my ability to **bring these stories to life** gave me the drive to see it through to the very end.

For that, I am **forever grateful.** This book is not just my achievement—it's a reflection of the **support and love from those who believed in me along the way.**

The Book Is Also Dedicated To Tulsa 1921